Gus diZerega offers a scholarly and eloquent foundation for inter-religious discussion. In clear and readable prose he compares and contrasts the Pagan and Christian worldviews, covering areas such as cyclic vs linear time, relationship with the natural world, spiritual authority and the nature of suffering.

Whether the reader is Christian or Pagan, this book will enrich their view of their own religion and promote understanding of the Other. This book is a valuable contribution to the discourse on religion in America.

—Rowan Fairgrove
Interfaith Activist, Wiccan Priestess, and author

In writing Pagans & Christians, Dr. diZerega has made a valuable contribution to the enrichment of interfaith dialogue. And even more, to the vibrancy and sustainability of our own precious Pagan faith traditions.

He articulates Pagan experience with clear vision, loving heart, subtlety of feeling, and solid facts. In accessible language, supported by documentation, he dispels many misconceptions. He draws upon his considerable erudition and experience to present clear, insightful, thought-provoking explanations. From this book, Pagans and Christians alike can gain a more balanced and complete understanding of our own diversity, and of our commonalities. May his open-minded and open-hearted approach serve to enrich us all, and dispel any remaining climate of intolerance based on fear of the unknown.

We Pagans are fortunate to have a Witch of Gus' distinction contributing to the enrichment of our culture. This book is an important addition to the curriculum of seminaries and chaplaincies, and useful to all who are engaged in interfaith work. As a Witch involved in the field of death and dying (a universal experience regardless of religion) I plan to use it in my own interfaith work.

—M. Macha NightMare
co/author, Pagan Book of Living and Dying

This is a provocative invitation to dialogue between Pagans and Christians. First, it is a challenge to Christians to understand the nature and goals of modern Pagans. Second, it is an appeal for dialogue. Nor is it merely a bland invitation to a polite cup of tea. DiZerega challenges Christians to rethink everything they have thought about paganism from antiquity to the present day.

What is especially appealing is the demonstration of both the author's grasp of Pagan and Christian theology and history as well as his personal insights into a possibly better relationship between Pagans and Christians. Christians may not always be happy with diZerega's arguments, but they are the stuff of real dialogue. This book will be especially useful for conservative and evangelical Christians who want to know more about their Pagan neighbors.

Also to be appreciated is a very clear exposition of why modern Paganism is often called a Nature Religion. The ecological sensitivity found in this version of Pagan theology ought to stimulate Christians to rethink and renew their own theologies in order to promote what our Buddhists friends call ecological sanity.

—Dr. John Berthrong
Boston University: School of Theology
Director, Institute for Dialogue Among Religious Traditions

*"How can two faiths apparently so dissimilar both be spiritually valid? This small book will answer these questions.*

—Gus diZerega

## Opposing Creeds or Complementary Paths?

There is no lack of animosity and mistrust between those of the Christian faith—one of the world's largest religions—and those of the Pagan way—one of the world's oldest spiritual paths.

Is there any hope for understanding and reconciliation? Gus diZerega says there is, and presents *Pagans & Christians* as a tool for promoting understanding and respect between the people of both faiths.

Within these pages you will find a clear picture of what Paganism really is; what its real roots are. The practices and beliefs of the modern Pagan are presented as they contrast and harmonize with those of their Christian counterparts. You will discover how Pagans relate to the Divine, and why Nature plays such a central role in their faith. You will also discover what Pagans believe about evil, suffering, and the devil.

You may be Christian, Pagan, or any other persuasion. Whatever you choose to believe, if you take to heart the commandment to "Love one another," this book will help clear away the roadblocks of fear and misunderstanding.

# About the Author

Gus diZerega is a Third-Degree Gardnerian Elder. He spent six years studying with Brazilian shaman Antonio Costa e Silva, and with other teachers in Native American and Afro-Brazilian traditions. With a Ph.D. in Political Science/Theory from the University of California-Berkeley, he has spent the past sixteen years in the academic field, teaching on the faculties of several universities and colleges. He is a frequent conference lecturer, panelist, or speaker and writer on topics such as environmental issues, community and society, contemporary politics, modernity, and religion.

As an author of both scholarly and spiritual material, his articles have appeared in numerous publications, both in the U.S. and abroad. His first book, *Persuasion, Power and Polity: A Theory of Democratic Self-Organization,* was published in 2000 by Hampton Press.

# To Write to the Author

If you wish to contact the author or would like more information about this book, please write to the author in care of Llewellyn Worldwide and we will forward your request. Both the author and publisher appreciate hearing from you and learning of your enjoyment of this book and how it has helped you. Llewellyn Worldwide cannot guarantee that every letter written to the author can be answered, but all will be forwarded. Please write to:

Gus diZerega
℅ Llewellyn Worldwide
P.O. Box 64383, Dept. 1-56718-228-3
St. Paul, MN 55164-0383, U.S.A.

Please enclose a self-addressed stamped envelope for reply, or $1.00 to cover costs. If outside U.S.A., enclose international postal reply coupon.

Many of Llewellyn's authors have websites with additional information and resources. For more information, please visit our website at http://www.llewellyn.com

---

For Llewellyn's free full-color catalog, write to *New Worlds* at the above address, or call 1-800-THE MOON

# PAGANS &
# CHRISTIANS

## THE PERSONAL
## SPIRITUAL
## EXPERIENCE

# GUS DIZEREGA, PH.D.

2001
Llewellyn Publications
St. Paul, Minnesota 55164-0383, U.S.A.

First Edition
First Printing, 2001

Book design by Donna Burch
Book editing by Connie Hill
Cover design by William Merlin Cannon

Library of Congress Cataloging-in-Publication Data
DiZergea, Gus.
    Pagans & Christians : the personal spiritual experience / Gus diZerega
    — 1st ed.
        p.     cm.
    Includes bibliographical references.
    ISBN 1-56718-228-3
    1. Witchcraft.   2. Experience (Religion)   3. Neopaganism—Relations—
    Christianity.   4. Christianity and other religions—Neopaganism.
    I. Title: Pagans and Christians.   II. Title.

BF 1566.D59    2001
299—dc21                                                           00-051449

Llewellyn Publications
A Division of Llewellyn Worldwide, Ltd.
P.O. Box 64383, Dept. 1-56718-228-3
St. Paul, MN 55164-0383, U.S.A.
www.llewellyn.com

Printed in the United States of America

This book is dedicated to Paul.

# Also by Gus diZerega

*Persuasion, Power and Polity: A Theory of Democratic Self-Organization* (Hampton Press, 2000)

# Contents

# Acknowledgments

My favorite proverb is from Africa: "I am because we are." Certainly this book reflects the wisdom and creativity of more people than myself alone. It is, because we are. Some have played a particularly vital role in stimulating my thought and encouraging my insight during its writing. Here I would like gratefully to acknowledge them.

I would like to thank in particular, D. H. Frew, who helped to write chapter 1, and whose comments and suggestions have influenced the rest of this work. The insights and wisdom of Kim Atkinson, Richard Ely, Rowan Fairgrove, Anastasia Fischer, Dana Hanson, Anodea Judith, Ph.D. (author of *Wheels of Life* and *Eastern Body, Western Mind*), Anna Korn, and Trish O'Malley have all played a vital part as well in adding to the strengths of this book. To all of them my most sincere gratitude.

## Introduction

# Spiritual Truth
# for Christians and Pagans
### *A Pagan Perspective*

Religious discussion can be either fruitful or a waste of time. I hope this volume will be fruitful to all who read it.

To be sure, in the final analysis, the value of a spiritual practice is determined by how well it brings us into a better relationship with what is Highest and most Sacred. If our spiritual practice does not help us in this task, it really is not important how many debates we win, how subtle our thinking, or how profound our insights. All these things, desirable as they can be, are simply icing on the spiritual cake. When the cake is good, the icing adds to its beauty and flavor. When the cake is bad, the icing is only a deceptive promise. So our personal practice within and without our spiritual community is primary.

Once we grant this point, there is a valuable role for Pagans entering into a discussion with other religious traditions, particularly Christianity. There are two broad reasons. First, and most importantly, Pagans live within a Christian culture, and our friends and neighbors view religion through lenses that have been crafted by 2,000 years of Christian thought and practice. This is so even when they do not consider themselves Christian. From such a perspective it is hard to enter into a sympathetic understanding of Pagan spirituality. Consequently, a forthright encounter of Pagan and Christian spirituality can only help us become better understood by others, and therefore less threatening to them. When people are ignorant they readily imagine the worst. Once they become informed those fears usually vanish.

Second, discussion of other perspectives can help us more deeply understand our own. The point of such discussion is not to determine whose approach is "best." Rather it is to probe more deeply into the nature of Spirit, and in doing so better appreciate both our own and other spiritual traditions. Such discussions will ideally have a similar impact upon those practicing other faiths.

Pagan spirituality is once again becoming well-known in the modern world. For many, Pagan traditions are challenging over 1,500 years of Christian hegemony, offering a different view of how we can appropriately relate to the Sacred. The implications of the rise of Pagan religion in the most modern countries of the West are puzzling to many. I believe these implications are profound. This book, written from a Pagan perspective, seeks to explore these questions and, in the process, help many Pagans better to see the deeper implications of our practice, while enabling those called to other spiritual practices better to understand our own.

Historically, in the West, the alliance of church and state served to suppress spiritual practices that were not in keeping with what had become orthodox interpretations of scripture. By the time tolerance returned again to Western civilization, all that most people knew of religion and spirituality was what they had been exposed to in standard interpretations of the Old and New Testaments. Christian or Jew, everyone saw religion in monotheistic terms, with ultimate knowledge about it revealed in sacred scripture. Most people accepted that there was only One True Way of worshipping the Divine, even if we could not agree as to what that way truly was.

As a Pagan in a society where most religious people are Christian, these common Christian attitudes are cause for some concern. Although our country's freedom of religion removes my worries about the worst historical manifestations of religious intolerance, it was not so long ago that Native Americans were prohibited from practicing their religion despite the Constitution's guarantee of religious freedom. Recently I witnessed a TV news program about a Wiccan Samhain celebration in North Carolina where a Christian minister reminded believers that the Bible commanded that Witches be killed.

Certainly murderous views such as this are not those of a majority of Christians, but many who feel the minister went too far nevertheless are ill at ease with the thought that Witches and other Pagans are a growing minority in the United States, and there are always a few zealots who concur. Even today there are many isolated acts of violence against American Pagans. I believe that we can only benefit by there being a wider understanding of Pagan spirituality and how it relates to the Christian tradition of the West.

## The Course of the Argument

Because Pagan spirituality is based upon personal experience as its ultimate standard of validity, I cannot pretend that my views are those of all Pagans. For every Wiccan it is personal experience—our own encounters with the Sacred—that give ultimate validity to our practice, but then, even Christians disagree about the meaning of Holy Scripture. Much of what I say here will be broadly true of all Wiccans, and some even of all Pagans. Where I cleave more closely to my own experiences, I will try to make it clear that that is what I am doing.

The first two chapters describe Pagan spirituality in a way that will win wide assent among those describing themselves as spiritually "Pagan." The third chapter will win wide assent among those of us Pagans who identify with traditional Wicca, or traditional Witchcraft, and to a large extent by those who are today called "Neopagans." Humankind being as they are, this assent will still not be universal.

The chapters that follow incorporate more personal experience and thought as to how Pagan spirituality relates to the perennial questions facing all spiritual practices as well as to Christianity itself. They will inevitably be more controversial. Parts Two and

Three are engaged in friendly conversation with widespread Christian beliefs regarding Pagan spirituality. The message of this book can be easily gained by reading the conclusion after finishing the first three chapters, but often it is through debate and examination that we and others gain deeper levels of understanding. That is the purpose of these middle parts.

Chapters 4 through 7 give Pagan responses to criticisms Christians have often made of our religion. Included here are discussions of evil and suffering, and the nature of spiritual authority. Chapters 8 and 9 focus on Pagan criticisms of Christian practice, focusing on the relationship of Spirit to the natural world and the implications of the common Christian claim to sole or ultimate spiritual authority. My object here is not to rebut Christianity, but rather to show that the Pagan view of nature is already present in Scripture, and that Christianity does not depend in any sense upon a claim to spiritual superiority.

The final chapter argues for the importance of *both* Christianity and Pagan spirituality within the modern world. Here I develop most thoroughly the underlying thesis of this book: that no spiritual tradition can give full expression to every dimension of the Sacred. Each focuses primarily on a few central dimensions, paying less attention to others, but taken together, humankind's core religions cover all the dimensions of Spirit that have manifested in human experience. Consequently, properly understood, each focuses on ultimately complementary aspects of Spirit, while not denying other dimensions more emphasized within different traditions. Both Christianity and Paganism are ultimately *enriched* by the existence of the other.

## What This Book Offers Pagans

This book is intended to be helpful to Pagans, Christians, and other faiths, although in different ways. I hope Pagans, and Wiccans in particular, will find it useful in understanding how our own spiritual tradition relates to the largely Christian ideas about spirituality that pervade the culture in which we live, as well as to the more inclusive mosaic of the world's religions.[1] The core realities of our practice are as beautiful and worthy of devotion as those of any other religion. In these pages I will explore a few of the deeper spiritual truths emphasized by our tradition, as well as within Pagan practices generally, going beyond the introductory discussions that are easily available today, but that only scratch the surface of Pagan spirituality.

In addition, many of us have Christian friends and family members. While there are a number of excellent introductory books on Wicca and Neopaganism generally, as well as some reliable short pamphlets to help explain our beliefs to others, there is nothing available that initiates a Pagan-Christian dialogue by means of a sympathetic view of both spiritual traditions. This work seeks to begin this task. As a consequence, I believe it will be useful for any Pagan who finds her or himself in frequent dialogue with Christians among their friends, at work, or in their family.

Although I am unwavering in my devotion to the Wiccan Goddess, and to the community that honors Her, my purpose here is bridge building, not spiritual battle. Here I hope to make an argument many Christians will find thought provoking: that Paganism and Christianity are both legitimate approaches toward a closer relationship with the Divine. To make such an argument I have had to criticize Fundamentalist claims that the Bible is uniquely objective and without error, and that Jesus' meaning was clear when he said no one could come to the Father except by him. I have also had to criticize the wider claim that Christianity, or perhaps Biblical and "revealed" religions generally, are the only genuine religions.

I believe that all of my criticisms are fairly made, and that none challenge the core insights about Christian spirituality. If there is to be lasting interfaith peace and good will, the high costs of, and false reasoning behind, all claims to theological exclusivity have to be acknowledged without thereby arguing that Christians should give up Christianity. No religion should depend for its survival upon claims of exclusivity.

I write this work as a traditional Wiccan who has extensively studied and to some extent participated in Native and Latin American Pagan spiritual traditions as well. Like the majority of American Pagans of European ancestry, my spiritual heritage is Christian. It is a background that profoundly influenced the ways in which I think about spirituality. Historically Christianity has made exclusive claims to providing salvation, and most of us coming from Christian backgrounds learned of this claim as small children and initially accepted it uncritically. Our Christian heritage continues to color our spiritual lives.

Loyola exaggerated when he said that if he could control the religious education of children he could ensure their life-long devotion to the Church, but he did not exaggerate by much. What we learn as children never really leaves us. Whatever our mature beliefs, we remain deeply and powerfully affected by the religion of our fathers and mothers, and cannot help but respond to it. It is in our bones.

Some Pagans' response to the Church is hostile. Christianity is the religion of "the patriarchy." It was responsible for the killing of countless Witches and other Pagans throughout the world. In its name, Pagan temples were leveled, books burned, and sacred groves hewn down. From this angry perspective Christianity continues to be a profoundly negative force in our lives and in human society as a whole.

Understandably, many Pagans who take such a view of Christianity define themselves against it. In doing so, they remain to some extent still within its power, even to the point of avoiding those Pagan practices that most overlap with Christian practice, such as prayer. By defining Pagan religion as different in all respects from Christianity, some Pagans unintentionally narrow their own spiritual lives. They also narrow their appreciation of Spirit, and of what we share in common with other people who sincerely follow Spirit as it has made itself available to them.

Christianity is multifaceted. There is much truth in the harsh indictment I described in the previous paragraph, but it is a one-sided truth and, like all one-sided truths, when rigidly adhered to it leads us into error.

All religions deal with entering into appropriate relations with the Sacred. Therefore it is inevitable that there will be much overlap in religious traditions. When we decide one tradition is bad, and so avoid everything that has any resemblance to it, we impoverish our own spirituality. Seeing what our spiritual practice shares in common with others enables us to come to a deeper appreciation of the fact that the Divine speaks to many people in different ways. This should be no a surprise to those of us who revere a world where even every snowflake is different.

For other Pagans, Christianity remains a source of continued fear and unease. They have left the fold of the Church not because they laid their beliefs in it permanently to rest, but because they decided if God was good, Christian doctrine could not be true. Christianity's view of the world, and of God, was too terrible to embrace. The Gospels were not "good news," but rather terrifying threats that most people were damned for eternity. This was my reason for leaving the church as a high-school student.

This attitude can linger among those who initially considered themselves believing Christians, who remain aware of their own fallibility, and who therefore feel threatened when confronted with many Evangelicals' absolute certainty that they speak in harmony with God's will, and that we are simply the dupes of Satan. In our humility we do not share such certainty. This book will show that the claim by many Christians to spiritual exclusivity has no rational basis, and that even its most common biblical justifications rest on very selective and arbitrary interpretations of Scripture, interpretations which ignore contrary scriptural evidence.

I have tried to provide sufficient scriptural evidence for the arguments that I make to give any Pagan an interesting and useful fund of information for employing in encounters with those Christians who are supremely confident that their path is the only valid one. For a Pagan book, there is a lot of Scripture quoted. My purpose is not simply to debunk claims to spiritual supremacy—however badly such claims need debunking. My aim is to help establish mutual respect, but to establish this respect, such debunking is necessary.

A much smaller number of Pagans grew up with no real acquaintance with Christianity. Sometimes our parents were themselves Pagans. Other times our parents were simply not religious, or were Jewish, Buddhist, or practiced some other faith. Many Pagans with these backgrounds find Christianity a strange but exceedingly powerful and threatening adversary. I hope that even this group will benefit from the discussion which follows.

Ultimately I will point to important bridges that can help link the understanding of Pagan and Christian alike—not to convert either to the other, but hopefully to enable each to have a greater appreciation for one another's spiritual strengths. I hope that it will help us all to acknowledge that different need not imply better and worse. It may only mean different. The spiritual path to which we are personally called often says more about us than about the superiority of our spiritual practices over those of others. A sunflower has yellow petals and a dark center. Neither color is superior, and both are needed to have a sunflower.

## What This Book Offers Christians

I have written this book for Christians as well. After discussing what Pagan spirituality and Neopagan Witchcraft really are, I confront common Christian criticisms of and questions about Paganism that I have frequently encountered. They have arisen over many years of discussions with devout Christians in formal interfaith contexts, as well as in the more personal and intense discussions that take place within families and between friends.

Many years after I had been called to a Pagan path, a family member became a devout Christian. His involvement in the Church turned his life around for the better, bringing more love and happiness to himself and his family, and involving him even more deeply in service within his community. He was, and remains, an inspiring testimony to the good the Christian Church can bring to a tortured life.

In time, he learned of my Pagan beliefs, and not surprisingly, tried to convert me to his own. He was concerned about the salvation of my soul and wanted to share the good news that had so transformed his own life. In response, I sent him a long letter, one that I had originally written to an evangelical friend explaining why I was not a Christian. This began a lengthy discussion by email and in person not only with my brother, but also with friends of his: a minister and other committed Christian laypeople who had read and pondered deeply the meaning of their faith, and with whom he had shared my letter.

In the course of this discussion I was impressed by the good will, generosity, and sincerity of many who sought so unsuccessfully to sway me from my devotion to the Wiccan Goddess. At the same time, while answering them, I was led to an ever deeper appreciation of what is most spiritually valid and beautiful in my own practice. I found the arguments I made in these discussions valuable for myself, and I hope for my Christian correspondents as well. Consequently I decided to offer it for others, Pagan and Christian alike. In preparing those letters for publication, their content has been broadened, deepened, and developed, but the basic arguments remain the same. *Pagans and Christians* is an ecumenically friendly argument for Pagan spirituality.

I hope these chapters will prove a convincing challenge to any Christian belief that our way is spiritually in error, or that theirs is uniquely true. In doing so I happily grant that Christianity does offer a unique and valuable path to the Sacred, but unique does not equal exclusive in the worth of religions any more than it does in the worth of people. We have increasingly learned to grant this point with respect to individuals. Why do so many people have problems granting it for those matters which most deeply address the nature of individuals?

I will also argue that the Wiccan path sensitizes us to spiritual truths that, while present in the Bible, have historically been largely ignored. My purpose is not to argue that Neopaganism is therefore better than Christianity. Rather, it is to demonstrate that when several spiritual traditions coexist with mutual respect, each can help the other to gain a more appropriate sense of how Spirit influences our world. Every path is partial, every view can become myopic, and it is in community with others having different perspectives that our own can become clearer.

Consequently I am *not* arguing for the superiority of Paganism among all religions. Pagan religions are fairly unusual to Americans in that they do not make claims to universal superiority. In this respect they differ from most historical forms of Christianity, which have supported missionaries. We have no missionaries, but ours nevertheless is a path of beauty and profundity, one to which a growing number of people are called. Pagan spirituality is both a very old practice, hearkening back to the dawn of humankind, and very new, speaking to many of us who, far from rejecting modernity, are among the scientists, entrepreneurs, and technicians of the computer age. Our world will be greatly enriched by its renaissance.

ENDNOTES

1. "Wiccan" is a technically more appropriate word than "Witch." It also has the advantage of not suffering the largely negative connotations of the latter word in the minds of most people, and of not implying that all practitioners are women. But Wiccans are Witches, and Witches can be men and women. I am a Witch.

# PART I

# The Nature of Pagan Spirituality

# What is Pagan Religion?

## *The World of Spirit*

Every year, around Halloween and May Day, newspapers and TV programs report on the activities of American Neopagans, for whom these days are special holy days. On Indian reservations around the country Native American traditionals are practicing their old ways with renewed confidence and openness. Sun Dance arbors have reappeared on hill tops from which they have long been absent. In Miami and elsewhere Santería celebrations witness dancers entering into deep trances, joined ecstatically to the spirits of African *Orishas* while *Umbanda terreiros* provide opportunities for healing and counseling by *Preto Velho* and *Caboclo* spirits. New immigrants from Latin America, Africa, and Asia bring their traditional spiritual practices with them, often perplexing Americans for whom, up until now, the local Unitarians and Pentecostals marked spirituality's extreme fringes.

For their part, Native American Sun Dancers, Neopagan Witches, Cuban Santeros, and Laotian animists rarely pause to wonder what they might have in common. Superficially they share little, other than not being considered part of the religious "mainstream" of America's monotheistic majority. Certainly most persons observing a Sun Dance, Witches' Esbat, Santería drumming ceremony, or Laotian shamanic healing ceremony would be hard pressed to find similarities between these different rituals and spiritual practices.

The adherents of monotheistic faiths such as Christianity, Judaism, and Islam have commonly referred to the followers of these "alternative" spiritualities as "Pagans," meaning primarily "poor benighted souls who have not yet been enlightened as to spirituality's *true* nature." For most Americans, "Pagan" means "not Christian or Jewish." Some even go so far as to call our modern secular society "pagan," denying to the word any spiritual connotation whatsoever. And yet, "Paganism" can indeed refer to a specific approach to spirituality; and America's Pagans share a number of fundamental beliefs and practices.

The word "pagan" (and the related word "heathen") did not start out as religious terms. Practitioners of the pre-Christian spiritualities of Europe would not have recognized these words as applying to their religious practices. There was no general term for the religious beliefs shared by these people. Instead, most people identified themselves spiritually in much more specific ways. For example, the classical writer Apuleius would have said he was a devotee of the Goddess Isis.

The Latin word *paganus* was derived from the word *pagus*, meaning "country district" or "shire." A paganus was a civilian and a local, the word emphasizing the association between the person and the place where they lived. In the heyday of the Roman empire, as Christianity was just beginning to expand, a *paganus* was a country dweller, usually with the connotation of being backward. It was similar in tone to the modern word "hick." When Christianity established itself in Europe, it first did so in large cities. Long after the cities had generally become Christian, it was the country dwellers who stubbornly held on to the old ways, bringing upon themselves the condescending term "pagan." A similar derivation appears to apply for the word "heathen," or people of the heaths, as country dwellers slow to adopt Christianity.

Over time, this association of pagans with people actually living in the country was lost. Consequently, today "Pagan" and "Heathen" refer to the religious practices of those pre-Christian peoples and to the enduring spirituality that is one of their legacies to us, along with similar practices in other parts of the world.

Despite its origins, then, the word "Pagan" has become a useful term for a particular type of spiritual practice. It is those aspects of the word focusing on connection with the land, tradition, and the old spiritual ways, that I wish to emphasize.

Other than not being Judeo-Christian, what do the practices of classical antiquity, Plains Indian Sun Dancers, Neopagan Witches, Cuban Santeros, and Laotian shamans have in common? As it happens, quite a lot. To be sure, Pagan has become a very different kind of religious term than Christian. No one refers to him or herself as a Pagan in the same way that other persons identify themselves as Christians, Jews, or Muslims. There is no universal Pagan spiritual leader, living or dead, to which such a term could refer, nor is there a universal Pagan scripture or holy book (although some Pagan religions, such as Hinduism, do possess texts they regard as particularly inspired). Nevertheless, to call a spiritual practice Pagan does indeed tell us more than that it is not monotheistic in its spiritual focus.

The metaphor of a rope may help us here. Usually no strand within a rope extends from its beginning to its end, but at every point along the rope there is sufficient overlap that we can identify the whole as a rope, and not simply a series of smaller ropes linked together. A cluster of family resemblances unites Pagan spirituality. Emphases within these traditions will differ, and occasionally a Pagan religion will lack one of these characteristics, but on balance we can safely say that a core set of beliefs and perceptions exists to unite and define the Pagan spiritual sensibility.

Pagan spirituality may be distinguished by the five following characteristics:

1. Pantheism or Panentheism
2. Animism
3. Polytheism
4. The Eternal Present (Primary emphasis upon spiritual reality's cyclical and mythical rather than linear and historical character.)
5. No equivalent of Satan or ultimate evil

# Pantheism and Panentheism

When modern Americans think of God, it is usually as a spiritual power fundamentally removed from the material world.[1] God created the world, like a potter creates a pot. The object created, be it a pot or the world, remains fundamentally separate from its creator. Such a view of the supreme spiritual power emphasizes its *transcendental* character. God is utterly and completely above us and the world in which we live.

When science and religion were not so far apart as they appear today, Sir Isaac Newton captured this transcendental vision with his striking metaphor of God as a clock maker and the material universe as a clock, obeying mechanical laws in a predictable fashion. Newton's metaphor allowed early modern scientists to dodge the theological implications of their research, arguing they were not investigating God, but only a material structure He had created. This wholly transcendental way of viewing God *desacralizes* the world. The material world becomes a soulless object. Taken on its own terms alone, it is not intrinsically valuable. A pot is without value unless someone values it.

As science discovered more and more about how the world appeared to work, God's role in His creation began to shrink. With the discovery of evolution, it seemed to many scientists and philosophers that God had become, as one put it, an unnecessary hypothesis. There is a subtle irony here. In an important sense, a strong family resemblance exists between the world as viewed by those who see Divinity as utterly transcendent and the world as viewed by those who see Divinity as utterly irrelevant. In both cases, the world is a collection of objects, devoid of intrinsic meaning. For many Christians, the world's value derives from its God-given utility to human beings in the process of carrying out His will and from the fact that God thought it worth His while to create it in the first place. For secular modern thinkers, the world is valuable solely because human beings value it. Both agree that there is nothing about the world that gives it intrinsic value.

Pagan spirituality takes a different view. For us, Divinity manifests *within* the world and in part *as* the world. The world is never completely separate from the Sacred, and therefore possesses intrinsic value that we are obligated to respect, and which is quite independent of our own preferences. Its value stems in part from the fact that the world is more intimately a part of the Divine than a mere creation. Ultimately, it is not an object.

This insight helps us understand why all Pagan religions recognize female as well as male aspects of Divinity. The image of the Goddess giving birth to the world is a much more intimate and interrelated conception of the creative process than the image of the Divine potter who is forever separate from his product. The child is separate from, but also a part of, its mother. To the extent the Sacred manifests through the world, the world is sacred.

Two similar theological terms describe this dimension of Pagan spirituality: *pantheism* and *panentheism*. The difference between the two words is that a pantheist conceives of the world (i.e. the physical universe) as Divinity in its totality, whereas a panentheist conceives Divinity's relationship to the world as being more akin to that of the mind or soul to the body. From a panentheistic perspective there is an aspect of God that is transcendent to the world in a way that is not the case with pantheism. Panentheism conceives the Divine as both transcendent and immanent, rather than merely immanent or merely transcendent.

At the level of mere words, the distinction between pantheism and panentheism seems clear, but these verbal distinctions become less certain in practice, not least because philosophers and theologians disagree as to what the mind and soul really are. Similarly, the physical universe as we now know it is not really physical in any sense we can grasp. Ultimately it is composed of energies, and we are not sure what energy is, either. Further, there is no adequate physical theory of consciousness, so it is not all that clear just what is meant by "the world" in pantheism. These are crucial questions for pantheists and panentheists, so it is hardly surprising that the matter remains unresolved. It shall probably always remain so. What *is* agreed among most Pagans, however, is that Divinity manifests throughout the world such that *nothing* in the world can be said to be truly and completely distinct from the Divine.

Thomas Yellowtail, a Crow Sundance chief, described the Crow's prayers to the Highest, which they term "Acbadadea":

> Grandmother Earth is a way of expressing that part of Acbadadea which is created in this world, because all that we have is created by and from Acbadadea, but Acbadadea is also above all things. It is the same for the Medicine Fathers. When I move the pipe in a circle to all of the four directions, it also has a similar meaning, because all the winds, the powers, and Nature, wherever you look or wherever you go, come from Acbadadea. . . .
> You might say that each of these things represents, in one way or another, part of Acbadadea, but always remember that Acbadadea is much more than all of these things.[2]

Yellowtail's spiritual views are in harmony with the primordial Pagan vision that began in the Paleolithic era, characterized the wisest philosophers of Greece and Rome, of China and India, and is shared by Pagan peoples down to the present day.

To be sure, when we survey Pagan spirituality as a whole, we will find a range of emphasis along this point. Some people will emphasize Divinity's transcendental dimension of Divinity, as with the late Classical Greek and Roman Neoplatonism of Plotinus. Others will emphasize more immanent spiritual dimensions, as is the case with contemporary Santería. But nearly all Pagan traditions acknowledge the existence of both dimensions. Plotinus viewed even the most refractory matter as an emanation of the One, and while Santería focuses most of its ritual attention on other subordinate spiritual powers, its practitioners recognize that all come from the supreme source of everything, who is called *Oloddumare*.

We do not need to try and discover where Divinity is, for there is *no place* where Divinity is not. Needless to say, few Pagans are ever troubled by existential *angst* over the supposed meaninglessness of existence. For us existence is sacramental, the world is sacred, and whenever we fail to live up to these insights the failing is ours, and not the world's.

When one believes that God is completely separate from the world, as is indicated with the common God as potter metaphor, then spiritual truth cannot be found *within* the world. Like the shape and plan of a pot, knowledge of God's truth has to come from outside Creation. God must intrude upon the brute material world with a revelation. Transcendental religions derive their authority solely from sacred revelations in which God "injects" His truth into the world for the benefit of humankind. From this perspective, the Bible, Qur'an, Book of Mormon, and similar texts provide the only reliable source of information about God's wishes. Individual spiritual insight is validated only to the extent that agrees with established scripture. A great deal of effort is expended in interpreting these texts, for the validity of the faiths they sustain would be shattered if the core of their texts were shown to be wrong.

When we see the world as one dimension of Divinity, rather than radically separate from It, we naturally look to different sources for legitimate spiritual knowledge and insight. While many Pagan spiritual paths do have traditional texts dealing with various aspects of their faiths, they are less concerned with interpreting scripture than are the world's monotheistic faiths. When Divinity is seen as manifesting within and throughout the world, it is absurd to argue that ultimate authority is within a text, especially one "revealed" in only one language to only one person, people, or tribe. Consequently, to a far greater extent than with transcendental religions, Pagan paths emphasize personal experience of the Divine and with Divinities through ritual, meditation, contemplation, trance, spirit incorporation, vision quests, and the like. Further, Pagan traditions often emphasize the importance of a lineage of practitioners able to train others and who incorporate the experience of countless generations within an ongoing living tradition.

In many Pagan traditions lineage replaces text as the source of spiritual authenticity. Were every priest and shaman in a Pagan tradition to disappear, that particular tradition would be fragmented and its inner meaning largely lost. The lineage will have died out. That is why so little is known today of the spiritual practices of the early Celts. While the beliefs and practices of the Druids were known, and often respected, throughout Classical Antiquity, Druids did not believe in writing down their spiritual practices. When the last Druid died, that variety of Pagan religion died with him.

On the other hand, since from a Pagan perspective Divinity is everywhere, the loss of a particular tradition, however terrible, would only be partial. New traditions would arise as people encountered the Divine in their own lives. For example, when African slaves were transported to Brazil and the Caribbean, their spiritual communities were shattered. Over time they rebuilt these communities, combining what they had preserved of their old practices with the experiences and inspirations that came to them in the New World. Santería, Candomble, Voudon, Obeah, and Umbanda have no exact African equivalent, but share much in common with the religions of the Yoruba, Congo, Fon, and other tribes, some of whose members had been transported as slaves to the New World.

A Pagan tradition's lineage focuses primarily upon lines of transmission through which people receive the right to conduct and teach certain practices. Compared to Christianity, there is not nearly so much focus on shared beliefs. What is at stake instead is mostly shared practices. Even here there is often room for substantial individual variation, once the lineage has been passed on. For example, Crow Sun Dance priest, Larson Medicinehorse, told me that were I, and others, to receive the right from him to conduct sweat lodge ceremonies, we would eventually each "personalize" them, doing them somewhat differently from how we were originally taught, *and that was all right*. In some Wiccan lineages, all that links different groups together are common initiations. Other than the initiations, there is substantial variation among groups.

The nature of spiritual authority thus depends on how we conceive of Divinity. Pagans see Divine teachings and lessons in the cycles of life and death, the phases of the sun and moon, the forces of nature, and indeed potentially in all experience, because that is at least one place where Divinity *is*. For us, the "sacred text" always surrounds us, waiting to be read. We usually do not deny direct Spiritual revelation in a more transcendental sense. Certainly in my experience such revelation happens, but when it does it neither erases nor denies the lessons that we find within the inspirited world of Nature.

Pagans also believe that some parts of the world are particularly powerful spiritually. It is in these special places that temples were built and the gods honored. Today it is often in these special places that vision quests take place, rituals are held, and healings done. Whereas a church becomes sacred because it is consecrated, often a Pagan temple is sacred because it was built in a sacred place. Fundamentally, the land, not the building, or the consecration, makes it special.

Wise practices in harmony with the powers of place and time can transform our minds. From an immanentist perspective the gap between the sacred and the profane is far more within the minds of the practitioners than within the external reality of the world. And when our minds are finally clear and our hearts open, we can grasp the full meaning of lines like the following from Rainer Maria Rilke:

> To praise is the whole thing! A man who can praise
> comes towards us like ore out of the silences
> of rock. His heart, that dies, presses out
> for others a wine that is fresh forever[3]

and from Robinson Jeffers:

> . . . the human sense
> Of beauty is our metaphor of their excellence, their divine
> nature—like dust in a whirlwind, making
> The wild wind visible.
> . . . And we know
> that the enormous invulnerable beauty of things
> Is the face of God, to live gladly in its presence, and die
> without grief or fear knowing it survives us.[4]

## Animism

Spirit is in all things. When Divinity manifests throughout everything, nothing is merely a thing or an object. Everything is an expression of the Divine. As divine emanations, everything is both an expression of the Sacred and a thing in itself, just as the child is both an individual and an expression of its parents. As the Divine is fully conscious and aware, so it follows that consciousness is universal. Everything partakes of awareness in its own way. The purest insight stemming from Pagan experience is to treat all things in an "I-Thou" relationship, with respect and, ideally, with love.[5] That this terminology comes from Jewish theologian Martin Buber underlines that one does not need be a Pagan to arrive at this insight. Nevertheless, it also flows directly from Pagan principles, however else it may also be derived.

At the same time, since we must consume other living beings in order to eat, find shelter, and the like, in its purest sense every aspect of life is sacramental. "Eat, this is my body" does not occur only at Communion. For the Pagan, *every* act of eating can be appropriately considered an act of holy communion. At the core of Pagan experience is a realization that life is sacred, and since maintaining life requires the taking of life, be it plant or animal, so every such act should be done mindfully, and with appreciation.

To conceive of all relations within the world as relationships between things that are in some sense aware is to be an animist. Pagans generally hold this insight to be true not only for animals and plants, but also for many objects which modern Westerners consider purely inanimate. We generally believe stones, mountains, the sky, oceans, and rivers, all to be in some sense aware and deserving of consideration as expressions and manifestations of the sacred. Since nothing is simply an object, everything should be treated with respect.

From such a perspective, everything of which we can conceive, be it a physical object, living being, or even an abstract concept, will generally have a spiritual power that is both the manifestation, and its overseer, or guardian. We can honor these powers, seeking to attain a special and personal relationship with them. We can try to avoid them, or even ignore them, but they exist nonetheless, and life flows more smoothly when they are not antagonized. We are immersed in a web of relationships with conscious entities, even when we are not aware of it.

It may seem to a modern Westerner that such primitive beliefs are unscientific. So long as science described reality in terms of force and inertia, and conceived atoms as mechanical building blocks, such a condescending attitude was justified, at least from within the scientific world-view. But one of science's most valuable characteristics is its ability to discover and purge its errors. With the coming of quantum mechanics and relativity theory, scientists no longer adhere to a mechanistic view of the world. Reality as revealed by quantum mechanics is paradoxical beyond the power of our minds to grasp, and consists ultimately of energy, not solid matter. Such a conception is more hospitable to entertaining the potential universality of awareness than conceiving a world ultimately to be made up of small impenetrable particles obeying mechanical laws of motion.

This is not the place to discuss in any detail the many exciting discoveries in modern physics and elsewhere.[6] All we need do here is note that the discoveries of modern physics are in basic harmony with pantheistic and panentheistic views of the world. No longer can those of us holding to such views be considered unscientific.

Because both are ultimately rooted in experience, Paganism and science are not in fundamental conflict. Pagans simply say that there is more to human experience and the wider world than can be encompassed by scientific methods based upon prediction, measurement, and deductive explanation. If the universe is Divine, then by telling us more about the physical universe, science adds to our appreciation and understanding of Divinity.

At the same time, from our perspective, scientific methods are designed only to investigate certain aspects of reality. Only that part of the world sufficiently invariant to be predicted or sufficiently limited or passive to be subject to experiment or human explanation is amenable to science. Indeed, for the most part, scientific methods deal only with aspects of reality in which the existence of awareness can be ignored. It goes beyond the evidence to argue that reality consists only of what can be produced or revealed by scientific methods.

Today it is no more scientific to deny the reality of animism than to affirm it. Science admits it can neither measure nor explain the nature of consciousness. Given the inability of science to speak meaningfully about consciousness, it is pretty arbitrary for some scientists and philosophers to argue that it exists in one place and not in another. I ask those who are so certain consciousness exists within human beings but not in trees or the wind: please show us your measurements of awareness in a human being that cannot be made with respect to trees or wind. Since science has nothing to say to this query, it has nothing to say about where consciousness may, or may not, be found.

There is an interesting resemblance between a Pagan spiritual tradition and a scientific theory. The vitality of each is determined not so much by its origins as by its utility and fruitfulness. Each is subject to and sustained by the test of practice. In each case allegiance is voluntary. Nevertheless, a spiritual practice is not a scientific theory, and the relationships developed with the spiritual world are not deterministic in the scientific sense. Hence, teaching

Pagan paths is primarily through example, practice, and oral tradition, rather than through texts and controlled experiments.

Lineage and initiation are important because only in this way can the wisdom and experience accumulated across generations be reliably transmitted. This is also analogous to the modern scientific community, where young scientists learn best by working with established scientists, rather than simply studying books and journals. In principle, both are open to new insights because neither claims adequate knowledge of the way things really are.

As with any human institution, however, in a Pagan religion there is a continual tension between tradition and change. Conservative adherents to existing traditions claim they should not be "watered down" by any accretion of new practices, but when closely examined, established traditions are themselves often found to be syncretistic in their origins, being composed of earlier practices combined by innovations inspired by contact with other traditions and peoples. Once they become established, successful new syncretisms become old traditions, their adherents as upset over new deviations as were their earlier critics.

I am not arguing that Pagan spirituality is simply a subjective mix-and-match amalgam. For any Pagan tradition the ultimate test of truth is experience—its capacity to satisfy the spiritual needs of its followers for meaningful contact with the sacred. This "quality control" is not dependent upon human argument, but rather upon human experience with the Divine. If those developing a spiritual practice are in contact with the Sacred, that approach will bear good fruit. If not, it will not. Change is channeled and shaped by this standard of success.

## Polytheism

Thales, an early Greek philosopher, wrote that, "All things are full of gods." Christians believe there is only One. Despite using the same word, "god," the two views cannot possibly be talking about the same thing. Because we have grown up in a Christian-dominated culture where virtually all that we take for granted about religion has a Christian flavor we need to tread carefully in trying to understand what other cultures mean by the word "God."

Polytheism is the most misunderstood characteristic of Pagan religions. Often people believe that polytheism implies denying the existence of a single source from which everything comes. Historically, it rarely has. A great many Pagan faiths acknowledge that there is an ultimate source for all that is, even while acknowledging other spiritual entities and powers with whom it is appropriate to relate. Some Native Americans call this source *Wakan Tanka, Orenda,* or the Great Mystery. Traditional Neopagan Wiccans refer to the *Dryghton,* "the original source of all things."[7] Behind the myriad Gods of Hinduism lies the Atman. Platonism, Neoplatonism, and Stoicism, the dominant philosophical/religious views of Pre-Christian Western Classical civilization, spoke of a One or Ultimate Source, often described as the Good, from which everything came, even the Gods. Yoruba spirituality recognizes Oloddumare as the ultimate divine ground of all that is.

The same way of conceiving the Ultimate even exists in the Christian mystical tradition. Some Christian mystics have termed the ultimate dimension of Divinity the "Godhead," which is beyond personality as distinguished from the more limited conception of "God" as a personality possessing some traits and not others. In Orthodox Christianity the Father within the Trinity is sometimes described as belonging to the realm of the inexpressible, which appears to be a similar conception.

We need to be cautious of whatever term we use in describing what is most Ultimate. Names carry with them the illusion of understanding what is named, but every name is an abstraction from the reality to which it points. In the case of the Most High, what we are attempting to name far exceeds our capacity for understanding.

Some Classical philosophers solved this problem by saying that terms like "the Good" simply described the impact of this Ultimate upon lower beings, but never really described itself. Others, as with many East Indian and some Neoplatonist and Christian thinkers, adopted the approach of "negative theology" whereby they would always say the Ultimate was not expressed by any particular description. My favorite name for the Ultimate is "Wakan Tanka," which is commonly translated as Great Mystery.

I like the incorporation of mystery, and therefore recognition that we are all finite and limited beings, into our conception of the Divine Ultimate. It teaches humility. Someone can say he speaks for God more easily than saying that he speaks for the Great Mystery. I will use a variety of terms in this work, to remind readers that there is no single term which is altogether adequate.

This Divine Source is not personal because any personality is necessarily limited. At best, personality manifests one dimension of excellence in a being. Other personalities manifest other dimensions. We cannot describe the "perfect personality." The same point holds for gender. Being male is no more perfect than being female, and so a perfect Source can be described neither in male nor female terms.

Using Christian terminology to make a Pagan point, the Godhead is beyond the power of human thought and perception to grasp. Upon this observation Pagan and monotheist mystics agree. It follows that any conceptualization of ultimate divinity must be necessarily partial, and a great many conceptualizations are possible.

With this foundation, we can begin to understand polytheism. The Pagan Gods and Goddesses are manifestations from out of the mystery and richness of Wakan Tanka. They are not ultimate deities, but rather are limited expressions of that Ultimate. Alain Danielou, writing about Hindu polytheism, makes a point I believe to hold for Pagan spirituality as a whole:

> Individual monotheistic worshippers . . . usually worship a particular form of their god and not his causal, unmanifest, formless aspect. There is a nearness, a response, in

the formal aspect which is lacking in the abstract conception. But a causal, formless, all-pervading divinity, cause and origin of all forms, cannot be manifest in a particular form and would of necessity be equally the root of all types of form, Divinity can only be reached through its manifestations, and there are as many gods as there are aspects of creation.[8]

In arguing against the early Christians' attacks on Pagan beliefs, the Roman Pagan Celsus pointed out that "where God is concerned it is irrational to avoid worshipping several gods," for the "man who worships several gods, because he worships some one of those which belong to the great God, even by this very action does that which is loved by him." Celsus concludes that, "Anyone who honors and worships all those who belong to God does not hurt him since they are all his."[9]

We are all limited beings. We cannot really grasp what is beyond all limits. Consequently, we can seek to make sense of our relationships with all things by reference to those dimensions of the superhuman which we can grasp to some extent. If we are successful, or blessed with the grace of personal experience, these dimensions, which I term "Gods," will respond to us. From a Pagan perspective monotheism is simply one means by which human beings seek to place themselves into right relationships with that which is most real.

Even within Christianity monotheism is a paradoxical concept, seeming often to combine different deities under a single name. For example, the Christian God in John Calvin's writings is an incredibly severe and utterly transcendental being. However, at least from what I have read of his writing, Calvin's God could hardly be described as a loving deity. Other Christian traditions emphasize God's love and desire to forgive our transgressions. Certainly this is how He has been presented to me by Evangelicals of my acquaintance. These two varieties of Christian monotheism describe what seem to me to be two different deities.

Even monotheists do not always agree about what constitutes monotheism. Some Jews and Muslims argue that Christianity is itself polytheistic. I have spoken with a rabbi who contended the Christian doctrine of the Trinity was polytheistic. I have no desire to enter into debate over the nature of the Trinity, but instead use this example to suggest that the simple dichotomy of religions as monotheistic and polytheistic does not find assent even among monotheists. Some consider others who claim the same label as being in fact polytheists, and the characteristics of the monotheistic God vary depending upon which monotheist we query. This is a natural outgrowth of trying to describe, and therefore limit, That from which all things come, That which is inexpressible and a mystery.

In what today can only be regarded as a supreme irony, many of the most important Pagan critics of Christianity during its early years charged that Christians were *insufficiently* "monotheistic"! The Ultimate, they charged, could not be divided into two or three separate forms, as Christians did when distinguishing between God the Father, Jesus, and the Holy Spirit. Few educated Pagans imagined a Divine plurality as the Highest, and most believed the Gods to which daily rituals were addressed were not the ultimate spiritual powers![10]

The contemporary relevance of these issues has not diminished. For example, the Western monotheistic God has until recently consistently been conceived as male. (The role of femaleness in Divinity is now a hotly contested issue within Christianity.) But it makes no sense to say that maleness is prior to femaleness, since either gender *necessarily* implies the other. This is particularly true of the male gender. There is no such thing as maleness absent femaleness. Ironically, parthenogenesis (giving birth without the involvement of a male) does exist in nature, with the offspring always being female. Even so, it still takes heterosexuality to enable the kinds of animals to have evolved that later became parthenogenic, such as aphids and some lizards.

Classical Pagans were free from these errors. They spoke and wrote movingly of the One from which all comes. But they also recognized the legitimate role played by other aspects of the Divine. As Plotinus explained, "Now every soul is a child of that Father, but in the heavenly bodies there are souls, intellective, holy, much closer to the Supernal Beings than are ours; for how can this Cosmos be a thing cut off from That and how imagine the gods in it to stand apart?"[11] Referring to those who belittled the Gods in supposed devotion to the One, Plotinus wrote "where there is contempt for the Kin of the Supreme the knowledge of the Supreme itself is purely verbal."

Within a culturally completely different tradition, that of the Sun Dance religion of many Native Americans, Thomas Yellowtail makes exactly the same point:

> So, when we pray for help to the Medicine Rock or to Seven Arrows or to any of the different Medicine Fathers, we are praying to them as representatives of Acbadadea, because they are closer to Him than we are, and they represent Him in this world that we live in. So when we pray to the Medicine Fathers, we pray to Acbadadea also.[12]

From Danielou and Plotinus and Yellowtail's perspective, the error of monotheists is not that they worship the "wrong" god, but that their conception of God, being limited, can in no way claim to be the only adequate one. Exclusive claims about the Ultimate are *inevitably* wrong and unjustified.

The Ultimate is infinitely creative. The physical world around us, that which is most readily accessible to our senses, is only one aspect of this divine creativity. There is also a spiritual world populated by a wide variety of beings—nature spirits, elementals, devas, ancestor spirits, deities, and the like. The polytheistic term "Gods" can refer to those entities or forces that are closest to the Source of all, or can encompass a greater or lesser number of these other spiritual forces and entities. Some apparently were once human, some apparently weren't. Sometimes these beings are anthropomorphized, as in the Greco-Roman pantheon or the West African Orixas. Other peoples, such as many Celts and more philosophical Greeks, Romans, and Africans, regarded such anthropomorphizing as naïve.

This conceptual vagueness arises from the nature of the phenomena. It is one source of the confusions that arise even when comparing different Pagan traditions. It takes only a brief acquaintance to demonstrate that there are usually no perfect cross-cultural correlations between the sacred beings of one tradition and those of another. Some can be close. For example, the Yoruba Oshun, their Goddess of beauty, is a rough equivalent of Venus in the Classical pantheon. But their God of war, Ogun, is also the God of metalwork, whereas Mars was not. For the Romans, Vulcan, quite a different deity, was associated with metalwork. For many of the Celts, Brigid, a Goddess of healing, was also the Goddess of metalwork.

Skeptics point to this variety of contrasting and contradictory Gods to argue that Pagan deities are simply social constructs. If Pagan religion were only a philosophy, seeking to impose an intellectual order on nature's diversity, such a criticism would be powerful, but Pagan practice is fundamentally experiential. Its philosophy and theology grow out of experience. In the Afro-Caribbean and Afro-Brazilian traditions Ogun can be invoked, and he will often come. The drum rhythms that call Ogun do not bring Chango or Oshun, Yoruba deities that respond to different rhythms, and are associated with different qualities. Different Gods appear experientially in other traditions as well.[13] Drumming or other specific invocational techniques are not always necessary to bring them, nor do such methods work infallibly. Gods can come quite unbidden, or refuse to come at all.

A *very* tentative way of making sense of the plurality of deities and experiences in Pagan religions is to suggest that awareness as it becomes more individuated becomes more focused on particular qualities. But these qualities all exist within the One. Encountering a deity is in some ways like tuning to a particular frequency that coexists with many others within a full spectrum of awareness. Our awareness also exists within this spectrum. We can therefore tune to such qualities of consciousness through ritual invocation, or other means, and they in turn can tune into us, which we experience as Divine revelation and insight. Unlike a radio or television station, such tuning in can create a reciprocal relationship.

Once we experientially encounter Divinity, we try better to comprehend it. In doing so we incorporate the context of the encounter and our own social and psychological framework. In addition, because the experience is of the superhuman, it is impossible to avoid metaphor when describing such experiences, as when I describe an encounter with a Wiccan Goddess in chapter 3.

Within this framework of interpretation Divinity responds to us, establishing a two-way relationship. While deities evolve with changing human understanding, deities themselves also can and do act to change that understanding. A God-form will always be associated with a particular cultural context, but still not be reducible to it. Because the Divine is more than we can conceive, any encounter will open outward in ways we cannot foresee.

Additionally, if the view of Ultimate Divinity I am presenting is accurate, and it permeates everywhere, then *any* bounded thing, from human being to tree to rock to wind to concept, is only partially isolated. It is also a manifestation of the sacred, and possesses a spiritual aspect. Perhaps this is why even our intellectual concepts often end up revealing implications that go well beyond our explicit knowledge or deliberate intent. They are, in fact, not simply ours.

This way of viewing the matter explains why conscious preparation and focused intent are such vital concepts in experiential spiritual traditions. It also explains why the content of our minds, our thoughts and feelings are considered of far more than personal significance. They are *not* simply confined within our skulls, but link to other forces, other frequencies, in ways that are spiritually important.

Whatever the ultimate explanation of the nature of their reality, polytheistic religions generally recognize a wide variety of spiritual beings, some well disposed towards human beings, some neutral, and some ill disposed. Thus, just as within the material world, within the spiritual world we are immersed in a community of relationships. A wise person strives to be a good and respectful member of that community, just as he or she strives to be a good and respectful member of the material community.

Perhaps at this point some readers will wonder about the common Christian charge that Pagans practice "idolatry." Nothing so captures the uninformed mind when thinking of Pagan religions as the memory of some Hollywood epic in which hundreds of scantily clad dancers cavort wantonly around some large, and usually monstrous, idol before which someone, usually the film's heroine, is to be offered up in bloody sacrifice. While, just as within the monotheistic faiths, there are instances of debased practices claiming membership in Pagan spirituality, such popular images are deeply misleading and distressing.

No Pagan believes that the Godhead dwells in an idol in any special way. Only rarely do they believe that *any* spiritual entity does. Many do believe that certain types of spirits are closely associated with certain things or places, perhaps in the sense that our soul is associated with our body, or in the sense that a musician's heart can be manifest in his music, but this can hardly be equated with confusing God with a physical object. To quote again from Celsus, who was answering the Christian charge of idolatry, "Who but an utter infant imagines that these things are gods, and not votive offerings and images of Gods?"[14] Statues and symbols of Pagan gods are no more confused by Pagans with the Gods themselves than is a statue of Jesus or a cross confused with Jesus Himself.

Anything that serves to guide our worship can be used badly, and thereby inhibit our spiritual comprehension. Any tool, symbol, text, image, name, or sacred object can be focused upon and elevated to the point of obscuring the deity it is supposed in some way to represent. In this sense idolatry is a danger in *every* spiritual practice.

Sometimes we can focus light on complex topics by looking at how they are treated in related traditions. In a meeting with the Dalai Lama, Jewish Rabbi Zalman Schachter made some comments that I think will be helpful to Christians trying to understand the character of polytheism. He, however, was describing angels from the perspective of Jewish mysticism and the Kabbalah.

> When we speak of angels . . . we mean by that beings of such large consciousness . . . that if an angel's consciousness were to flow into my head right now, it would be too much for me. . . . There are all kinds of angels. So that higher and higher for instance, we think each nation has an angel. . . . There are angels for rewarding people and for imparting wisdom and angels also for punishing and for testing. This is in our tradition. . . . They say not a blade of grass grows without an angel saying, "Grow, grow, grow". Angels are pushing fruit to ripen. So they speak of all kinds of beings, but when we use the word angel, that is only human speech because the number and variety of these beings is beyond being able to count. . . .[15]

Angels as described in the traditional mystical Jewish view have a great deal in common with many Pagan conceptions of Deities. In both cases they are innumerable. In both cases they are connected with specific forces of nature, people, groups, and concepts. In both cases they are emanations or creations of the Most High. To a remarkable extent, the differences between Jewish angels and at least a great many Pagan deities appear to be purely verbal. The chief substantive difference appears to be that Pagan spiritual practice has less compunction about dealing with them directly. Never, it seems to me, has so much confusion grown out of what in many cases are simply semantic differences.

# The Eternal Present

Today's monotheistic faiths both hold and are dependent upon a linear view of time. It is an essential part of their cosmology that the world was created, exists now, and will end some time in the future, all as part of some overall plan of salvation by a Creator-god. This monotheistic conception of time is much like the sequence of events in a novel. There is a single, unifying story behind all things. It is necessary for faiths holding this view that past events be demonstrably part of this overall pattern. Thus, it is essential to most Christian faith to assert that Christ did indeed exist; that He was crucified, and that He did rise from the dead, all as concrete historical fact.

Few Pagan traditions have such a linear view of time. Instead, Pagans tend to view time in terms of a series of repeating cycles or spirals. One age follows another; death is followed by rebirth as spring follows winter. The sun, moon, and heavens repeat their cycles regularly. Different Pagan religions may emphasize different cycles. Agricultural cultures are acutely aware of seasonal cycles relevant to successful planting and harvesting. Hunting cultures focus on the cycles of scarcity and abundance most relevant to their sustenance. Practitioners of Yoruba spirituality from tropical Africa will emphasize different manifestations of this insight than will European Pagans living with a very different cycle of seasons.

In this Pagan conception of time, the historicity of events is less important than their mythic significance. For example, the Classical Pagan myth of Persephone, who goes to the underworld and returns ever after, plays a different role than does the Christian story of the divine son who was killed and resurrected, although both embody themes of death and resurrection. For most Christians, Christianity depends upon the actual historicity of Jesus' personal death and resurrection. For Pagans, the loss and return of Persephone is manifest every year, first with the dying at fall, and then the arrival of spring when the green plants return to the earth and the days grow longer. Persephone's departure and return is not an historical event. She exemplifies an eternal truth, existing in what mythologists call the "Eternal Present."

Mythology is not primitive science, nor is it the meaning *of* life. It serves quite different purposes. Pagan mythology illuminates the meaning *in* life. Permeated by Spirit, all life carries meanings below the immediate surface. Myth explicates these meanings. For Pagans, life is more a poem than a novel. Its living is more an art than a technique.

With this insight we can address a common misunderstanding of Pagan as contrasted with Christian conceptions of time. We frequently hear that Western civilization's belief in progress is due to its Christian heritage. Christianity's linear and historical view of the world holds open the prospect of improvement in a way that the Pagan cyclical view allegedly does not. This contention idea of progress was very well-known in the Pagan West. As early as the end of the sixth century B.C., the Greek Xenophanes observed that, "The gods did not reveal to men all things in the beginning, but, in the course of time, by searching, they came to find better." Aristotle noted that, "Those who are now renowned have taken over as if in a relay race (from hand to hand, relieving one another) from many predecessors who on their part progress, and thus have themselves made possible progress." The Roman Pagan Seneca wrote in the first century A.D. that, "The time will come when mental acumen and prolonged study will bring to light what is now hidden. . . . The time will come when our successors will wonder how we could have been so ignorant of things so obvious." These examples show beyond doubt that the idea of progress for societies as well as individuals is scarcely unique to Christian civilization in the West.[16]

At the same time Christian civilization is by no means universally associated with Western conceptions of progress. Byzantine civilization never developed that frame of mind and neither did other Orthodox cultures. Nor is Christian Ethiopia very impressive evidence that the internal logic of Scripture teaches, let alone uniquely, that we can indefinitely better our situation.

*The West is not simply Christian.* That this term is used so often to describe our culture is simply another instance of the victors writing the history books. I want to be fair here. Separating the Christian (and Jewish) strands in our heritage from the Pagan ones is very difficult. Furthermore, the Christian part of our heritage is itself quite varied in its perspectives on the role of progress and history in human life. Certainly the Christian Middle Ages, while hardly the abysmal pit of ignorance implied in the term "Dark Ages," did not give much credence to the idea of progress. That was to come only with the Renaissance and Enlightenment, and in both these periods the initial inspiration for the idea was not Christian.

From the Renaissance to the Enlightenment, the rise of Western modernity is vividly associated with the extraordinary revival of interest in and admiration for Classical Pagan culture and philosophy (but not usually religious practice), as with the widespread admiration for Cicero, Seneca, and other Classical Pagans, by men such as Montaigne, Voltaire, Montesquieu, Hume, and Adam Smith. America's founders also thought highly of Classical thinkers. Their opinion symbolized by the use by many educated Americans of Classical names as pen names. Alexander Hamilton, James Madison, and John Jay wrote as "Publius" to defend the proposed Constitution in the brilliant *Federalist.*

Indeed, the underlying philosophy of the U.S. Constitution itself is rooted in a concept of natural law which Montesquieu traced to the Classical Pagan Plutarch's conception of God's role in the universe—as a source of reliable law rather than frequently intervening from outside by means of miracles.[17] The association of Classical Civilization with the rise of much that we most treasure about Western modernity is undeniable. Western modernity is at least as indebted to Classical Pagan civilization as it is to Christianity.

Having said as much, there *is* a difference between a Christian and a Pagan outlook on the role of progress and of cycles. Because Pagans experience the Divine in the world around us, and this world is characterized by cyclic change, Pagan spirituality *emphasizes* the world's cyclical character. Human beings can progress, both individually and as societies, but at the deepest level these recurring divine patterns continue to manifest. We progress within a divine framework which encompasses change but is not fundamentally altered by it. These eternal patterns are signs of an underlying sacredness. Consequently they, and the world which manifests them, are not experienced as fundamentally flawed and needing redemption. Therefore, progress in no sense requires devaluing the present. Indeed, from this perspective genuine progress requires honoring and respecting the present.

When the intrinsic meaning in the world is devalued and we focus *only* on progress, the value of the present is measured solely by how it contributes to the future. Even what is good in the present is expected to be surpassed. Everything is compared with a not-yet-existent future, and found wanting. The cult of youth denigrates the elderly because the young were born "further along" the progressive road. This is a myopic overemphasis on progress and upon the allegedly inferior nature of the present compared with the future. My point is not that progress is bad, but that a Pagan view emphasizes that the present is a good in itself. Let us progress—but let us also honor the time and the place where we are now.

Disparaging the present in the name of the future is, I believe, a powerful contributing factor to the millennial utopianism that has afflicted the West, and led to so much suffering and bloodshed. The first violent Western revolution to seek to remake humankind was that of the English Puritans. The most radically utopian of Enlightenment and post-Enlightenment philosophers, from advocates of the French Revolution to modern communists, often thought they were writing in complete opposition to the Church. Ironically, while classical writers helped free them from unthinking acceptance of religious domination, their own habits of thought were still deeply influenced by their Christian upbringing. Their belief in the complete overthrow of the old order, to be followed by a time of milk and honey, is often a secularization of

Christian apocalyptic beliefs in Armageddon and the Second Coming. This sort of thinking was largely absent in Pagan antiquity.

Today's lack of concern for the environment is another example of disparaging what exists in the name of a promised future. Indeed, the strongest reason many people can give for destroying forests, rivers, canyons, and ecologies is, "You can't stop progress." *But what kind of progress?* That vital question is rarely asked, and the value of the present is never acknowledged.

When Classical Pagan philosophers discussed the Godhead underlying the cyclic world, they often described it as changeless. An alternative conception sees it as eternally creative, but not in the sense that later creations are better or worse than earlier ones. They are simply different. As the Wiccan chant goes, "She changes everything She touches, and everything She touches changes."[18] From either perspective, progress is simply one dimension within a greater whole which denies the claim of any part, including the future, to ultimate value. So I would contend that the Pagan idea of the world as *already* sacralized, *already* worthy of respect and admiration, and *already* a good home for human beings is an important corrective for a modern conceit run rampant.

The Pagan emphasis on the significance of recurring patterns leads most to recognize some form of reincarnation in their beliefs regarding the afterlife. Like everything else, human life is a cycle of birth, death, and rebirth. Unlike at least some schools of Buddhist thought, however, as a rule, most Pagans do not see this endless cycle as a problem to be overcome, but rather a process within which to harmonize.[19]

This point can be expanded upon. Since everything exists within the context of the Sacred, nothing in itself is truly complete. Not being complete, nothing can be without change, for all things exist and are maintained by virtue of their relationships, and all relationships are subject to change. This change, however, takes place within that ultimate context which, when we experience it, is always described in terms of the Good, Perfect Love, and the like. Change in this respect is like the shifting light of a sunset or dawn, where new beauty come from movement, rather than seeing change as a sign of universal decay and decline.

This insight is often reflected in Pagan rituals and symbols. For example, the Neopagan "wheel of the year" emphasizes that there is an eternal cycle of birth, growth, maturity, decline, and death. The phases of the year symbolize this process, repeating itself over and over again. The focus in many Pagan perspectives is not to get off this wheel, or abolish it, but to harmonize with it.

The Pagan view of cyclic time leads us to focusing more on process than upon goal, upon the road traveled rather than to where it may end, upon continuity rather than upon point of origin. True wisdom comes from traveling well, not from traveling quickly.

## Evil and Dualism

Along with its beauty, our world is characterized by enormous suffering. Every person suffers, and some delight in harming others, or worse. Often suffering appears unrelated to whether the victim did anything to deserve it. Spirituality helps us cope with suffering, and here is a deep mystery indeed. Encountering the most inclusive dimension of divinity always brings with it experiences of beauty, love, harmony, and divine order. So why are our daily lives characterized by so much pain and suffering? Why do we so rarely manifest the love that characterizes the Divine? Most of us, most of the time, are not consciously surrounded by divine epiphany. If these transcendent experiences disclose the nature of divinity, why are we cut off from experiencing it all the time? Why do we suffer? Why do we cause others to suffer?

The world's Pagan traditions offer a variety of answers. However, without exception, and in marked contrast to traditions emphasizing a single transcendent creator, they do not have a place for a Satan, or Devil, nor do they generally see suffering as evidence of something being fundamentally awry within the world. They do not see the world as primarily characterized by a titanic struggle between good and evil. Interpretations such as these seem confined to monotheistic traditions, and for good reason.

When a perfectly good, omnipotent, and omniscient divinity creates a world that is fundamentally its artifact, there would seem to be no room for suffering. Since suffering exists in abundance, it must come from somewhere else. Within monotheistic traditions two main perspectives have dominated. The Judeo-Christian-Islamic view is that at one time a divine subordinate rebelled against God, and this rebellion hatched all the subsequent suffering that has taken place in the world. An alternative Gnostic belief was that the God who created the world, with all its suffering, was inferior to a more perfect God who was radically separate from the world. From the Gnostic perspective, people were spirits trapped in flesh by this evil god, and salvation required somehow escaping from fleshly form and from rebirth. The implication of such a view is that we are *already* trapped in hell. Either way, evil was seen as radically distinct from the ultimate God, and in implacable opposition to Him. The most extreme form of this view is theological dualism, wherein the two principles of good and evil are of virtually the same power, eternally battling one another. Our spiritual task is choosing sides.

Pagan spirituality denies that there is a fundamental evil principle or force at work in the universe. There are spiritual forces well worth avoiding, to be sure. Some are quite terrifying, or even lethal, but none are so central to the character of spiritual reality as the Christian Satan. No force equivalent to Satan stands in fundamental antagonism to the highest spiritual reality. Because of the central importance of this issue, I shall return to this important subject in later chapters.

ENDNOTES

1. I refer to "God" in masculine terms when speaking of the Jewish, Christian, and Muslim conception of Divinity. I will use the more generic "Divinity" and similar terms to refer to ultimate spiritual reality as a concept.

2. Michael Oren Fitzgerald, *Yellowtail: Crow Medicine Man and Sun Dance Chief, An Autobiography as told to Michael Oren Fitzgerald* (Norman, Okla.: University of Oklahoma, 1991), p. 102.

3. Rainer Maria Rilke, *Selected Poems of Rainer Maria Rilke: A Translation from the German and Commentary by Robert Bly* (New York: Harper and Row, 1981), p. 207.

4. These lines of Robinson Jeffers are taken from *Not Man Apart: Lines From Robinson Jeffers, Photographs of the Big Sur Coast,* David Brower, ed. (New York: Sierra Club and Ballatine Books, 1965), pp. 46, 52.

5. Indeed, the vital role of love, or agape seems to be a common feature of all religions. See Peggy Starkey, "Agape: A Christian Criterion for Truth in the Other World Religions," *International Review of Mission,* vol. LXXIV, No. 296, October, 1985, as well as Martin Buber, *I and Thou,* trans. by Walter Kaufmann (New York: Charles Scribner's Sons, 1970).

6. A vigorous and fascinating literature has arisen presenting in lay terms what appear to be the deepest implications of modern science. I suggest starting with Nick Herbert, *Quantum Reality: Beyond the New Physics* (New York: Anchor, 1985). Herbert discusses the major interpretations.

   Physics is not the only area of modern science that appears compatible with an animist perspective. See also Ilya Prigogine and Isabel Stengers, *Order Out of Chaos: Man's New Dialogue With Nature* (New York: Bantam, 1984), and Paul Davies, *The Cosmic Blueprint: New Discoveries in Nature's Creative Ability to Order the Universe* (New York: Simon and Schuster, 1988). All the authors referred to in this note are practicing scientists. I do not suggest, however, that they are also animists!

7. As named in the "Blessing Prayer" of the Gardnerian Tradition of modern Witchcraft.

8. Alain Danielou, *The Gods of India* (New York: Inner Traditions International, 1985), p. 9. Those monotheists who focus on a transcendent deity, and who have abandoned the anthropomorphizations which characterize lay practice, are still subject to Danielou's point. They focus only on one aspect of deity.

9. Celsus is quoted in Robert L. Wilken, *The Christians as the Romans Saw Them* (New Haven: Yale University Press, 1984), p. 118.

10. Wilken, pp. 105–8.

11. Plotinus, *The Enneads,* Stephen MacKenna, trans., John Dillon abr. (London: Penguin, 1991), p. 128. While the word "Father" appears in this quote, in fact Plotinus held the Supreme Being to be beyond any particularity, such as gender.

12. Fitzgerald, op. cit., p. 101.

13. Although its psychological reductionism is off the mark and its title off putting, E. R. Dodds' *The Greeks and the Irrational* is an excellent study of this

experiential dimension in Greek religion (Berkeley: University of California Press, 1951).

14. Celsus, op. cit., p. 119.
15. Roger Kamenetz, *The Jew in the Lotus* (San Francisco: Harper Collins, 1994), pp. 78–80.
16. See Robert Nisbet, *History of the Idea of Progress*, (New York: Basic Books, 1980), pp. 10–46.
17. See Thomas L. Pangle, "The Philosophic Understandings of Human Nature Informing the Constitution," *Confronting the Constitution*, Alan Bloom, ed. (Washington, D.C.: American Enterprise Institute Press, 1990), p. 25. Pangle obviously doesn't like this Pagan foundation, which makes his recognition of it all the more significant.
18. This chant may be found in Starhawk, *The Spiral Dance* (New York: Harper and Row, 1979), p. 89.
19. Thich Nhat Hanh, *Living Buddha, Living Christ* (New York: Riverside Books, 1995), p. 133.

# Spirit and Humanity in
# Pagan Religion

There is a fascinating relationship between our beliefs about the nature of reality and how we act. This observation is as true of our spiritual as of our more secular beliefs. Different spiritual communities conceive of men and women as being in different relationships with the sacred. These differences are reflected in peoples' practices.

I do not mean to suggest that our beliefs are easily and clearly reflected in our practices. Human beings are too complex for such simple correlations. Each of us only imperfectly practices our deepest beliefs. Often we fall short. Our actions and our communities reflect our weaknesses as well as our strengths. In every spiritual community, Christian, Pagan, and otherwise, there are those who for reasons of anger, ambition, or fear fall far below the values of their traditions.

Nevertheless, beliefs do matter. They help determine our actions, and the actions of others. They shape our societies, and help us see some evils better than others. Growing up as we have within a Christian civilization, we will not understand Pagan practices using only the conceptions of spiritual action with which we are familiar.

For a modern Westerner, Pagan spirituality differs in three major ways from traditional Christian beliefs, ways reflected in our Pagan and Christian societies. These distinctions are:

1. Religious pluralism, that is, Pagans recognize and respect many spiritual paths
2. Emphasizing harmony rather than salvation as the primary religious focus for women and men
3. Greater respect for personal experience rather than faith or others' experience as a valid criterion for spiritual truth

## Religious Pluralism

Most Americans have come to associate religion with claims to exclusivity, and active missionary work, but these images are largely characteristic only of Christianity and Islam. With Islam, Christianity is a proselytizing religion. Christians traditionally believed that only *their own understanding* of God is correct, and correct for all the peoples of the world. Islam, the other major Abrahamic religion, makes similar exclusive claims and, like Christianity, seeks to spread its faith. Their common ancestor, Judaism, generally does not seek converts, but as a rule its orthodox adherents are equally certain theirs is the only really true faith.

Most other religions do not seek converts or hold to exclusive views of spiritual reality. This is true of almost all Pagan religions. Some, particularly many practices generally lumped together under the label Hinduism, often argue that you cannot really convert to their faith at all. You are either born into it or you aren't.[1] It is all a matter of karma. Currently traditional Native Americans are vigorously debating among themselves the propriety of teaching their spiritual practices to European Americans who increasingly seek them out. Among Pagan religions people usually have to go to some trouble in seeking out teachers in order to learn and practice these faiths in any depth. This is certainly the case with Wicca, where refusal to proselytize is an all but universal central tenet.

The aversion of nearly all Pagans to the imposition of their faith on others is grounded in their pan(en)theistic conception of the world. If Divinity is everywhere, manifesting in countless ways, it makes little sense to argue that one particular spiritual path is somehow better than the other religions. Nature exults in breathtaking individuality and diversity. From snowflakes to people, nothing is simply a duplicate of something else. Even fundamental particles can change into one another and are not entirely predictable. If Nature teaches us anything at all about the intentions of the Divine, it is that variety and unpredictability are treasured.

How could *any* Pagan, basing his conception of his Gods in the geography, seasons, and culture of, for instance, the Mediterranean, insist that his or her Gods were the only correct Gods for brethren living in the Canadian arctic or the Amazon rain forest? The more a thoughtful Pagan learns about the world, the larger his or her conception of Divinity grows and the wider the range of manifestations of the Divine become acceptable. This is so even though that person may cleave to a particular path in his or her own spiritual practice.

The response of most Pagan societies to encountering new Gods has been either to incorporate them into their existing pantheon ("Oh, your Jesus must be another avatar of our Vishnu, just like Krishna and Rama are"), or to find equivalencies between the new and old deities ("I see, your Thor is the Norse manifestation of our god Mars"). Consequently, conflict between Pagan societies has rarely been based upon religious disagreements.

Today many Wiccans consider all female deities to be different aspects of the Goddess, just as all male deities are aspects of the male God, mirroring beliefs of earlier devotees of Isis and other Goddesses whose followers made universal claims during Classical times. Yet from Classical times to the present, such universalistic conceptions have not denied the legitimacy of other ways of honoring the universal Goddess. For example, Apuleius in *The Golden Ass*, quotes Isis as saying:

> I, the natural mother of all life, the mistress of the elements, the first child of time, the supreme divinity, the queen of those in hell, the first among those in heaven, the uniform manifestation of all gods and goddesses . . .

I whose single godhead is venerated all over the earth under manifold forms, varying rites, and changing names. . . . But those who are enlightened by the earliest rays of that divinity the sun, the Ethiopians, the Arii, and the Egyptians who excel in antique lore, all worship me with their ancestral ceremonies and call me by my true name, Queen Isis.[2]

For followers of Isis, their deity prefers this name over others, but does not turn Her back on those using other names, or condemn their error. As to whether Apuleius understood Her correctly as preferring that name, the question can only be answered experientially.

Other Wiccans believe that individual deities are distinct, with some geographically situated, others overseeing different qualities and dimensions of life. In my case, a particular Goddess is overwhelmingly associated with my experience of Wiccan ritual, but my experience of Her is different from Goddesses I have experienced in other Pagan traditions, and also seems distinct from other female deities that in my experience are less frequently invoked within traditional Wiccan rituals. Contrasts among deities can be as striking as the similarities.

In addition, the rise of universalistic Pagan claims about Goddesses, such as this late Classical view of Isis, appears strongly associated with a growing popular rejection of the goodness of the physical world and a corresponding search for salvation, a way out of widespread misery. The lives of many people during Hellenistic times were not enviable. The Roman Empire was frequently oppressive and often the land itself was declining in fertility due to prolonged warfare and poor farming practices. Poverty and disease were widespread. It seemed to many as if a general decline in all things had set in.

If people think the world is deeply flawed, they will look for a way out. If there is such a way, it must not be obvious, or it would already have been taken. In a Pagan context this view sometimes took the form of claiming to know the one best way to honor the Supreme Goddess, although as the passage indicated, in Her eyes She was legitimately, if not always competently, honored by other names and in other ways.[3]

Most Pagans will *prefer* the particular God-forms to which they are accustomed over those of another culture, but rarely deny the validity of other people's Gods. Speaking for myself, perhaps the situation with respect to Divine Femaleness and Maleness is analogous to that which exists with respect to the Source of All with its polytheistic implications. Deities, like everything else including ourselves, are manifestations, or emanations, from the ultimate Source of All. The closer to that Source, the more universal their qualities. Greater distance is accompanied by greater individuality. Whatever the ultimate reality of their relationships to one another, there is no sense in any Pagan tradition that only their Gods and Goddesses are valid deities for worship.

By contrast, monotheistic faiths, believing that they possess the one true religion, have all too often adopted a "convert or die" attitude toward Pagan faiths. Yet with few exceptions Pagan traditions have generally been accommodating toward monotheistic ones. This has led some monotheists to accuse the Pagan approach of being either opportunistic or simple-minded and illogical. I hope the previous arguments have demonstrated instead that our openness to other Gods and forms of worship is a direct outgrowth of our own deepest spiritual insights.

## Persecution of Christians

The counter example to Pagan tolerance that is most frequently cited is the Roman persecution of the early Christians. While I neither defend nor condone the atrocious actions of those emperors and their supporters, Christians were never persecuted for being monotheists. The Roman government's politicized view of religion saw their gods as intimately involved in the affairs of the state and in the well-being of the country. The Christians denied that these Gods existed (which is why early Christians were called "atheists" by Roman writers). They refused to swear oaths of loyalty to the state in their name, and refused to make offering to the emperor's *genius* or spirit, which was considered different from the living Emperor himself.

From the perspective of those times, what the Christians did seemed disrespectful and even subversive. For a rough contemporary equivalent, imagine the reaction of today's patriotic Christians to someone who desecrated the flag, spat upon the Bible, and argued the Founding Fathers and all existing churches were inspired by absolute evil. I think such a person would sorely test their tolerance—and many would fail the test.

To the Roman authorities, early Christian attitudes and behavior appeared dangerously treasonous and subversive. This was particularly the case because Christians proselytized among the general population of Roman citizens, creating an ever larger group of people whose loyalty to the imperial authorities was suspect. Consequently they were attacking support for the deities whose good favor upheld the success and prosperity of Rome.

Roman persecution of the Christians is one of the few examples of religious intolerance within Pagan societies. For the persecutors, the problem was not so much that Christians only worshipped one God as supreme, for many Pagans did the same. It was the rejection of the Deities of that community and place. Since Pagans of the time believed the well-being of the community depended upon honoring its Deities; such activity was a direct assault upon the community itself.

Biblically, this belief was analogous to the Old Testament's God threatening Israel if He was not obeyed. According to the prophets He continually made such threats. Christians might answer, yes, and he fulfilled those threats, but this answer cuts both ways. Pagans retorted that only after Romans abandoned their protective Gods, and its government became predominately Christian, was Rome invaded and pillaged.

In Pagan societies the nature of the obedience the Gods required was much less demanding than that of ancient Israel, and they never forbade honoring other Deities. Often Roman magistrates would beg accused Christians to at least go through the motions required by Roman law. They did not care what the accused really believed. The fundamental reasons for Roman persecution of the early Christians were more political than religious in the modern sense. The best evidence that my argument is true was Rome's treatment of Jews within the Empire.

Roman Jews also refused to make offerings to the Emperor's spirit. They were *not* persecuted. In fact, they were officially exempted from making such sacrifices. As official tolerance of Judaism demonstrated, strict monotheism as such was not in any sense a crime in Pagan Rome.

Roman toleration of Judaism was not unique among Pagan societies. Some Jews entered India as refugees in A.D. 70, and were never persecuted in the nearly 2,000 years which followed. A similar story prevailed in ancient China, except that Chinese toleration was so great, and opportunities to the community open enough, that many Jews took the imperial exams, and entered into the government. Eventually the community was completely assimilated. Pagan Rome, India, and China offered more toleration for their Jewish residents than did Christian Europe until the last fifty years of Christianity's 2,000-year history.

As early Christianity grew in adherents, but still lacked the political power to compel a particular understanding of Scripture, it fragmented into Arians, Catholics, Marcionites, and many other sects. Some factions often formed angry mobs which frequently harassed other Christian factions. It was not uncommon for such mobs, sometimes inspired or even led by bishops, to attack and lynch one another in the streets. Many Roman laws later deemed "oppressive" by Christian historians were in fact attempts to restore order and make the streets safe to walk.

Indeed, the co-Emperors Licinus and Constantine (while Constantine was still a sun-worshipper and before he became a Christian and sole emperor), recognizing the growing religious diversity in the Empire and the tensions it could create, enacted the following edict in February A.D. 313:

We resolve to grant Christians and all other men freedom to observe whatever religion they think fit, so that
the divinity, who has his abode in heaven, be propitious
and benevolent as well for us as for any of those living
under our rule. It seems to us a very good and very reasonable system to refuse to none of our subjects,
whether a Christian or a follower of some other cult,
the right to observe the religion that suits him best . . .
We leave Christians the fullest and most absolute freedom to celebrate their cult; and as we grant Christians
that right . . . other people also must enjoy it. It is fit for
the era we live in, it suits the peace which benefits the
Empire, that full freedom be given to all our subjects to
worship the god they elected, and that no cult be deprived of due honors.[4]

By contrast, the actions of the early Church to suppress Paganism were specifically directed to stamping out by any means the
last vestiges of the old faiths. Going through the motions was
never enough.[5] Nor did things get any easier for those suspected of
heresy or unorthodoxy, even after the Church had triumphed.

## Harmony and Salvation

Speaking broadly, a great divide separates two distinct approaches to spirituality. The one that most of us take for granted sees
spirituality as primarily a vehicle for salvation. Life is a vale of
tears, a time of trial, or a place of suffering. We are trapped, endangered, or otherwise poorly served by the world, and need salvation
from it. While hardly unique to Christian, or even monotheistic spirituality, this is the basic theological understanding most religious
Americans have of our relationship to the spiritual.

Yet such a perspective is by no means the only one possible.
Other spiritual teachings emphasize attaining harmony within
the world, not salvation from it. When the Divine is conceived in

panentheistic terms this perspective arises naturally, for the world is seen as permeated by the Sacred. It therefore cannot be fundamentally fallen.

From such a perspective our actions, and not our reality, are the major source of our separation from the Sacred. This view characterizes spiritual traditions associated with American Indians, Africans, Japanese Shinto, Taoism, all shamanically rooted practices, and contemporary Neopaganism, including Wicca. When our actions are brought into complete harmony with reality our spiritual task is done.

The Pagan Greeks called nature *kosmos*. Their word is obviously the ancestor to our "cosmos," but the meanings are significantly different. "Cosmos" is usually defined as "world order," but for the Pagan Greeks order included beauty. According to Peter Manchester, for the Greeks, "The orderliness of nature is not just law-like but beautiful, not just beautiful but powerful, not just powerful but living. The great cosmentic array of things is not a fact but a Presence."[6] This profound sense of the world's order and beauty is a continual theme in almost all Pagan experience. It is as present in the beliefs of the traditional Navajo as in the Classical Greeks.

I will have much more to say about this focus on harmony instead of salvation later, when I deal with specific Christian criticisms of Wiccan religion. For now I will simply use this difference in emphasis to lead into our final point of distinction: the very different roles played by faith and experience within Pagan and Christian spirituality.

## Emphasis upon Experience Rather than Faith

The emphasis upon harmony rather than salvation that differentiates so many Pagan traditions from Christianity, and from religious monotheism in general, leads to a final distinction. Christianity has always been characterized by its central emphasis upon faith. Faith is a difficult concept to treat briefly, but it usually means placing confidence in a religious teaching, even in the absence of personal experience that it is true. Usually Christians are asked to have faith in the Resurrection, the Virgin Birth, and more generally, faith in Jesus and in God. The teachings in which Christians are to have faith are written down in Scripture, where they were first revealed to someone else.

Personal experience within most Christian traditions is always subordinated to Scripture. Any experience that does not appear to verify a scriptural point is suspected as demonically inspired. Historically, this elevation of the authority of the written word led many Christian denominations to distrust spontaneous expressions of Spirit during their services, or elsewhere in the lives of believers.

Obviously, within a tradition as rich and old as Christianity there are exceptions to this pattern. Ecstatics and mystics such as Theresa of Avila, Meister Eckhart, and Hildegard von Bingen had powerful and transformative personal experiences of Divinity. In different ways, modern Pentecostals and Charismatics frequently experience powerful manifestations of Spirit, but historically these practices have been on the outer fringe of the larger Christian community. Perhaps the most common personal spiritual encounter in Christianity is the conversion experience, where contact with the Holy Spirit leads a person to Jesus. Powerful as these can be, they are still subordinated to Scripture. In Christianity as a revealed religion, the test of personal experience is its conformity to scriptural understanding. Faith in scripture is supposed to trump any personal experience within the Christian community.

Pagan traditions usually differ profoundly in this regard. Because Spirit is immanent, it remains accessible in ways a purely transcendent Deity can never be. Further, emphasis upon harmony rather than salvation leads to a much stronger emphasis on spiritual transformation or connection in this life rather than bliss in the next. Many Pagans expect to have some direct experiential contact with at least some Deities, and expect that this contact pay off in this life through greater harmony, healing, and inner peace. More superficial Pagan approaches expect pay-offs in material terms, but this misunderstanding is equally prevalent in Christian communities.

At this point many Christians will say that Christian practice also leads to greater harmony, healing, and peace. No doubt this is often true, but when we go through those times when these benefits appear absent, or withdrawn, in the Christian context we are enjoined to have faith in God as revealed through Scripture. Pagans also go through these dark nights of the soul. But at least in my case, when that happens what sustains me is memory of personal spiritual experience, combined with a community of teaching that says these periods of suffering are ultimately transformative for the good. And my case is hardly unique. My faith is with an experience that I have personally had. By contrast, for many Christians, faith is in experiences other people have had, and written down.

This is why one issue frequently discussed among Christians, how to prove God's existence, has never been of interest to me or many other Pagans. That it historically has been an important part of Christian theology suggests to me that many Christians never had a powerful experience of the Divine, whether in or out of harmony with Scripture. After all, once someone has experienced the superhuman two things are usually settled for good. One is its existence. The other is that, precisely because the experience is of the *super* human, there is no reason to take too seriously human attempts to prove its existence.

Pagan traditions have developed a wide variety of practices to facilitate contact with Divinities. Shamanic journeying, trance drumming where Deities enter into the bodies of their devotees, drawing down the moon in a Wiccan Circle, vision quests, fasting, and many other means as well all encourage such experiences, although they by no means guarantee them, but for many of us they do work. In addition, occasionally a Deity or Spirit will manifest itself without any preparatory work, or even expectation, on the recipient's part. The most important spiritual experiences are often the least expected. That has been the case with me.

I believe that the common Christian concern with proving God's existence may be connected with a relative dearth of spiritual experience within the community. If so, I suspect this relative absence is brought about, at least in part, by a refusal to encourage contact with intermediate levels of Spirit, whether they are called Gods or angels. If one believes the world is fallen, filled with evil, a snare for the unwary, and so forth, cultivating an awareness of spiritual entities, or even simply being open to their presence, can seem a risky business indeed. And so, many Christians appear to experience life as a kind of spiritual exile in a fearsome world. When our minds and hearts are closed to Spirit's manifestations, it should be little surprise that we rarely encounter it, at least in ways we recognize.

Whatever the explanation, it is clear that faith and experience play very different roles in Christian and Pagan spirituality, and these distinctions appear linked with the other differences I have discussed above. I think, these distinctions come down most fundamentally to whether God is conceived as purely transcendent, or as panentheistic. I suggest this is the fundamental issue because many reports of Christian mystical experience have much in common with accounts of Pagan mystics. In short, at the level of transcendence, Christian and Pagan mystics appear to have similar encounters, but within the manifest world we may as well live in different universes.

These features, taken together, comprise a family of spiritual tenets constituting the Pagan religious outlook. Among Pagan traditions these tenets will be emphasized in different ways, but all will generally share them to some extent. Within this framework there is room for much variety. Considered as a whole, they paint a very different picture of our relationship with spiritual reality compared to that taken for granted by many people in the West.

## Neopaganism

The most rapidly growing Pagan practices among modern Westerners are often termed "Neopagan." This means that they constitute a renaissance of Pagan spirituality from within the dominant Christian and secular culture. Unlike the Paganism of Native American peoples, for example, the lineage of Neopagan traditions is not an unbroken one.

As far as we know Hindu, Shinto, and Navajo practice extends backward in an unbroken tradition whose roots lie in the origins of humankind. This was also the case with the Classical Paganism of Greece and Rome. For the most part, the same is not true for the resurgence of European Paganism. A thousand years and more of cooperation between church and state extirpated most Pagan practices indigenous to Europe. What survived is at best fragmentary, the merest echoes of past practices.

Only in Eastern Europe, particularly in Lithuania, might much more remain. Lithuania was the only significant European Pagan political power in the Middle Ages, a people forced to unite in order to defend themselves against military attack by the Christian powers to the West and Tartars to the East. Reportedly the last sacred groves in Lithuania were finally cut down in the nineteenth century. Its subjection to the alliance of Catholic Church and state was far briefer than elsewhere in Europe. Even here, however, subjugation, followed by the hideous terror of Stalinism, left precious little behind.

In addition, and as importantly, Neopagans have been strongly influenced by Christian insights. This heritage is by no means all bad, and a number of its strengths have found their way into Neopagan practice. Had the Pagan West survived, these insights may have come to fruition anyway, for they certainly existed in Classical times, but the Pagan West did not survive, and so these insights came to influence our society through the authority and within the context of the Church. In this sense, modern Westerners who are drawn to Pagan spirituality are in some ways much different in their outlook than their distant Pagan ancestors.

I will discuss the genuine spiritual contributions associated with Christianity at greater length later. Here I simply want to list what I believe to be the two most important: a belief in some sort of spiritual equality among people; and a greater emphasis on love and forgiveness as spiritual qualities. These insights were hardly lacking in pre-Christian times, and in my view the political and economic changes that have transformed the world since then are at least as important as the Church's teachings in helping these insights to take what root they have. Nevertheless, they give to contemporary Neopaganism a flavor somewhat different than that prevailing in pre-Christian Classical Europe, and in many traditional Pagan traditions. In good Pagan tradition, the modern revival incorporates Christian as well as Pagan insights into its spiritual practice.

The flourishing young tree of Neopaganism has many different branches, from attempts to resurrect previous European practices to those acknowledging that all, or nearly all, of their practices are of recent lineage. If there is one tradition that has had a disproportionate influence on Neopaganism, however, that tradition is what we today call "Traditional Wicca." It is that complex of spiritual practices that Gerald Gardner discovered on its last legs in England, and enriched, in order to lay the foundation for what today is called "Traditional" or "Gardnerian" Wicca.

Many Neopagan groups distinguish themselves from those who work in a direct line of descent from groups founded by Gardner. However, most of them have also adopted many of Gardnerian Wicca's central practices. They celebrate eight Sabbats throughout the year, define sacred space by casting a circle, invoke guardians at the four cardinal points of their circle, and then invoke the Goddess or the God's presence within that circle. Today it is this complex of common practices that unites many, though not all, Neopagan traditions.

Now that you have a clear sense of what broadly constitutes Pagan spirituality, we are able to turn to considering specifically Wiccan Paganism. In doing so I focus on Traditional, or Gardnerian, Wicca. There will often be variants and differences of emphasis between Neopagan groups, but most will adhere more or less closely to the tenets and observances that I discuss in my next chapter.

1. The Hare Krishnas are one of the few Pagan traditions making claims of religious exclusivity, even against other Hindus.

2. Apuleius of Madauros, *The Golden Ass,* Book 11: 5, from Marvin W. Meyer, ed., *The Ancient Mysterias: A Sourcebook, Sacred Texts of the Mystery Religions of the Ancient Mediterranean World* (San Francisco: Harper and Row, 1987), p. 179.

3. This paragraph owes much to Luther H. Martin's, *Hellenistic Religions: An Introduction,* (New York: Oxford University Press, 1987).

4. As quoted in Pierre Chuvin, *A Chronicle of the Last Pagans* (Cambridge: Harvard University Press, 1990), pp. 25–26.

5. The popular image of Pagan-Christian relations during classical times suffers from the fact that for over a thousand years only the winners wrote the histories. Hollywood epics have not helped. However, good histories by modern writers do exist. I suggest Ramsay MacMullen, *Christianity and Paganism in the Fourth to Eighth Centuries* (New Haven: Yale University Press, 1997); Robin Lane Fox, *Pagans and Christians* (San Francisco: Harper and Row, 1986), John Holland Smith, *The Death of Classical Paganism* (New York: Charles Scribner's Sons, 1976), Pierre Chuvin, *A Chronicle of the Last Pagans,* op. cit., and Robert L. Wilken, *The Christians as the Romans Saw Them* (New Haven: Yale University Press, 1984).

6. Peter Manchester, "The Religious Experience of Time and Eternity," *Classical Mediterranean Spirituality, Egyptian, Greek, Roman.* A. H. Armstrong, ed. (New York: Crossroads, 1989), p. 387.

# What Is Wiccan Paganism?

Most varieties of Wicca have been influenced powerfully by the writings and teachings of Gerald Gardner, and those around him, who made Witchcraft public in England after repeal of the anti-Witchcraft laws. Gardner's influence has been vast, helping to inspire not only traditional Wicca but the many variations and spin-offs that have arisen since. As Chas Clifton put it, "'Gardnerian Witchcraft' has acted like a powerful magnet and polarized all the iron and steel in its vicinity."[1] While most of what follows is true of Neopaganism generally, no complete generalization is possible. Whenever I have to choose, I focus primarily upon the traditional, or Gardnerian, element in Neopagan practice, for it underlies, in more or less modified form, most Neopagan traditions.

As we might expect in trying to trace activities that were proscribed under penalty of death for over 1,000 years, Wicca's antiquity is subject to sometimes very heated debate. Some argue that it was mostly or entirely made up in recent times, largely by Gardner himself, in post-war Britain. Many of us who have seen Gardner's handwritten manuscripts doubt this is true. There is too much evidence that he was copying from another text, and that he was only exposed to this text in piecemeal fashion, but if Gardner did not make it up, that only pushes our confirmed past back another generation.

Some give primacy to Wicca's Celtic roots, claiming it is inherited from the practices of pre-Christian Celtic peoples. Others, and

I am among them, argue that while much Craft ritual is of recent origins, other elements are much older, having powerful similarities with Neoplatonic Theurgical traditions of the late Roman Empire. Whether in this case there is an unbroken line of practice, or simply that these traditions were transmitted and only occasionally practiced, will probably never be known.

It should be apparent by now that the origins of Pagan practice are ultimately of secondary concern. If people have personal encounters with a Divinity or Divinities, and these encounters fulfill their spiritual needs, the tradition works. If not, its antiquity does not matter. How such an approach addresses questions of "true" and "false" spirituality must wait for a later chapter. For the moment we need only acknowledge that it is personal experience of the Divine, or "gnosis" which is the basis for validity in a Pagan path. Faith, in this context, is trust based on past experience. It is not "blind."

## My Path to Wicca

About fifteen years ago a friend invited me to a Midsummer Sabbat, a celebration of the summer solstice in the beautiful hills east of Berkeley, California. It was at that celebration that I had an experience that set me on the path I now follow, but how I ended up there is also a part of this story.

I first met the man who was later to invite me to that Sabbat while selling my artwork in Berkeley. I was completing my Ph.D. dissertation in political science and was using my artistic skills to help make ends meets while I did my research. Don soon became a repeat customer, and in time we began having conversations when he would come by. At one point I asked him what he did. He said he was a magician. "Where do you perform?" I asked.

"I'm not that kind of magician," he answered.

Berkeley is a city with far more than its share of unusual and even weird people. And I liked this guy. Now, it seemed to me, Don was also one of the nuts. But he was also a good customer, and it is never good practice to tell your customers you think they're crazy. I just nodded, and said, "That's interesting."

About a year later I was in the midst of Christmas sales. I had just completed my dissertation and was feeling pretty cocky. When Don came by to make some purchases I asked him if he would "show me some real magic?" I was curious as to how he would get out of it, since I knew the entire subject to be fantasy.

His answer was unexpected. "Sure. How about tonight?"

I was unprepared for *that* response. I muttered something about it being Christmas season, that I was busy with my holiday sales, was tired, and really didn't have time. After he left, I also felt very foolish. I decided if the opportunity ever repeated itself, I would take him up on his offer.

About a month later I did see him again. I asked the same question, and when he gave the same answer, I said "OK—you're on."

"Show up tonight at my place around 10:00," he replied, and gave me his address.

That night was the most amazing night of my life, at least up to that time. When I finally returned home my entire world-view had been decisively overturned. Not only that, I had also become Don's student.

Over the next several months of study I learned a great deal, but never asked him anything about religion. My many years in Berkeley had left me deeply uninterested in anyone's religious ideas. Christian missionaries with bull horns, Hare Krishnas passing out copies of the Gita, and "Moonies" inviting me "to dinner" had thoroughly inoculated me. Further, if I had been interested in religion, it would have been either Judaism or Buddhism, because both respected learning. But neither had interested me enough to investigate their teachings and practices in any real depth.

Shortly before Midsummer, Don asked me if I was interested in attending a Witches' Sabbat. While uninterested in Witchcraft as such, I was intrigued. How many people get invited to a Witches' Sabbat? I wondered. Not many, I guessed. And so I decided to go.

At the time I was on guard. What little I knew of Witchcraft did not inspire much confidence. It seemed connected with black magic and nasty spells, neither of which interested me. As the date drew closer I found myself wondering whether I would survive the experience. Maybe Don's friendship was merely feigned, simply to draw me in. Maybe they planned a sacrifice! I worried enough about this possibility that, the day before the celebration, I told a couple of friends that they should tell the Berkeley police who had invited me, if I disappeared.

Looking back today, my fears seem enormously paranoid and incredibly silly, but at the time they seemed simply to reflect judicious caution. Now I often have to remind myself that others may still feel the same way I once did.

It was with a mixture of excitement, anticipation, and fear that I followed the directions I was given, taking me to an isolated glade in Tilden Park, high in the Berkeley Hills, where the Sabbat was to take place. When I finally arrived my nervous anticipation vanished in a flash. The smallish crowd I encountered seemed neither exciting nor mysterious, let alone dangerous. The warm summer day seemed like any other; the faces around me not much different from any random Berkeley crowd.

My deflated expectations turned to dismay as the announced time for the Sabbat came and went, with no noticeable effort on anyone's part to get anything started. I was compulsively punctual, and I had run head first into what is called, tongue firmly in cheek, "Pagan Standard Time." PST means scheduled events will be held late, sometimes very late.

After perhaps two hours had passed, with nothing much happening except for chit-chat. I was trying to figure out how to go home gracefully, without disappointing Don, who had invited me. Fortunately as it turned out, a good excuse never came to mind, and then the ritual finally began.

We formed a circle in the wooded glade. Something seemed strangely archaic and also comfortingly familiar about that circle, but at the time I paid these feelings little mind. Mostly I was relieved that, at last, something was happening. The circle was cast and the powers of the elements and directions were invoked, neither of which seemed to me more than simple theater. At that point the priest and priestess walked to the circle's center, and began their invocation of the Goddess.

His voice filled the circle:
She is white; She is red; She is black.
She is dawn; She is daylight; She is darkness.
She is joy; She is fullness; She is sorrow. . . .

His invocation concluded:
Come down Lady. Come in Lady. Come through Lady. . . .
She is coming. She is here. She is All.

As the invocation came to an end I was suddenly enveloped in a presence of incredible power, beauty, and love. While nothing was visible to my eyes, the closeness of that presence was palpable. There was a sense of nature, of forests and streams and meadows. At the same time, there was a pervading sense of beauty beyond words, power beyond imagining, and love beyond conception. And the presence was feminine, in the most perfect way.

Most important of all to me was Her love. It was unconditional, all embracing, all comprehending. She saw me fully and completely, with nothing hidden, and Her love poured forth anyway. In those brief moments within Her presence I realized that I had never really understood what love was, never deeply comprehended compassion, never truly grasped what acceptance meant. For the first time I experienced Divinity. Her qualities so far exceeded my experience, that it was akin to seeing the light of the sun after having lived in darkness illuminated by candles. Only the light was gentle, not painful. It was a gift and a blessing that, if it never happened again, was enough to leave me grateful for a lifetime.

"Here is a religion where they ask their God to come, and She does!" Soon thereafter I began study for formal initiation into Wicca. But my real initiation had taken place that Midsummer, on a sunny afternoon in Tilden Park.

Every Wiccan with whom I have discussed the reasons for their involvement has referred to personal experiences. No one mentioned the persuasive power of a text or the example of a friend. Those things may have led some here, but I haven't heard about it. At most, some people have said that when they first read something accurate about Wicca they realized, "Why, that's what I've always felt! I'm not alone after all." The argument was not persuasive because they were already convinced. It only assured them they were not alone. Involvement in Wicca comes from a very deep connection, one more fundamental than intellect and deeper than friendship, and it makes no claims to speak to everyone.

Wicca focuses on Divinity as it manifests in male/female duality, and in the basic forces and cycles of nature. The Goddess and the God, often referred to as the Lady and the Horned Lord, together symbolize the basic dualities characterizing embodied existence: female and male, life and death, growth and decline, light and dark, and change and stability. While seemingly opposites, they depend upon one another. For us, these dualities are manifestations of the sacred.

Many Wiccan traditions generally conceive all Goddesses as aspects of the Great Goddess, and all Gods as aspects of the male God. The Charge of the Great Mother, in my opinion the most beautiful of our liturgies, begins with the call to, "Listen to the words of the Great Mother, who was of old also called amongst men Artemis, Astarte, Dione, Melusione, Aphrodite, Cerridwen, Diana, Arianrhod, Bride, and by many other names."[2]

Other Wiccans distinguish between different deities as self-aware manifestations of the Sacred. For all practical purposes Hekate is not Brigit is not Diana. Regardless of how these theological points are understood, however, common to all Wiccan belief is a focus on the basic dualities of the Divine in their male and female aspects, whether as two or many.

Although both Goddess(es) and God(s) are equally central to our beliefs, in most rituals the Goddess takes her place as first among equals. In part, Her prominence redresses thousands of years of spiritual practice which have de-emphasized the female aspect of divinity in favor of the male. But this rectification, justified as it is, hardly accounts for Her primacy.

Today, the female aspect of Divinity better addresses the experience of Spiritual immanence, where the world is ultimately of the same substance of the Divine. For thousands of years male deities have generally been conceived in purely transcendental terms. We are predisposed by history, culture, and our dominant theologies to conceive male deities as distant. This need not be, but is. By contrast our dominant metaphors for our material world are female. For this reason, and likely many others, we seem most receptive to immanent deities as female.

In my opinion, it is contact with this dimension of Spirit that many moderns desperately need. For two thousand years Spirit has become progressively more invisible within the Western world. As our vision has improved in some things we have become blind in others. We desperately need to learn to see where we are now blind. and, today, the world has seen more than enough of such stern and distant role models. The Goddess' enhanced presence widens and deepens our conception of Divinity in ways that can help guide us toward more appropriate ways of living with the world and with one another.

In the final analysis, all this reasoning is simply a human attempt to explain the superhuman. The basic truth of the matter is that She came to me that Midsummer afternoon, and my life was never again the same.

In the traditional Wiccan Charge of the Goddess, the Great Mother identifies Herself:

> I am the gracious Goddess who gives the gift of joy unto the heart of man; upon Earth I give knowledge of the Spirit eternal; and beyond death I give peace and freedom and reunion with those who have gone before; nor do I demand sacrifice, for behold I am the Mother of all living, and my love is poured out upon the earth.

She also describes how She can be most appropriately honored:

> Let my worship be within the heart that rejoiceth; for behold, all acts of love and pleasure are my rituals and therefore let there be beauty and strength, power and compassion, honor and humility, mirth and reverence, within you.
>
> And thou who thinkest to seek for me, know thy seeking and yearning shall avail ye not, unless thou knowest the mystery; that if that which thou seekest thou findest not within thee, thou wilt never find it without thee, for behold I have been with thee from the beginning and I am that which is attained at the end of desire.

These words reflect the common Pagan view that the Divine is immanent as well as transcendent. From this distinction flows a basic difference in how we understand the nearly universal sense of separation between human beings and the sacred. Our different understanding leads to another approach for bridging that separation.

If the Divine is purely transcendent, our separation is complete, and nothing on our part can bridge it. The only way a bridge between the human and the Divine can be built is through the agency of the Divine. In Christian theology John Calvin expressed this point of view with uncompromising rigor. According to Calvin, salvation can come about only through God's grace. Nothing we do can merit that grace, and even to try is, in a way, an affront to Him, for it supposedly manifests our pride. Jonathan Edwards, the famous New England Calvinist, reminded his flock that God "holds you over the pit of hell, much as one holds a spider, or some loathsome insect, over the fire . . . you are ten thousand times so abominable in his eyes as the most hateful venomous serpent is in ours."[3] Fortunately Martin Luther, and most other Christians, found such doctrines too severe. From their perspective God still granted grace, but our own efforts and good works could help to win it. Either way, however, the gulf between humanity and the Divine is fundamental and qualitative.

Traditional Wicca takes a different view. The Divine is within us, but hidden. So hidden in fact that it can *appear* completely separate. Who, after all, is able to manifest the perfect love that Wiccans attribute to their deity? Certainly no one of my acquaintance. On what grounds then, can we say Divinity is within us? Before my encounter with Her I was not even able to imagine what a deity really is.

When I first encountered the Goddess the most memorable aspect of that experience was Her unimaginable love. In retrospect I realized I did not know what that word really meant before I experienced it from Her. Perfect love involved genuine acceptance and total compassion and concern. There was no need on Her part that Her love be returned, although during the encounter it was impossible for me not to respond completely with my heart. Her love was superhuman. For me there is no denying that the difference between the human and Divinity is extraordinary.

Yet, at the same time, and this point is crucial, great as was the difference between us, in my view the difference between human love and Divine love was ultimately quantitative, not qualitative. To use a metaphor, the acorn contains within it in some sense the oak tree that it has the potential to become, improbable as such an outcome may appear when comparing an acorn with an oak. There are two reasons for my argument that the gulf between the human and the divine is not total.

First, if the Divine were completely Other, how could we feel at home in its presence? Surely no one could feel fulfilled by an experience with Calvin's God, to whom we are loathsome. Such a Deity is completely alien. No human being who said he was motivated by love would create beings preordained to damnation for eternity, but such is the behavior of Calvin's God. By contrast, reports of human encounters with Divine love in spiritual traditions worldwide emphasize the sense of completion, fulfillment, and being at home that accompany the encounter. This is as true of Christian reports as of other faiths, and it is true of my encounter with the Goddess.

Second, the distance between Divine and human love is along a continuum of more and less, not a leap to a completely different state of being. We could not even identify love as a quality of the Divine if it were completely foreign to ourselves, for it would have nothing in common with what we mean by love. We may as well describe color to someone who sees only in black and white.

We are all aware that insofar as our love for another comes with conditions, it is in part selfish, and so not genuine love at all. To the extent we are able to love, the other is *intrinsically* valuable. Many, perhaps most, of us have experienced times when we approach feeling genuine love in this sense, but we all fall short of it much of the time. We are beings who are too subject to our own needs and fears consistently to act in this way. Even so, the concept is not alien. We understand it when we encounter it, we can recognize it as a *perfect* manifestation of something we manifest imperfectly.

An analogy helps us better to grasp this point. If I have never enjoyed good health I can still begin to get an idea of what it is like to have it, so long as my debilities vary over time. I can then imagine being without illness or fatigue or pain. There is nothing about being human that enjoins us from having good health, even if none of us maintain that state perfectly. Similarly, though I may never have practiced perfect love, I can get a sense of what it is like even without encountering a deity. However, my intellectual model of good health will be nothing like actually feeling the exuberant vitality and energy it brings to my body, and my intellectual understanding of perfect love will be nothing like actually experiencing it from a deity.

When we are spiritually embraced by a loving deity, a dormant potential is awakened. A quiet seed is watered and encouraged to sprout. Our comprehension is no longer intellectual, it is experiential, and so we can begin to build on it in a way intellectual comprehension cannot accomplish.

Yet the skills we acquire are not alien to us, even if we would never have acquired them in the absence not only of a teacher, but of a teacher who engaged us on many different levels during our apprenticeship. Great teachers bring out potentials of which their students were themselves unaware.

I think these examples help illustrate how we learn to open our hearts to others through following a spiritual path. We are in a special relationship with deities who manifest these qualities far beyond our own capacities. If we truly explore the teachings within our spiritual tradition, we can grow more along these lines than we may at one time have ever thought possible.

To return to the Goddess's words in the Charge, to the extent that I can love, She is within me, for perfect love is open to everything, rejecting nothing. This view, by the way, is identical to Paul's views in 1 Corinthians 13, 1–7, for without love there can be no true charity, and indeed in this passage "charity" is sometimes translated as "love":

> Though I speak with the tongues of men and of angels, and have not charity, I am become as sounding brass or tinkling cymbal. And though I have the gift of prophecy, and understand all mysteries, and all knowledge; and though I have all faith, so that I could remove mountains, and have not charity, I am nothing. And though I bestow all my goods to feed the poor, and though I give my body to be burned, and have not charity, it profiteth me nothing. Charity suffereth long, and is kind; charity envieth not; charity vaunteth not itself, is not puffed up, Doth not behave itself unseemly, seeketh not her own, is not easily provoked, thinketh no evil; Rejoiceth not in inequity, but rejoiceth in the truth; Beareth all things, believeth all things, hopeth all things, endureth all things.

A person utterly without the capacity to love would have no point of access to Her. But I doubt whether such an unfortunate individual truly exists, although there are far too many people doing little or nothing to nourish the most sacred quality they possess, and when our fears and ignorance have truly been laid to rest—"at the end of desire"—then we discover that She has never truly been gone from us. I write this not because I have attained such a state. I have desires aplenty, but when I approach it more closely than usual, Her presence seems closer as well, not so much as a gift from above, such as when She manifested to me during that Sabbat, but as a certainty of connection.

## Living Within the Wiccan World

Ours is a celebratory path whose framework of spiritual observance follows two complementary cycles: the phases of the moon and the turning of the seasons, known as the "wheel of the year." Wicca also honors and works with the various symbolic dimensions of fertility in all its aspects. The lunar phases and seasonal cycle symbolically represent the basic rhythm of embodied life, from birth through adulthood to death, followed by rebirth. These cycles are celebrated particularly on the full moons, or Esbats, and during our eight seasonal celebrations, or Sabbats.

Since the world is divine, we are continually living within a temple, or the body of the Ultimate. At its best, our spiritual practice reflects this insight. The Wiccan attitude toward spirituality is captured in an insight by the Pagan Roman writer, Plutarch. Referring to Diogenes the Cynic, who had observed, "But is not every day a feast for a good man?" Plutarch answered:

> Certainly, and even a brilliant feast, if we are properly informed. For the world is a very holy temple and most worthy of God; man is introduced to it by his birth . . . [The material world has within it] by nature a principle of life and of movement: the sun, the moon, the stars and the rivers constantly renewing their water, the earth from which comes food for plants and animals. Our life which is an absolutely perfect admission and initiation into these mysteries must be full of confidence and joy.[4]

Today most of us live within a secular society where almost everything has become incorporated into organizational hierarchies and the market order. Virtually nothing is recognized as possessing intrinsic value. Natural beauty and sacred days alike are appropriated as aids in selling. Often they are used to promote values completely at odds with what they truly are. Images of the fresh air of spring sell cigarettes. Wide-open spaces sell cars. Just after Halloween stores put up decorations encouraging people to spend money on Christmas although it is still almost two months away. It seems as if nothing escapes being a tool for making money. Everything has been desacralized into a tool for financial gain and personal power.

Of all the world's peoples, we moderns have traveled farthest from the harmony of the world and spirit, and a daily perception that our world is sacred. We are almost completely surrounded by our own artifacts, and we see them through the lenses of our own preoccupations with power, profit, and pride. We also feel the emptiness that results.

Our situation is not really so bleak. While our society has obscured the sacred in everything it touches, we moderns can still reconnect with Spirit, with the sacred and divine, in honoring and pondering the lessons contained within what is most timeless in nature, and therefore least susceptible to our manipulation. It is here that Wiccans, and most other Pagans, find their scripture, a scripture that is renewed with every seed that sprouts, every droplet of rain that falls, and every day that dawns.

In seeking to experience genuine spiritual value we are increasingly drawn outside human society, into the timeless cycles of nature, and of life, in order to grasp that which is larger than us all. Doing so puts the frantic hustle and bustle of our lives into a different, and more fitting, context. So long as we are infatuated with the promise of technology and power, we remain largely deaf to the realm of Spirit. We are entranced, instead, by the narrow realm of ego, a fragment thinking it stands alone and seeking endlessly to be a whole while simultaneously turning its back on that from which it manifests and which sustains it.

Once we realize the ultimate emptiness of seeking power and possession, we are open once again to the more subtle but infinitely deeper truths graspable through nature and nature's cycles. We discover the true and sacred context which gives meaning to our lives. This context encompasses not only the cycles of nature where in many cases they are most apparent, but underlies all existence, even enobling and lifting up the secular world as well.

As a manifestation of Spirit, Nature becomes a source of wisdom. The cycles of the seasons are owned by neither corporation nor government. The phases of the moon are unrelated to either Madison Avenue or Washington, D.C. No human purpose mediates our encounter with them. They are available to all. They directly manifest value, and we need access to copyright or cash in order to perceive it.

Wiccans do not deny the value of other spiritual paths that find their inspiration by other means or that share with us recognition of nature's divinity, but interpret it in other ways. We wish those following them well. For us, it is in and through nature's processes that we most directly find our inspiration and our home. Those of us who have been blessed by the Goddess's presence know beyond doubt that this world is sacred, that it is permeated by Her love, and that this path can be one of shining beauty and profound wisdom.

## The Wheel of the Year

Sabbats such as Midsummer play a central role in Wiccan practice. Through our observance of the eight Sabbats, every dimension of physical existence is honored in its place, recognized as holy, and celebrated as a manifestation of the Divine. Properly conceived, the Sabbats provide a meditative cycle on all of life, a cycle that can be repeated and deepened with every year of their observance.

The four great Sabbats are Samhain (pronounced "SAOW-win"), Imbolc (pronounced "im-OLk"), Beltane, and Lammas or Lughnasadh (pronounced "LOO-na-sa"). They honor the Celtic seasonal cycle as it was observed in Western Europe. The four "cross quarter" Sabbats are geared to the solar cycles. They consist of the Winter Solstice, or Yule; the Summer Solstice, or Midsummer; and the Spring and Fall Equinoxes. Together these eight Sabbats comprise the "wheel of the year," eternally turning, the constant foundation supporting life's wonderful variety and complexity.

Our new year begins October 31, with Samhain, or Halloween. On this night, darkness triumphs over light, for in the Celtic world night precedes rather than follows day. This is similar to the Jewish day, which also begins at sunset. Samhain marks the triumph of the forces of death and decline. Night comes early, and will come earlier still in the rapidly shortening days between now and the Winter Solstice. A chill is in the air nearly everywhere.

Within our tradition, Samhain is one of two times when the boundary that separates the human and spirit worlds is said to be most permeable, and so Samhain is a time for honoring our ancestors, both literal and spiritual. Like Mexico's Day of the Dead, which also occurs around this time, our honored dead are invited to come be with us, if they choose. Far from beings an evil or terrifying time, Samhain is a celebration, but as befits its subject, it has solemn, somber, and serious tones as well. Those who have passed on are physically lost to us for the remainder of our lives, and we miss them. Death is a sacrament, but not one actively to be pursued. It will come in time to all, a fitting and inevitable end to life. For life's end to be truly fitting life must be lived well.

Our second Sabbat is the Winter Solstice, or Yule, on December 22. It marks the year's longest night. Solstice night brings with it the symbolic death and rebirth of the sun, and of all for which it stands. With its rebirth the inexorable triumph of night over day, of decline over growth, and of death over life, is reversed. The increasing light brings with it the slow renewal of life's currents.

Even here, near the northern California coast, where life-bringing rains usually return earlier in the fall and continue through spring, the branches of our maples, alders, and deciduous oaks are bare and almost no flowers bloom before Winter Solstice. Here, where our Western European celebratory cycle does not quite fit the rhythms of our climate, the match of light with leaf and bloom still reminds us of the vital truths that no darkness is total, no night endures endlessly, no death lasts forever. Mythically, the Great Mother gives birth at this time to the Lord of Life, the male aspect of Divinity. Other Neopagan traditions mark the same observance with the mythical felling of the Holly King of Winter by the Oak King of summer, who will increasingly dominate the year until the summer solstice brings his end in turn. Both of these images are metaphors for the eternal interrelationship of life and death.

On February 2 we celebrate Imbolc. The cold of winter is still the dominant presence and new life and light are both in their infancy: small but growing promises of the year to come. Our celebrations emphasize this growing light, but light without much heat, of candles, not bonfires, of promise and not fulfillment. Imbolc is a good time to make promises and vows for the coming year.

We also celebrate the Feast of Brigit at this time. Brigit is the Celtic Goddess of fire, poetry, learning, metal-working, and healing. A Goddess so beloved by her people that they sought to honor Her even as they adopted Christianity, Brigit was canonized as the Mother Saint of Ireland, second only to Saint Peter in stature. A fanciful legend was promulgated that She was Christ's wet nurse. No evidence exists that a human equivalent of Saint Brigit lived during that time, and historians have concluded that behind her even-armed cross stands a much loved Celtic Goddess. We find, some of us, that She is still with us.

On or around March 21 comes the Spring Equinox, a time of balance between the growing light and declining dark. Like all balance in this world, it is transitory. The Equinox is also a time of promise, for the days to come now tilt decisively in favor of light over dark. Plants are stirring from winter's dormancy. In much of the country the signs of spring are unmistakable and here in northern California the flowers of spring have begun to bloom brightly. In colder climes this is a time for sowing seeds for the coming year.

Beltane, on April 30, and the following May Day, mark the beginning of summer. Beltane honors life's vitality and fertility. Fields are green and flowers abundant. Breezes are often warm, carrying the scent of nectar. All traces of winter have faded from most places. This is a joyful time, a time of love and sexuality, and of the celebratory power of Spirit. May Queens and Maypoles, dancing and feasting, and Morris dancers dancing up the sun at dawn make this the most joyous of Sabbats—a time honoring youth and physical beauty. If the Equinox celebrated the fertility of plant life, Beltane and May Day honor animal and human fertility. Today, however, human fertility is often more a problem than a blessing, and so we honor and celebrate fertility in all its forms: artistic and intellectual, as well as physical.

With Samhain, Beltane is the other time when, myth has it, the veils between the physical and spirit worlds are thinnest. The Otherworld, the land of faerie, is close at hand, and ceremonies acknowledging and honoring that proximity take place. Magical workings, particularly those in harmony with the meaning of this time, are considered especially efficacious if done now. It is a good time indeed to use magic to assist in getting pregnant.

June 22 brings Midsummer, the Summer Solstice, the year's longest day. More than any other day, Midsummer honors the most complete expression of nature's bounty of light and warmth. As Beltane honored the energy and fertility of youth, Midsummer focuses on the achievements of maturity. In some Wiccan traditions it is here, at the height of his power, that the Oak King of summer, symbolizing life, is felled by the Holly King of winter, who symbolizes death. In this enactment, Midsummer is the mirror image of the Winter Solstice myth. Midsummer reminds us that all things in this world are transitory, for at the height of its power, day and all that it symbolizes becomes increasingly subject to the influence of night, and the world it symbolizes.

Lammas, or Lughnasadh, on July 31 is the pre-eminent celebration of harvest. The abundance of summer gardens symbolizes the fulfillment of human effort and creativity in harmony with the world. They represent also the fruition of the energies honored at Beltane. But with the joy of a bountiful harvest is simultaneous recognition that it comes at a price, that life rests upon death, that grain and fruit and beast must die, so that our own lives may continue. Abundance and loss are linked, and more than other Sabbats Lammas recognizes this sacrificial aspect to all life, and embraces it. Lammas thus serves to remind us that worldly achievement is not permanent, that to truly last it must become in turn become wisdom, the harvest of love and experience.

With the Autumn Equinox around September 21, what only the discerning eye could see at Lammas is now apparent everywhere, though the days are still warm and life abundant. The declining energies of summer surround us. The harvest continues bountiful, but its end is in sight. In contrast to Lammas, the Autumn Equinox takes on a more poignant tone. Like the Spring Equinox, it is a time of balance, but now the coming transition will be in the other direction. Night begins to dominate the year, though at first only subtly. The triumph of the powers of death and physical decline is rapidly approaching, to rule again at Samhain. Colors are beginning to appear on leaves that once were exuberantly green. Far from being a sad time, in many ways fall is the most beautiful season, the culmination of the period of growth that preceded it. Its beauty symbolizes for me the final gift of wisdom that is perhaps the greatest blessing of the many gifts that life provides to us, if we will only grasp them.

Our Sabbats help each of us understand our continued participation in cycles bearing many levels of meaning. Honoring these cycles helps us to harmonize ourselves with the most basic currents that animate our world, our lives, and our loves, and to recognize their sacred character. The Sabbats can be celebrated simply as the coming together of community in celebration and commemoration.

There is nothing amiss in such an approach. Like all religious practices, the Sabbats can also take us ever more deeply into communion with Spirit.

To some, the tone of our cycle may seem bittersweet: if darkness is never completely triumphant, neither is light, but this is to misunderstand the meaning of the dark—as I once did. For the darkness symbolizes that which lies beyond life, and that is much more than death. We are material beings, and it is appropriate that as such, we prefer to live and flourish abundantly. We are also beings of Spirit, and our flourishing is of little moment if it does not ultimately deepen our awareness, our love, and our wisdom. When our time comes that is what we will take with us, our life's true and final harvest.

# Wheel of the Year

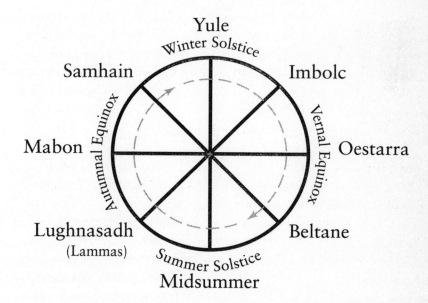

The same basic symbolism accompanies our Esbats, or celebrations of the lunar cycle. Most commonly, we meet on the full moon, as befits a practice which, while honoring all stages of life, affirms the essential goodness of life itself. As with Midsummer among our Sabbats, the Full Moon Esbat symbolizes the height of abundance, with the Goddess at the peak of Her power as the Source of life. Whereas within traditional Wicca the Sabbats emphasize both male and female energies, our lunar observances are far more focused upon the Goddess.

Other times than the full moon are also sometimes chosen for meeting, but they are correlated with the lunar cycle as well, such as horned moons and dark moons. In such cases the character of the observance is in harmony with the cyclic symbolism of that lunar phase. So, in a way, each lunar month recapitulates the deeper cycles of the year, just as each year symbolizes the still deeper cycle of a life, and each life in turn mirrors the basic nature of physical reality. This symbolism helps us focus on the basic meanings within life itself.

To understand myth as history, or as explanation in the modern sense, is not to understand myth at all. Myth is not primitive science. Wiccan myths encapsulated within the wheel of the year are not nostalgic efforts to recapture an era that is long dead. Myth is more a tool of meditation than explanation and leads to insights that defy literary description. Myth illuminates inner meanings, not external observation.

## On Death

Wiccans generally believe death leads again to life, with return considered more a blessing than a curse. Here we are in harmony with many Pagan traditions from other parts of the world. For example, in *The Education of Little Tree,* the Cherokee boy, Little Tree, returns to find his ailing grandmother has passed on, as had his grandfather not long before. She left him a note: "Little Tree, I must go. Like you feel the trees, feel for us when you are listening.

We will wait for you. Next time will be better. All is well. Grandma."[5] The Hindu *Kaushitaki Upanishad* describes a choice the deceased can make as to whether to pursue rebirth, with those choosing to return obviously not regarding the wheel of rebirth as a misfortune.[6] In traditional Wicca a beautiful teaching says that "to fulfill love you must return again at the same time and place as the loved one, and you must remember and love them again."[7]

In our focus on living in harmony with the world rather than seeking salvation from it, our point is not that the world beyond death is unimportant. Most Pagan traditions, including Wicca, say it does exist and is important. Instead, the point is that the afterlife need not be our ultimate concern in this life.

In a beautiful and sacred world it seems both ignorant and ungrateful to seek to leave it for good. Better far to learn to live in loving harmony with it, and let the afterlife take care of itself. If people could learn to treat one another with kindness and compassion, it is hard to imagine a more blessed existence. Wicca's and other nature religions' emphasis on the basic goodness of embodied life, and upon Spirit's immanence within it, places us in a different relationship to the world of Spirit than is the case with Christianity and other spiritual paths emphasizing that life is best lived as a preparation for death.

Spiritual fulfillment is found with others, within a community which is itself a reflection, or emanation, of Spirit. This community is not limited to human beings. Far from separating itself from the world, our spiritual community *is* the world. By contrast, Western Christianity in particular emphasizes the isolated individual, separate from the human and natural community alike, who must solve the problem of his or her salvation. This is clearly the case with Protestantism, but even the more community-oriented Catholicism views itself as radically distinct from "the world." By contrast, a Wiccan perspective would endorse my favorite African proverb, "I am because we are."

From this it follows why our primary spiritual emphasis is on direct spiritual experience of our Gods and their teachings, rather than relying on verbal or written instruction. The world is sacred and so a grove or other natural site for worship most appropriately constitutes our cathedrals. With sacred teachings surrounding us on all sides, we need no written scriptures.

## Sexuality and the Sacred

Perhaps the most powerful, and for non-Witches often the most controversial, of those teachings concerns sexuality. Sexuality, that divine mystery wherein individuality finds its fulfillment in union with another, is the physical manifestation of the creative energy that makes the world possible. Out of union comes renewed diversity and creativity.

Our honoring of sexuality leads many non-Pagans to their most lurid fantasies about what we do, but this prurient attitude focuses solely upon sexuality's profane dimension, divorced from a deeper context, and so misses everything important about our practices and beliefs. At the sacred level, sexuality is recognition of the truth contained in an immanent experience of the Divine: that the Great Mystery gives birth from out of itself as an act of love, flesh of its flesh, spirit of its Spirit.

Like all sacred powers, sexuality can be either flagrantly abused or ignorantly feared. In its usual pattern of excess, our society accomplishes both. Sexuality's enormous power, its capacity to overrule our minds and will, can make it seem very frightening indeed, and it is frightening to all who have not come to terms with it. I think this is why spiritual paths that emphasize leaving the world try so hard to deny, distract, or avoid sexuality. Few powers tantalize us with such promise, and reward us with such delight, as sexuality, and few powers can so easily leave us feeling alone and isolated.

In Classical times the God Pan was identified with sexuality. Pan can be translated as "All." Sexuality is the force behind virtually all physical beauty. It creates and shapes the forms of flowers; colors of birds and fish, and horns of stags; and the beauty of men and of women. To debase sexuality is to reject the world and life itself, and to reject these is, from our view, to reject the Divine. Better to sacralize it, recognizing its sacred mystery, and so honor the Divine.

The English writer D. H. Lawrence grasped this insight and was able to put it into words perhaps better than any other writer of our language, and so I will quote him extensively in this section. In *Sons and Lovers*, Lawrence describes the power of sexuality for two lovers:

> They had met, and included in their meeting the thrust of the manifold grass stems, the cry of the peewit, the wheel of the stars . . . To know their own nothingness, to know the tremendous living flood which carried them always . . . If so great a magnificent power could overwhelm them, identify them together with itself, so that they knew they were only grains in the tremendous heave that lifted every grass blade its little height, and every tree, and living thing, then why fret about themselves? They could let themselves be carried by life . . . [8]

Sexuality is not love. The two can exist separately from one another. Love comes in many forms, all characterized by caring for the other as being intrinsically of great value to be treasured and honored, but I believe there is no greater blessing in earthly existence than the union of sexuality and love. Lawrence had wise words on this subject as well—words different from what many who have only heard about him at secondhand might expect.

> Oh, what a catastrophe, what a maiming of love when it was made a personal, merely personal feeling, taken away from the rising and the setting of the sun, and cut off from the magic connection of the solstice and equinox! This is what is the matter with us, we are bleeding at the roots, because we are cut off from the earth and sun and stars, and love is a grinning mockery, because,

poor blossom, we plucked it from its stem on the tree of life, and expected it to keep on blooming in our civilized vase on the table.[9]

Lawrence does not deny the vital personal element in love. But it is not *merely* personal. Through love in all its forms, we participate in something greater than ourselves. And this is as true of sexual love as of any other. Writing of married love, Lawrence observed that most marry:

> With their soul vibrating to the note of sexual love . . . but love is much finer, I think, when not only the sex group of chords is attuned, but the great harmonies, and the little harmonies, of what we call religious feeling (read it widely) and ordinary sympathetic feeling.[10]

Lawrence has got it right, I think. It is when we are most in harmony with life itself, its great and little harmonies, that sexuality finds its most appropriate context, and becomes most sacred and beautiful for us. He did not, as some think, reduce love to sex, but rather argued that we rarely did justice to either. Love and sex are both sacred, both holy, and conjoined, they bring a blessedness that is perhaps unique to embodied existence.

From our perspective, one cannot truly honor the sacred immanence of the world without honoring its cycles. The wheel of the year, its greatest cycle, is the cycle of life and death, and central to the cycle of life and death is sex, its energy, its mystery, its beauty, its creativity. It is the most profound and most frightening challenge to all who would divorce Spirit from body, for it is the strongest expression of Spirit through body.

To return a last time to Lawrence, who in my opinion is ahead of many contemporary Pagans in his understanding of these matters:

> It is a question, practically, of relationship. We *must* get back into relation, vivid and nourishing relation to the cosmos and the universe. The way is through daily ritu-

al, and the re-awakening. . . . To these rituals we must return: or we must evolve them to suit our needs. For the truth is, we are perishing for lack of fulfillment of our greater needs, we are cut off from the great sources of our inward nourishment and renewal, sources which flow eternally in the universe.[11]

The Wiccan emphasis upon sexuality as a sacrament is a dimension in the spiritual healing of our lives as beings on this earth.

## Diversity and Unity

Superficially, at least, there appears to be more variation in Wiccan than in Christian practice. Many Christians have been bothered by this variety. Once, one wrote me about what he regarded as "the distressing number of practices, beliefs, and views of Wicca." He, and many others, find a weakness where I find a strength.

Certainly there is variety. Myths of Oak and Holly Kings seem not to fit with myths of the Goddess of Winter and the God of Summer. Different covens use different names for their chief deities. Sometimes people decide to come together and found a coven after reading a book, whereas others carefully trace their lineage back generations. Some believe the Gods were once people, some that they are forces of nature, some that they are creations of the human mind. Some accept all these beliefs about the Gods, and all such views may be represented within a single coven. To those who strictly honor and seek to follow a written scripture this diversity piled upon diversity can all seem quite incoherent.

Emphasis upon personal experience, lack of a written scripture, and lack of an umbrella ecclesiastical organization all contribute to this variety. May it always be so! In my opinion, the supposed unity of religions based upon scripture has little to do with scripture's objectivity and much to do with the power of organizations to impose a common meaning.

From the beginning of its legalization, the early Church appealed to the state to punish those who read Scripture differently. For ages lay people were forbidden to even read Scripture, leaving authority for its interpretation solely within the hands of those approved by organized authority. With the coming of Protestantism, competing interpretations of Scripture proliferated. Once religious freedom was established, the number of sects ballooned again. I think the reason for this abundance is in part because Spirit speaks to each of us individually. Once we are free to think for ourselves, diversity blossoms.

This diversity can be an embarrassment for a revealed religion, because its Scripture is supposed to provide the one true revelation of divine truth. Different groups read that revelation in different ways, all claiming to have the one true understanding. Within this framework it has proven difficult even for many Christians to tolerate one another's interpretations, unless they first admit that Scripture is not objective.

By contrast, common ritual unites Wiccan groups with each individual free to interpret that ritual's meaning by her or his own lights. Because the world is not viewed as fallen, there is no perceived need for a special revelation for all to help find our way to salvation. We believe Spirit can communicate more clearly when Its message is not continually filtered through a central human authority.

Covens stay together so long as they satisfy their members' spiritual needs. When they cease doing so, they dissolve or divide. Many Wiccans are not even members of covens. They are what we term "Solitaries," who encompass a very wide range of practices and involvement within the Pagan community.

Compared to the stability of institutionalized Churches, this variety can seem superficial, possessing only the shallowest of spiritual roots. The objection can then be raised to Neopagan practice that individuals often do not know their own spiritual needs. Institutionalized spiritual authority is needed to help guide them along their path.

The first part of this claim is true: often we do not know what we need. Certainly this has often held true for me. Individuals who honestly seek are ultimately led by Spirit to paths appropriate for them. Those who do not honestly seek are unlikely to do any better with an ecclesiastical organization to guide them. Worse, they may have the political skills to rise within the ecclesiastical organization itself, thereby creating difficulties for others who are more sincere.

Lack of formal structure has characterized most Pagan religion throughout history. In describing the spiritual practices of the ancient Greeks, Classical scholar A. H. Armstrong writes "all pieties of the older kind, which are bound up with and live in worships and rituals, are intensely concrete, particular, and indefinitely various. . . ." He adds that in the ancient piety of the Greeks and their neighbors:

> The rites of worship were not deliberately designed to express doctrines or even mythic imaginations. They were there, and the most varied ways of feeling, imagining, and thinking about the beings to whom they were directed grew out of them, and were compatible with them. And they were there all the time for everybody. No religious reformer ever seriously attempted to embody a new way of thinking or feeling about the gods in an intrinsically different kind of ritual.[12]

Another example demonstrates the truly cross-cultural character of this dimension of Pagan spirituality. In his study of the Crow Indians, Rodney Frey writes:

> Because [their] Sun Dance religion recognizes, and even encourages, individual interpretation and realization within the spiritual, no dissonance generally arises when individuals hold contrasting understandings of the nature of the cosmos. The Apsáalooke [Crow] may disagree among themselves on such issues, but the need

for a consensus on cosmology is subordinate to the
function of the religion as a means to the spiritual. . . .[13]

Any Wiccan would feel right at home regarding Frey's description. Neopagans can, and usually do, celebrate together without
even asking whether they agree as to theological or ritual interpretation. For example, I believe there is an ultimate spiritual
unity to existence. Some other Pagans believe in a ultimate multi-
plicity. We do not let such disagreements undermine our ability to
work together, or to recognize one another as Pagans. When creating a ritual, whether a proposal feels right is far more important
than its doctrinal orthodoxy.

This characteristic of Pagan spirituality is so widespread that it
must be regarded, I think, as a fundamental feature of this spiritual tradition. The early disputes in Christian theology, particularly
their viciousness and acrimony, concerning whether Jesus was
wholly a man, wholly divine, or some mixture of the two, is
deeply alien to Pagan spirituality. Pagans prefer, in the words of an
elderly fourth-century Pagan writing to Saint Augustine, to worship in "concordant discord."[14]

The deeper meanings of Pagan religion are experiential. They
necessarily vary from person to person. I have given some of my
own experiences to help explain why Pagan spirituality makes
sense to me, but neither I nor anyone else can claim access to its
"true" meaning. This book is the best I can do in making a Pagan
perspective accessible to others. It makes no claims at all at being
canonical or prescribing the One Right Way. Other Pagans will
endorse or argue with it, and the best of both will be based upon
their spiritual experiences rather than any devotion to dogma.

In chapter 1, I compared Paganism with a rope. At any point
along its length many strands will make up a rope, but at any two
points some distance apart on that rope, some of the strands may
be different. Yet we still clearly have a rope. Just as among Pagan
religions there will be a cluster of overlapping qualities, without
any particular quality being absolutely definitive, so within a Pagan

religion, or at least many of them, practitioners will share practices and many beliefs without there being any orthodox interpretation of the whole.[15]

To be sure, Traditional Wiccans have written traditions and teachings such as the Charge of the Great Mother, which are passed along to initiates in "Books of Shadows." But Books of Shadows are not much concerned with doctrine. They are more akin to "spiritual cookbooks" of ritual techniques, the precise interpretation of which is left to each initiate. Even those parts of them that do give doctrine are not regarded as divinely inspired in the sense of being a unique revelation binding on all practitioners. Revelation can always happen, anytime, to any one.

## Secrecy

Books of Shadows are generally kept secret. Although many parts have been published, usually by people who have broken their oaths in order to do so, no complete and unaltered Book of Shadows from a Traditional Wiccan lineage has been made available to non-initiates that I am aware of, as of 1999. It is done only rarely within less traditional Wiccan lineages. As a person becomes more experienced within our tradition she or he may be offered additional initiations, during which times more of their coven's Book of Shadows will be made available to them. It is this graduated unveiling that has, for the moment, kept Traditional books from being made fully public, but it is only a matter of time until this happens. When it does, those expecting to discover something lurid will be profoundly disappointed.

Our secrecy leads to misunderstandings. Many people assume that if we have something to hide, it must be bad. Because I am oath-bound not to reveal certain things, I and many other Wiccans find ourselves in a frustrating situation. We know we have no horrible dark secrets that would appall decent people. At the same time we cannot reveal the secrets we do have to prove our point.

Groups as long established in our society as the Masons often seem evil to the paranoid, simply because they have secrets. That George Washington was high enough in the Freemasons to be offered the post of Grand Master of all American lodges while Benjamin Franklin was Grand Master of the Philadelphia Lodge does not seem to have satisfied the paranoids. Presumably Washington was plotting against the not-yet-established United States at Valley Forge. If the Masons can suffer attacks of such imbecility, it is hopeless for Wiccans to expect to fare any better with their most implacable critics. Even so, I will try to explain why secrecy plays an important role in Wicca.

There are several reasons. First, secrecy is a way of acknowledging our past, when anyone publicly accused of practicing Witchcraft was subject to long torture and a gruesome death. More enlightened times substituted imprisonment. Wicca became public in England only in 1951, when the Witchcraft Laws were finally abolished.

Shortly before abolition they were still enforced. The last person convicted under them was in 1944 (her particular "crime" was making *accurate* predictions of a ship sinking, something the British government wanted kept secret). Today, with the end of most forms of legal oppression, we are able to be far more public than before.

Even so, today there are many accounts of Wiccans who have lost their jobs, and even their children, because of others' ignorance about our beliefs and practices. Some communities have tried to outlaw the practice of meeting at a member's home to celebrate the Sabbats and Esbats. Bob Barr, one of America's most idiotic Congressmen, has encouraged military discrimination against Wiccan servicemen and women. Too many people still believe the hysterical accounts of our enemies, and so, for many people in many parts of the country, secrecy remains wise and prudent. Somebody, after all, votes for Bob Barr.

Second, because Wicca is ultimately rooted in spiritual experience rather than dogma, the less a prospective initiate knows of the next level of insight before his or her initiation, the better. Ultimately the Gods, and not human beings, provide the real initiation. In this sense we are a mystery religion, with strong affinities with Classical mystery religions of the ancient world. No book learning or verbal teaching can substitute for experience of the Sacred, but we can assist by minimizing the prospective initiate's knowledge of what she or he can expect.

The mystery of initiation is something that can only be experienced, not explained. We could publish everything, yet not truly reveal the mystery, but its truth is more likely to be experienced if initiation is approached with uncertainty as well as reverence.

Third, there are secrets that pertain to one's skill in working within a Wiccan context. For example, some kinds of psychic healing can rebound badly upon the would-be healer if he or she is careless or ignorant. We learn, in my case sometimes in hard and painful ways, that psychic energy in its various forms is very real and very powerful. There are things I was more open about when I knew less about them.

Because of its reputation, Wicca often appeals to people who are initially attracted more by the lure of obtaining magickal powers than in demonstrating growing compassion and love. Witches in popular movies emphasize this image. Nor is spiritual and psychological maturity any more abundantly distributed in the Pagan community than any other. As in any community, maturity comes only with time and experience. My first teacher once told me he would not teach certain things I asked him about because I would only really merit knowing them when I could discover them on my own. I know now that he was right.

We believe secrecy is important for our practice. But we acknowledge that in the context of a society without respect for privacy, some on the outside will assume we have shameful things to hide. We don't. The above reasons are more than adequate to explain our reasons for secrecy. They will not convince the paranoid—but then, nothing convinces the paranoid. The more open we appear, according to them, the more devilishly dissembling we really are. Still, while oath breakers have exposed substantial portions of various Books of Shadows, nothing shameful has come to light. This must rest as evidence that we are truthful in our assurances.

I like this approach to spirituality, and not only because it works for me. It is also about as immune to fanaticism and dogmatism as any vital human endeavor is likely to be. It exemplifies personal responsibility, for no one can hide behind scripture and disclaim responsibility because of its supposed objectivity. And for many of us, we are blessed with direct experience of our Gods.

ENDNOTES

1. Chas Clifton, "Leland's *Aradia* and the Revival of Modern Witchcraft," *The Pomegranate: A New Journal of Neopagan Thought*, February, 1997, p. 15.
2. This and other quotations of the Charge are taken from Vivianne Crowley, *Wicca: The Old Religion in the New Age* (Wellingborough, England: Aquarian Press, 1989), pp. 160–161.
3. Jonathan Edwards, *A Jonathan Edwards Reader,* John E. Smith, Harry S. Stout, and Kenneth P. Minkema, eds. (New Haven: Yale University Press, 1995), pp. 97–98.
4. Plutarch, *De tranquillitate animi,* quoted in Jean Pépin, "Cosmic Piety," in A. H. Armstrong, *Classical Mediterranean Spirituality, Egyptian, Greek, Roman* (New York: Crossroad, 1989), p. 431.
5. Forrest Carter, *The Education of Little Tree* (Albuquerque: University of New Mexico Press, 1976), p. 214. Some have questioned the authenticity of Carter's story. I gave the book to a traditional Cherokee, who said it was an accurate account of their beliefs.
6. Wendy Doniger, "Who Lives, Who Survives?" *Parabola*, Winter, 1998, p. 28.
7. Janet and Stewart Farrar, *The Witches' Way: Principles, Rituals and Beliefs of Modern Witchcraft* (London: Robert Hale, 1984), p. 30.
8. D. H. Lawrence, *Sons and Lovers* (New York: Viking, 1958), chapter 13 quoted in Dolores La Chapelle, *Sacred Land, Sacred Sex, The Rapture of the Deep: Concerning Deep Ecology and Celebrating Life* (Silverton, Colo.: FinnHill Arts, 1988), p. 266. LaChapelle's discussion of Lawrence is in my view perhaps the best discussion of sexuality from a Pagan perspective that I have encountered.
9. D. H. Lawrence, "A Propros of Lady Chatterly's Lover." In Harry T. Moore, ed., *D. H. Lawrence: Sex, Literature and Censorship* (New York: Twayne Publishers, 1953), p. 109.

10. D. H. Lawrence, in H. Moore, ed., *The Collected Letters,* Vol. I., p. 23. Quoted in LaChapelle, p. 266.
11. D. H. Lawrence, "A Propos of Lady Chatterly's Lover." op. cit., p. 116.
12. A. H. Armstrong, "The Ancient and Continuing Pieties of the Greek World," in A. H. Armstrong, ed., *Classical Mediterranean Spirituality, Egyptian, Greek, Roman* (New York: Crossroad, 1989), pp. 66–67.
13. Rodney Frey, *The World of the Crow Indians: As Driftwood Lodges* (Norman, Okla.: University of Oklahoma Press, 1987), p. 67.
14. See Robin Lane Fox, *The Unauthorized Version: Truth and Fiction in the Bible* (New York: Vintage, 1993), p. 154.
15. A very suggestive study of relevance to the United States is Diana DeG. Brown's *Umbanda: Religion and Politics in Urban Brazil* (New York: Columbia University Press, 1994). Brown's study, while a bit reductionist, nevertheless gives a good picture of how Paganism, when given the opportunity, develops within a modern society.

# PART II

# Christian Criticisms of Wicca

# Suffering and Evil
# in the Material World

The existence of evil and suffering is a perpetual challenge to any religious perspective, as pressing for Pagans as for Christians. As with Christian perspectives, no single Pagan approach will satisfy everyone. Liberal and Fundamentalist Christians certainly view this issue in different ways, and the same is true among Wiccans and Pagans in general.

I have encountered searching criticisms from Christians as to whether the Wiccan approach to spirituality can handle the problem of evil. Our religion celebrates and honors all basic dimensions of existence. Some Christians ask whether in doing so we demonstrate a naive or even willful blindness to human suffering. Some Christians argue that if our Goddess is truly the Goddess of this world, then the suffering and evil we experience are Her creation. Therefore, far from being devoted to Her, we should reject Her in every respect.

From a Christian perspective this criticism rebuts itself. The Biblical God explicitly takes credit for creating evil. Amos 3:6 asks rhetorically, "shall there be evil in a city, and the Lord hath not done it?" Yet Christians do not abandon their faith because of this admission. By reminding them that their own God admits He created evil, this Biblical passage should alert Christians to the possibility that evil may prove more paradoxical than first meets the literal eye.

Other Christians have argued that our denying Satan's existence points to our spiritual simple-mindedness. We are describing the world as if the Fall never took place, blinding ourselves to the hellish conditions that afflict so many people on this earth, and to the evil that people do to one another. This criticism deserves a reply. I offer mine here.

Christian critics are correct in pointing out that we Wiccans do not focus much on evil. We do not regard this lack of emphasis as a failing. Our understanding is simply different, and our view of evil's role agrees with that of Pagan spirituality more broadly conceived.

We can begin to grasp a Pagan perspective by considering how many people in ancient Greece thought about the matter. In describing the Greek tragedians' view of the relationship of the world and the Divine, Classical scholar A. H. Armstrong wrote:

> the [general] perception of human life [was] in terms of the rhythm of the natural world, the rhythm of day and night and the seasons and birth and death, the rhythm of an endless dance rather than a march to a goal. This is neither an "optimistic" nor a "pessimistic" way of looking at life. It does not issue in absolute hope or despair, because one can always look at it either way up . . .[1]

This paragraph could have been written as a description of many contemporary Wiccans' views on the matter. The world is not heading toward a la-la land of earthly delights, certainly not in the foreseeable future, but neither is it a fallen place. We do see beauty and folly, wisdom and suffering, life and death, acceptance and transcendence—and, in our clearer, stronger moments, accept all, embrace all, as ultimately good, no matter how well disguised. Like all people, sometimes our confidence weakens, and we feel beaten down by adversity. Even so, we see no fallenness here.

If our world is a manifestation of the Sacred, why does it contain so much suffering? And why does so much of this suffering seem gratuitous? Any possible answer takes us deep into core issues concerning the nature of spiritual reality.

From a Pagan perspective a number of answers have been suggested and it is beyond the scope of this chapter to examine them all. When Spirit is immanent valid insights may be found in many spiritual traditions, and modern Pagans have often been enthusiastic students of other traditions as well as exploring their own. Rather than attempt a comprehensive survey, I will focus on the arguments I have found most satisfying, based upon my own experience both spiritually and in coping with the vicissitudes of daily life. I believe these answers demonstrate there are *reasonable* responses to this question from within the framework of Pagan spirituality.

In my view, a wide variety of fundamentally distinct things and events are too frequently lumped together as "evil." If the world is an artifact, produced by a master potter, then it may make sense to combine all sources of suffering into a single category. Presumably the pot, flaws and all, is testimony to the skill of the potter. Such an approach is alien to a Pagan perspective that delights in and is open to the world's diversity as well as its goodness. For us, this indiscriminate amalgamation into a single category of everything we don't like, from tornadoes to cancer to serial killers, hampers our capacity to come to terms with them.

The evils we encounter in life can be divided into three broad, and very different, groups: (1) suffering that is the natural result of embodied existence, (2) accidental suffering that is the result of unintended human actions, and (3) deliberately inflicted suffering, both human and spiritually caused. My argument in these next two chapters does not claim to solve the problem of evil. We are limited beings, and any human answer to the deepest issues of human life must be tentative and provisional. I do claim that it is at least as reasonable as *any* Christian alternative.

In the Christian perspective, death is usually regarded as a divine punishment resulting from human sin. Even those of us who do not judge death this way deeply mourn the passing of our loved ones. Nor, as a rule, do we seek swiftly to follow them. Disease, drought, earthquakes, floods, the pain and decrepitude arising from our aging, and more, all add to the roster of natural causes of human suffering. Such experiences lead us to ask whether a world with such events is in fact a truly good place.

From the point of view of many Christians these events are the result of human or demonic agency upsetting a previously perfect world. Some have even told me, based on their reading of the Bible, that before the Fall there were no carnivores nor were there storms or earthquakes. Animals were vegetarians and heavy dew watered the earth. After all, storms and carnivores frequently cause death, often to the innocent. If the world was made by a perfect potter, these sources of misfortune can have no truly acceptable place. They are a sign that something is amiss.

## A Mystical Experience

As with Christians, my understanding of evil is intimately connected with my grasp of the ultimate spiritual nature of the universe. In common with many Pagans, my understanding is based more on personal experience and spiritual encounter than philosophy or theology.

The event that proved most fundamental to my understanding of the world occurred during a "dark night of the soul" where everything in my life seemed jinxed, and my strongest efforts to accomplish any goals important to me appeared utterly in vain. I had suddenly lost a research job with no opportunity to find another to take its place. I was also having to move from a cabin in the woods back to a large city to begin selling my artwork again as a street vendor. Any prospects for having a good relationship with a woman seemed pointless exercises in wishful thinking. Broke, having to move, with no ready prospects of any sort, my life appeared deeply cursed, as I bumbled and stumbled through middle age, every touch turning all I sought to dust and ashes.

My only remaining hope for happiness, I felt, was based upon my earlier experiences of the Goddess, and of Her unconditional love. It seemed to me that if I could cultivate that feeling toward others, I would be less vulnerable to the continual pain arising out of disappointments and rejections from so many avenues of my life. Love can be its own reward, but I had a lot of cultivating to do. I was depressed, often in despair, and all too aware of how far short I fell from my ideals.

One morning, while glumly driving down to the city where I was moving, I was suddenly surrounded by a Presence of perfect love. Unlike my encounter with the Goddess or other high deities, no other qualities were present. I sensed neither maleness nor femaleness, neither a feeling of nature nor a feeling of disconnectedness from nature—or rather, all such qualities were present, but none definingly so. This loving presence was neither personal nor impersonal, or rather, it was completely personal but without any of the limitations we associate with personhood. In attempting to describe that experience such limiting terms did not make sense. There was nothing but love, for all things, everywhere, with perfect understanding. From this presence poured forth an infinite immensity of care for each being, each in its own unique individuality. Accompanying my experience was the insight that perfect love was the fundamental quality of All that Is, of the Godhead, of the Source from which all Gods and Goddesses and everything else manifests. In traditional Wiccan terms, this is what we call the Dryghton.

Within the context of this infinite love, suffering and misfortune acquired a context that redeemed them. At the deepest level of reality it was clear that everything was all right, all beings were loved, none were truly alone, and they really did matter. Lilies of the field, falling sparrows, and deeply despairing Pagans were not living meaningless and futile lives, nor was the meaning of their lives located solely in parts they played in a larger drama whose meaning and outcome they could never grasp, although that was also true. In addition, each being was personally valued at a spiritual level.

My experience of Divine Presence passed all too quickly, but my ability to recall a pale glimmering of that love and beauty decisively changed my view of existence. Since this experience I have no doubt that a Divine Source exists for the material world, that this Source is characterized by superhuman love, compassion, and goodness, and that it transcends the dichotomy of personal/impersonal. The Divine as love embraces all beings. It is unconditional, and permeates everything. In the Jewish philosopher Martin Buber's sense, it is the ultimate "Thou," within and for which everything else is a "Thou" as well.

Deities partake of this same quality, but in a more individualized way. The Wiccan Goddess, for example, is female, and carries with Her a sense of nature, of sun-dappled meadows, dark groves of trees, merry brooks, and brilliant flowers. By virtue of possessing these characteristics She does not possess those of maleness or ethereal detachment. She is therefore a more limited expression of that ultimate Divinity which is beyond limits.

Judging from what I have read, experiences such as mine provide the panentheistic core to many Pagan spiritual traditions, both contemporary and ancient. Nor are such experiences unknown within monotheistic spiritual traditions, where they are often expressed as encounters with the Godhead. Within the nontheistic Buddhist tradition, a friend to whom I described my experience said that it resembled the experience of enlightenment. (*Having* an experience of enlightenment is quite different from *being* enlightened!)

Many spiritual traditions talk of experiences such as this in somewhat different ways. Most importantly, some describe it in personal terms, others in impersonal ones. But all who wrote of such experiences described what happened to them in the context of their own spiritual traditions, using, as best they could, concepts familiar to their audience. Judging from my own experience, terms such as "personal" and "impersonal" ultimately fail to do these experiences justice. Those having such experiences universally say that words can not adequately describe the encounter. Words point to, but do not define.

We need to remember that in trying to analyze such events we run the risk of confusing particular descriptions with the experience itself. If we do, we substitute human comprehension of the Sacred for the Sacred Itself. Insofar as it may help Christians better to appreciate the spiritual validity of Pagan practices, and help some Pagans think more deeply about their own traditions, these efforts are worthwhile. The limitations of any human mind or language are fundamental when describing the Great Mystery. Even so, those having the experience universally conclude that suffering is ultimately not a fundamental aspect of reality and infinite and unconditional love and goodness are such an aspects.

## Love and Reciprocity

Love manifests as caring and delight. The greater the love, the greater one's desire for perfect understanding and treasuring of the beloved. There is no greater nor more perfect love than that from the Ultimate.

The world Spirit manifests in beautiful and abundant individuality, down even to snowflakes. From a human perspective this divine Source apparently delights in the extraordinary variety of things. At the same time, we have discovered profound connections among things, even at the subatomic level. It seems evident that variety, abundance, connectedness, and creativity are obvious and essential aspects of our world, aspects that the Divine finds at bottom to be good and worthy of unconditional love.

Some readers might challenge my argument by saying that because the Divine is far beyond human understanding, *any* verbal description is misleading. In one sense I agree. The experience I had was beyond the power of words to grasp, and my experience was unavoidably limited by my humanness. When I use the word "love" there is no guarantee that what I mean by the term is what you mean. Because "love" is a complex word in our language, there cannot help but be differences in how we use the word, but while we can never be sure our communication is totally clear we manage well enough, because we share a common humanity.

If the Divine were completely other, we could not describe it, even imperfectly. Nor would we have reason to worship or honor it. Perhaps love, which we first learn about within a human context, is only a metaphor for describing the encounter with the Highest, but love is universally recognized as the *best* metaphor. I believe it to be a reliable metaphor because the kind of love reportedly experienced is not simply human love. The experience encompasses complete understanding and unconditional acceptance, neither of which are purely human capacities. It does not reduce the Sacred to the human, but opens the human more widely to the Sacred.

A perfect and limitless love would delight in the existence of enormous variety, manifesting every way in which a good life can be lived. Because Divine love is unconditional, each being would be treasured and cherished, regardless of whether that love was returned. For the Divine to enter into a maximum of loving relationships there must be a breathtaking number of beings, each exemplifying one way for love to manifest, that Spirit may be even more abundantly fulfilled.

If this is so, why do these beings suffer, rather than simply exist in bliss? Any reasonable answer will be complex. Mine starts with the experience of individuality.

Individuality implies variety, both of beings and how they choose to act. For choices to be genuine there must be the possibility of some choices being better than others. If a choice doesn't matter, it is not much of a choice. Consequently, from the chooser's perspective, choice involves the possibility of better and worse, and therefore of error and of regret.

If we begin with Divine perfection, and believe that this perfection is everywhere and complete, individuality can only emerge when that perfection becomes limited in some way. One way is through manifesting a world of matter. When matter exists, boundaries exist. All matter is limited and, insofar as it provides a vehicle for individuated consciousness to manifest, that consciousness must also be limited.

Self-aware material beings are inevitably aware of boundaries, for selves are defined by boundaries: there is "me" and there is "not me." With that awareness comes recognition of individuality. Different limitations create possibilities for new kinds of individuality. With every new individuality comes a new way of manifesting love: for every being in its uniqueness.

The question arises whether these limitations are radical shortcomings, or whether perhaps their presence makes something good possible that might not otherwise exist. World-denying religions emphasize the shortcomings of such limitations. I think this view is not so much mistaken as one-sided. It also raises the perplexing question of why a truly loving Source would create or manifest entities whose chief properties are limitation and the suffering that comes from such limitation.

When we directly experience the Sacred context within which we exist, we grasp ourselves and our world as lovable and as cherished. The Divine does not disapprove of our shortcomings or limitations. We can therefore conclude that, from the perspective of Spirit, it is not necessarily a misfortune to be a limited being. I think we can go still farther.

## Change and Stability in the Sacred

The Divine takes pleasure in our happiness. In Classical European Pagan philosophy this statement would often be challenged as implying an incompleteness on the part of the Ultimate. Desire, they would argue, implies a lack, and God does not lack. Venerable as it is, this view is an error. It relies on the assumption that all possible value can be actualized in an ultimate being in solitude. Not only does this assumption beg the question of why anything else exists, it also implies that perfect love is uninvolved with what is loved. Philosopher and theologian Charles Hartshorne, among others, has persuasively argued this view is an error.

According to Hartshorne, perfect completeness that cannot be improved upon is a purely abstract idea that breaks down when applied to anything concrete. The idea is a product of our language, not our experience. When we speak of the Divine as perfection we can mean either that nothing else is more perfect or that It is absolutely perfect, and cannot even surpass itself. The former concept has room for a perfect being changing, the latter does not. The former concept applies to a loving God, the latter does not. The former does not end in confusion, the latter does, because when we think of absolute perfection we end up in confusions such as claiming the most perfect being lacks the capacity to increase perfection. Yet a God that loved others would by all conceivable accounts be more loving, and therefore more perfect, than a God that did not.[2]

Love can only be fulfilled by the existence of the beloved. It is even more fulfilled when the beloved in turn is also fulfilled. A being loving unconditionally will therefore find delight even in the beloved's loving another. This is why the concept of a jealous God is utterly incomprehensible to me, as it has long been to many Pagans.

Consider the alternative. It makes no sense to say that the Absolute loves conditionally. If conditions must be met for love to exist, then to that extent the would-be beloved is treated as a tool or means to something separate from itself. Such a being is a subject, and neither purely a means nor a tool. Conditional love is for "its," not "Thous," in Buber's sense. Because conditional love is rooted in a misperception of the loved, it cannot be a divine attribute. Indeed, this is a far more limiting conception of the Divine than the alternative I have presented.

If we must choose, it is better to love than to be loved, because love is complete in itself. No matter how complete that love, though, it is even better to be loved in return. This enhanced and deepened joy arising from love reciprocated need not arise because of any lack on the original lover's part. It is a creation of something genuinely new, something that depends upon a new relationship between the beloved and the lover. In this sense it is a *joint* creation. Because the Divine is aware of everything, its existence is enriched without thereby implying that it was previously impoverished. Here is the ultimate expression of the phrase "to him who has is given." The Ultimate has everything, but when we love, everything is enlarged, and the Great Mystery is thereby enriched.

Even among limited beings such as ourselves, there are times when we freely love another even if she or he does not return our love in the same way. Often our own needs and fears ultimately erode or confuse this love. Even so, many of us have felt it to some degree. When the love we give is returned by our beloved, our joy is greater still. The relationship has changed, and with that change both parties are enriched, but before it is returned, the love we previously felt was neither defective nor necessarily limited. Reciprocal love is different from unreciprocated love because the relationship is different and enriched.

Love is only genuine when given freely. Free beings, particularly ones of limited knowledge and wisdom, will return that love in different ways and at different times. They will not be predictable. Each takes its own path. Each is uniquely itself. As each comes to reciprocate that love, the delight of that Ultimate source of reality is enhanced, and because the Ultimate is aware of everything, when we become more loving towards one another, that too enhances God's well-being. From fullness comes even greater fullness. Hartshorne quotes Jules Lequier as saying, "God, who sees things change, changes also in beholding them, or else does not perceive that they change."[3] I think there is much truth in Rainer Maria Rilke's insight that it is "inside human beings is where God learns."[4]

The world of freedom is a world where each of us, slowly, hesitantly, often fearfully, and perhaps over many lifetimes, grows in our capacity to love and wisely care, thereby enriching ourselves and All That Is. Along the way we take plenty of detours, venture down plenty of byways, and given our limitations, make plenty of errors.

The world's spiritual traditions offer us maps that can take us farther along this road than we might otherwise travel. The test of the value for any particular map is how far it carries us. Some of us may read one map better than another.

This observation leads to another: the map is not the territory. We would pity a person who saves travel time and money simply by looking at maps and photos taken by others. Those equating Spirit with the religion they are taught make an even greater error.

In my experience, the Divine attracts us not through fear, but by being so supremely loving and compassionate that once we have encountered the Ultimate we will seek better to express and dwell in those qualities ourselves. In this most fundamental of senses, love is more powerful than power as we normally conceive it.

I have never met a human being who comes close to these qualities as I experienced them, either with the Divine, or with the Goddess and other high beings. Perhaps earth, sacred and lovely as it is, is but a stage along our path in developing ever greater love and wisdom, each in our own way. Ram Dass, a teacher in the Hindu tradition, once memorably described this possibility. When asked if the world was getting better, he answered: "The world is a lot like the fourth grade. People enter the fourth grade, and they graduate from it, but there is always a fourth grade." If Ram Dass is right, graduation may require learning to love this world in all its magnificent beauty and mystery. Otherwise we have not learned its lesson.

The remainder of this chapter is my attempt to make sense of the existence of suffering and despair in a world that, at its core, is an expression of perfect love. I do not mean to imply that I am now free from suffering, and even from despair. That is very far from true. There are still times when my memory of these experiences consists only of the thinnest of threads. To be human is to be no stranger to suffering. However, at some deeper level I know this suffering occurs within a sacred context, and that my periods of despair reflect my own weaknesses in understanding, faith, and patience rather than being justified by the true nature of the world within which I live. The failings, which can be substantial, are my own, not the world's.

## Death

Let us begin with death. Death is far from the greatest source of suffering. There is much worse, hence the enduring allure of suicide. Even so, we are all deeply pained by the passing of loved ones and of the innocent. Often we fear our own passing. Yet at the same time death accompanies life, and apparently plays an essential role in its development and continuation. If the world is good, death can not be a sign of its imperfection. It is too central a feature to our existence.

So how are we to think about it? Nothing seems more directly to undercut the value of individuality than the death that destroys its physical existence. Individuals are filled with extraordinary potential in countless ways. Death brings it to an end. On a billboard in the town where I live is the photo of a happy young boy. It reminds all viewers that he was killed by a drunken driver. If life is good, how can death be good as well? How can a young child, with nearly all his life ahead of him, be killed by a drunk driver in a good world?

We can take two approaches. Both are valid. First, we can ask what role death plays in the existence of those conscious beings for whom we care and whom we know will inevitably die? Second, we can ask why physical death exists at all?

Regarding the first question, most Christians and Pagans alike can agree that consciousness need not be dependent upon physical bodies. The destruction of a body need not imply the destruction of awareness. This is a commonplace belief for any spiritual practice that encourages, and even teaches, its adherents how to have contact with the world of spirits, as does traditional Wicca. Seeing a spirit effectively ends any worry that consciousness must be attached to a physical body. Although for different reasons, Christians will agree. What is really at stake is not whether awareness is extinguished so that the person we love no longer exists. Christians and Pagans agree there is no compelling reason to believe this is the case. Were I writing primarily for secular readers I would explore this question. Here I need not do so.

From a Wiccan perspective, death does not appear to be a time when those we love disappear for good. It seems instead to be a moving on, a shedding of one's skin, a change of abode, to a new dimension of existence. If the Source of All is supremely good, and our universe receives its love without condition, then only our partial vision and self-centeredness makes death appear to be a tragic cutting down of vital, loving, and beautiful beings. We are not aware of the complete context in which a being dies. Our perspective is limited and to an unavoidable extent, self-centered.

If life is a blessing, why move on? Why experience death at all? There are many possible reasons, and life's irreducible mystery will prevent us from knowing for sure which are true. An analogy may help us to understand the one I find most satisfying.

Each time I backpacked to the bottom of the Grand Canyon and out again, at some point I questioned why I was doing it. Sore and blistered feet, the fatigue of carrying a heavy pack up 5,000 feet of trail to the rim, and the relentless draining heat of the sun are not my ideas of fun. Once, as I began my climb out, one of my knees went bad, just after crossing the Colorado River on a suspension bridge. I could not bend my leg without excruciating pain. I think the rim never looked farther away than it did when that happened. It was a *very* long hike to the top! Even when my knees were fine, more than once I have wondered why I am doing this. More than once on my way up I have thought of nothing but the restaurant on the rim, with its comfortable chairs, good food, air conditioning, great views, and table service. When I get to the top, I go there, and I enjoy that restaurant immensely.

But, and this is my point, I am also very grateful to have been at the Grand Canyon, to have backpacked into its immensity, to have experienced its beauty and peace in ways fundamentally unavailable to those who view it from the rim or by airplane, unavailable even to those who take a mule to the bottom. Trips such as these are transformative, in ways less challenging explorations are not. I and others who do these things are enriched in ways those settling for a comfortable restaurant view are not, no matter how good the wine, the service, and the food. Once I have been away for a while, I am ready for another trip, to do it again. I am looking forward to another descent into its serene and awesome chasm, next time with fewer blisters and better knees.

These trips inevitably entail suffering, and there have been times when my physical suffering was by far the greater part of what I experienced. However the suffering is the price of the experience, and in my view ultimately one worth paying. Of course, abstracted from the experience as a whole, the pain is not worthwhile, but the pain is not abstracted. It is part of the package. I can reduce my suffering through wise preparation, or make it worse (or even terminal) through foolishness or bad luck. Either way, suffering is an avoidable part of the trip. Such adventures pay off in ways not available to those who have never done anything similar. Perhaps life is in some ways akin to a backpack into beautiful, but rugged and challenging country. It is strenuous and tiring, while also enriching in ways unavailable without the experience, and death is a time of relaxation.

From this perspective, our religions are simply trail maps, ideally good ones, to guide us into and through life's terrain. Good maps avoid the worst cliffs and swamps while leading us to the best views and campsites. This view is in harmony with Pagan spirituality because it is grounded in spiritual experience of goodness and beauty, not dogma written by some and interpreted by others, to be listened to and believed by us.

There are many other possible reasons for each of us having eventually to die. To fully manifest and develop our own capacities we may need to live more than once. Being a man and being a woman are in many respects very different experiences. Perhaps we each need to live both roles. As a rule our individual gifts and talents vastly exceed the opportunities available to us to develop them within a single life. Our lives are continually filled with fateful choices where we take one path rather than another, becoming different people than we otherwise would have been. Our world offers far more ways to live in fulfilling ways than a single life can ever grasp. Perhaps to fully develop all that we can be we need many lives—to backpack not just into canyons, but high into mountains and exploring coasts and valleys and forests and plains as well. Perhaps.

For those whom we particularly love, is there not a special blessing in loving them in many ways over many lifetimes—as lover and as friend, as parent and as child? If there is a deeper purpose in our lives, I suspect it lies principally in perfecting our hearts as self-aware beings, for love is the most basic quality of the Divine to which we have access. The myriad ways we can live may constitute a vital part of this process of developing our capacity to love. As a teaching in traditional Wicca puts it, "To fulfill love you must return again at the same time and place as the loved one, and you must remember and love them again."[5] For those of us who love life, and one another, reincarnation is a blessing, even if sometimes a painful one. It is like yet another trip into the sacred beauty of the Grand Canyon.

There are also more concrete, and less immediately theological, reasons for our not seeing death as a problem in an ultimately good world. Death appears to be a necessary accompaniment to physical growth. Only a form of life that no longer reproduced itself would need to be freed from the hand of death. Immortal material beings that reproduced would sooner or later fill up all available space. One need not be theistic in any sense to shudder at the prospect of a world wherein death was unknown.

If physical life is good, it is appropriate for other beings also to have the experience of living. Part of life, and certainly part of love, is sharing. Divine love includes unconditional respect, concern, regard for, and delight in others. We who do not fully embody this quality nevertheless find ourselves in a world where ultimately each life form cannot help but provide for the existence of others. The attitude with which we confront this eventuality is important. Part of life is learning to be in harmony with the sacred rhythms that make embodiment possible. This includes being in harmony with death. Part of this harmony is concern for the well-being of generations to come—perhaps the most unselfish type of love which we as human beings can easily practice.

Gary Snyder made a wise observance in this regard. Snyder is a Buddhist, but his sensibility is often close to that of many Pagans, including my own. Considering the role of death, Snyder writes: "'What a big potlatch we are all members of!' To acknowledge that each of us at the table will eventually be part of the meal is not just being 'realistic.' It is allowing the sacred to enter and accepting the sacramental aspect of our shaky temporal personal being."[6]

Death is a sacrament. When we acknowledge the dependence of virtually all living things on other living things, our tendency to oversentimentalize life, and be offended by its sometimes gritty reality, is healed. So long as we deny the sacredness of death, we cannot truly embrace life.

Our society denies death's sacramental character, treating it as an unjust and embarrassing intrusion upon human goals. When we die, our bodies are usually filled with chemicals, painted, and sealed within caskets protecting them from the forces of decomposition; forestalling as long as possible their inevitable return to the earth. This seems to me a grudging and miserly response to a world whose cycles and processes have given us physical life.

Disapproval of death also motivates many who attach a deep moral significance to vegetarianism. There are good reasons for some people being vegetarians, but I do not think refraining from killing is one of them. Human beings cannot avoid killing—or at least delegating that task to others on whom we depend. This point is as true for vegetarians as anyone else. To grow crops a farmer must displace countless animals from their homes as he or she prepares fields for sowing. Many more animals, gophers and rabbits, crows and sparrows, countless insects, and more, may be killed to protect the crops, so that they can be harvested for our use. The best farmers minimize this, but I doubt whether any can eliminate it altogether. After this killing is done (out of our sight but for our benefit) some vegetarians then feel virtuous for not eating animals as food. They miss the point. There is plenty of blood hidden in a plate of spinach and sprouts.

My criticisms of the moral self-righteousness of *some* vegetarians in no way justifies contemporary factory farming, where chickens, pigs, and other animals are confined to simplified mechanical environments, and treated merely as protein producing machines. Neither animals, nor anything else, are simply inert objects to be shoved and manipulated solely for human ends. There is no respect for life in a factory farm. But the evils of such practices can not be equated with eating meat. These evils are rooted in ignorance, callousness, and greed, not in being a carnivore.

To live well, life requires us to integrate a paradox. In unconditionally accepting life's value and beauty, we must also accept the existence of death, which appears as the negation of all beauty and value. This paradox reminds us of the limits to human logic and desire, and confronts us continually.

How we come to accept both life and death is one of the challenges facing all spiritual paths. Christianity promises salvation on the other side, redeeming this life and enlarging the context of our perceptions. Pagan spirituality often takes a different approach, but one that also enlarges the context, providing a way to embrace *both* poles of the paradox within an unconditional affirmation of life.

This is one of the gifts Wiccan spirituality can offer us today - an acceptance of death as part of a world that is good. In almost every dimension Western culture exists in fear and denial of death. It needs this insight of accepting and honoring death, for its fear and denial are ubiquitous—ultimately both self-defeating and spiritually harmful.

When we fear death as the greatest of evils, we desperately utilize any and all things in a futile attempt to prevent it. In doing so we devalue the world around us. Physicality itself becomes an enemy we need to conquer in order at the same time to preserve what? Our physicality! In honoring death in its appropriate place we embrace life more fully. In rejecting death we retreat from life itself.

Those seeking to banish all risk from life are a sad example of how this morbid fear of death impoverishes and circumscribes the life it supposedly preserves. The physical world is always in a state of change. Things come into being, manifest, and then pass away. In seeking to arrest that change we try to make the physical world something it is not. Trying desperately to preserve our physical existence against all change, we find ourselves unable truly to accept or appreciate it. We end up acting not so much from a love of life as from a fear of death, thereby committing a double error, for life is to be loved and death not to be feared. To do less with either is not to trust the Divine nor to act with gratitude for the life we are given.

We Wiccans honor death as part of life. On October 31, at Samhain, its presence is invited. It is not that we seek to die. Far from it. But we know that for each of us our time will come, and we seek to grow in wisdom and insight to the point that when it does come, we will pass into its realm without fear. When I first read Socrates saying philosophy was a preparation for death, I thought his words pessimistic, even depressing. I was much younger then, and not a Pagan. Not I better grasp his profundity. Ideally at that time we can say, as would the wisest of the Plains Indians confronting the chance of death, "Today is a good day to die."

## Spirit and Matter

Classical Pagan philosophy knew that in many ways the material world was a recalcitrant medium for expressing compassion and tranquillity. Many Classical Pagan philosophers considered matter to be the "densest" manifestation of Spirit, or as that dimension of Spirit farthest from the Source of ultimate Goodness and Love. Often Pagan philosophers, such as the late Classical Neoplatonist Plotinus, seemed to condemn the existence of the physical world almost as strongly as did the ancient Gnostics, who often considered the world the creation of an evil God who used it to trap souls into material bodies. The major difference was that Pagan philosophers knew the world was still a Divine manifestation and therefore worthy of respect and love, but their praise could be very faint indeed.

I take a happier view of the matter of matter. I think this difference between my view and that of the ancients is due to two facts. First, the place and time in which I live enables most people to enjoy at least modest prosperity and freedom. Second, as I explained, I reject the Classical Pagan error, for error it seems, of equating perfection with imperviousness to change, a position which radically devalues matter.

Yet there is an important sense in which our Pagan ancestors were correct. Embodiment situates us in a world where *need* is endemic to existence. All living things live in a state of continual need. Physical embodiment requires us to seek physical sustenance. We must take in energy to survive. We require food, water, safety, shelter, and more. Much of life is oriented around satisfying these and other needs, or suffering in the absence of their satisfaction.

Consequently, material existence seemingly stands in stark tension with our experience of the Ultimate, which manifests perfect and unconditional love while being itself perfectly fulfilled.

As self-aware physical beings with memory and foresight, we are aware that our needs might not be met. From this possibility comes a fear of doing without. Today in particular, our suffering often comes as much from our fear of lack as from any genuine deprivation itself. I think that most human suffering and cruelty has its deepest roots in a universe characterized by the ubiquity of need, and our fearful response to it.

In our world awareness is mediated through our physical structure. Every individual is characterized in part by the limitations and possibilities its physical characteristics provide for manifesting awareness. The structure of our eyes determines what we can see, the sensitivity of our ears what we can hear. Most fundamentally, every being is powerfully shaped by all the external forces that have influenced how it and its ancestors survived and reproduced. This is so even if all awareness is, at its core, perfect love—for physical structure is needed to manifest awareness in material form.

Modern biology and fossil records alike indicate that throughout most of life's history on earth natural selection was the final editor, determining which forms of life flourished, and which did not. Those that survived were relatively adept at acquiring the energy needed to flourish. Earthly evolution encouraged and rewarded creativity, subject only to the need to survive and reproduce.

If life is free to explore how to acquire energy, survive, and thrive, some beings will ultimately investigate possibilities of living at the expense of others. Once some organisms discovered that other beings could provide more readily accessible energy than could nonliving processes such as sunlight, the path to a far greater complexity of living entities opened wide. The road to this wonderful variety began with the first munching of a plant—and accelerated enormously when an early muncher was munched in turn. The richness of earthly life grows out of death at the hands of others. If there was a "Fall," this was it, but from this "Fall" has come incredible beauty, variety, and goodness. This was the price paid for consciousness to develop in material form.

Less-aware forms of life seek sustenance with no concern other than maintaining their existence, and reproducing. Within these limitations life flourishes. The resulting variety of life forms are a source of wonder and delight, as well as providing the foundation making our own existence possible. Life seems capable of occupying every possible niche, including rocks thousands of feet underground and adjacent to superheated thermal vents at the bottom of the oceans. Life even creates new niches for itself through complex dances of predation and symbiosis. The very cells of our bodies are symbiotic partnerships of formerly independent entities. Long before they can make moral choices, living organisms simply take advantage of the opportunities they encounter.

Animals eat plants in order to exist. If they are not ultimately to eat themselves into universal starvation, something must eat them. Hence the sacred role served by predators. In seeking to avoid the fate of becoming someone's meal, the successful embody new traits calling forth in turn new capacities on the part of predators. In the absence of carnivores, the world would have remained no richer in life than a planet of blue-green algae. The overwhelming evidence of the fossil record is that predators and even disease provide important spurs for change and development.

An embodied consciousness such as our own can only arise if beings were continually subject to pressures to change and adapt to new opportunities, gradually enriching and diversifying the forms life takes. Before a physical organism can become complex enough to manifest self awareness in individuated form, it must have evolved from out of a long series of simpler forms. Competition between predators and prey, and with one another for desirable mates, encourage diversity, and so, complexity.

If divine creativity enables countless possibilities for life to explore, with the immediate criteria for success being the capacity successfully to reproduce, not all avenues pursued by others will add to our own comfort. For physical consciousness to evolve to where it can act with self-aware, loving kindness, it had to manifest many levels of more opportunistic behavior, taking advantage of whatever chances existed to obtain the energy needed to survive. Most beings are completely unconcerned with our well-being. The very same world that makes our physical existence possible can make that existence brief. However, if physical life is a place for the free development and exploration of creative possibilities, the existence of our uncomfortable and even dangerous kindred appears less spiritually confusing than it would if every-thing was created once and for all by some cosmic potter.

The shape of our bodies, and the complexity of our brains, are the result of millions of years where natural selection edited what was possible, and what was to be cast aside. Spirit had to mani-fest in many ways to lay the groundwork for such a complex physical awareness as we possess. Human awareness has a fantas-tic pedigree, one shaped by all those forms of life from which we descend.

I do not suggest the earth's purpose is to manifest us. Long be-fore human beings existed, the physical world was already com-plete. In our absence it still manifests peace and beauty, variety and the delights that come from the senses. It is sacred in its own right. Today we can make contact with this perfection when we enter attentively into wild nature. The perception of nature as beautiful is found in every society. We do not import beauty into nature as our subjective reaction. It is there, and we discover it.

Robinson Jeffers caught this point perfectly when he wrote of the natural world: "The human sense of beauty is our metaphor for their excellence."[7] Until we finally develop our capacity for genuine love, Nature will remain that manifestation of Spirit that is most fulfilling for us, because it is complete, and we are still in-complete. Once we have become adept at manifesting love, far from disparaging the world of nature, we will love it all the more.

Because our existence is necessarily rooted in need, self-con-scious beings capable of genuine love become so obsessed with meeting their needs and avoiding their fears that they lose sight both of nature's perfection and their own inherent possibilities. As more complex beings than our less self-conscious relations, we are also more prone to error than they. We can make all the mistakes other kinds of life can make, plus many errors that they cannot. My cat, Kiki, can make mistakes, but she probably will make no mistakes about theology.

As the most self-aware life forms, human beings depend upon physical and emotional intimacy and affection in order to prosper.

Babies deprived of loving human contact rarely live to adulthood. Nor does this appear true of human babies alone. Other relatively aware life forms also need nurturing in more than purely physical ways in order to survive. Experiencing gentleness, care, and intimacy appear to be requirements for living beings whose minds have developed beyond a certain threshold of awareness. The more self-aware the being, the more it needs and desires intimacy, trust, affection, and delight in the affectionate reciprocation of others. In the absence of these feelings such beings often die, and those that survive emerge deeply scarred. This continuum of need is what we would expect to find if full awareness is love, and if we are the most self-aware of material beings.

## Self and Love

With self-awareness the tension between our subjection to the realm of need and openness to spiritual awareness free from need becomes a defining feature of who we are. By contrast, animals apparently live largely in the moment. They do not appear to worry about their future. It seems reasonable to hold that they relate to the Ultimate in ways in keeping with their nature, and their nature may be less likely to go awry than ours.[8]

In our greater self-awareness we have separated from them, and often suffer from our inability to maintain a similar spontaneity within a human context without long and disciplined effort. That very self-awareness that so easily separates us from living in the beauty of the moment also deepens our capacity for love. If self-awareness was our peculiarly human fall, it was also our rise. *Self-awareness is a necessary element in the development of a loving awareness of others as unique beings.* Our awareness of self, and of a depth to self, brings with it awareness of other selves, and of similar depths on their part. It makes possible a differentiated and reciprocated love between individuated beings.

To root the human capacity for love in our self-awareness seems a paradox. It is more often used to explain human selfishness. It is true that only self-aware beings can be selfish, but this observation only scratches the surface of what it is to be self-aware. By itself that scratch misleads.

To have a self is to have a self-interest. To act in my *future* self-interest requires me to have a conception of my *future* self, which does not yet exist. It is my capacity for empathy with others that enables me to identify with this future self, because from my present perspective this anticipated future self is an "other." Without my capacity to put myself in the place of another I could never overcome the temptation to seek immediate gratification at the expense of my long-term well-being, because the temptation is always for seeking pleasure now. Future pain, after all, will not come to the "me" with which I currently identify. However, if I can empathize with my future self, that is, if I can project myself into an experience that is not happening to me, but which might, I can refrain from that temptation. Every student doing homework today to avoid embarrassment tomorrow accomplishes this.

The same empathetic capacity that helps me act for my own long-term well-being enables me to identify with other selves. From empathy and understanding the uniquely human love of individuality can grow, both for myself and for others. Many years ago the Russian poet Yevgeny Yevtushenko beautifully captured this insight for me:

> In any man who dies there dies with him
> his first snow and kiss and fight.
> It goes with him.
>
> They are left books and bridges
> and painted canvas and machinery.
> Whose fate is to survive.
>
> But what has gone is also not nothing:
> by the rule of the game something has gone.
> Not people die but worlds die in them.[9]

Yevtushenko expressed his insight on individuality as a materialist, but his truth here is greater than his error. I know of no one who has better expressed the precious value of every life. It is through human nature that Spirit as a realm beyond need and matter as characterized by need can together create values neither can accomplish by themselves.

D. H. Lawrence made a perceptive observation about the peculiarly human kind of love possible between limited individuals:

> Only in the conjunction of man and woman has love kept a duality of meaning. Sacred love and profane love, they are opposed, and yet they are both love. The love between man and woman is the greatest and most complete passion the world will ever see, because it is dual, because it is of two opposing kinds. . . .
>
> Sacred love is selfless, seeking not its own. The lover serves his beloved and seeks perfect communion of oneness with her. But whole love between man and woman is sacred and profane together. Profane love seeks its own. . . .
>
> But the love between a man and a woman, when it is whole, is dual. It is the melting into pure communion, and it is the friction of sheer sensuality, both. In pure communion I become whole in love. And in pure, fierce passion of sensuality I am burned into essentiality.[10]

Such a relationship is only possible with beings who are both subject to need and aware of that kind of love which is free of need. It is not possible with beings who are free from need, for they are fulfilled with spiritual love alone. Nor is it possible with beings who are not self-aware, for they are satisfied with sensual love alone. This is the kind of love that is most uniquely human. If it opens us up to agonizing pain when thwarted, it also gives us unutterable joy when it is not.

Our self-awareness provides us an additional gift. Implicit in human nature is the capacity to love in ever-wider circles of inclusion, and the more we develop our humanity, the wider those circles of inclusion become. Our capacity for ever-expanding circles of love that enables us to love one another as individual beings of intrinsic value. We can even grow to love diversity rather than simply being threatened by what is different from us. With self-awareness the expression of love and compassion within the physical world becomes potentially much greater. It also makes it possible for us to reciprocate Divine love in a way apparently distinct from other earthly beings. Only compassionate and loving human beings are fully human beings.

The American ecologist Aldo Leopold made this point with rare insight. Leopold wrote that while we can mourn the extinction of the passenger pigeon, whose flocks once numbered in the millions before being destroyed by market hunters, no passenger pigeon would have mourned our passing had it been human beings who disappeared from the scene. He concluded that, "For one species to mourn the death of another is a new thing under the sun."[11] It is this quality of unselfish care, care that blossoms into love, that we can bring into the world, and so manifest the Sacred in a way most truly fitting for us. It is our unique gift to life.*

Here is a still deeper meaning of the Wiccan teaching "to fulfill love you must return again at the same time and place as the loved one, and you must remember and love them again." With each incarnation the possibilities for loving relationships can be deepened. Such a view of incarnation cannot see it as a curse.

A world of change and creativity will of necessity also be a world where everything that exists in material form is inevitably subject to decline. All change is a passing away as well as a coming into being. Everything that exists changes. This is the world we experience. As with our Midsummer Sabbat, at the peak of

---

* As an aside, Leopold's insight means that those who care about the fate of endangered species, far from being opposed to human values, as their detractors argue, exemplify them in a very strong way.

---

physical vitality and success the seed of transient mortality sprouts. All material forms always pass away.

A good model of our reality may be a kaleidoscope, or perhaps a sunset. Each moment of beauty must pass if new beauty is to arise, and the full cycle of such a process far surpasses that available in any freeze frame, for change is part of the beauty. To enjoy either a kaleidoscope or a sunset we do not fixate on a single moment, but instead allow ourselves to become enchanted by the beauty of the changing patterns, as well as each moment in the process. The same is true for life itself.

For living matter to exist a tension between need and sufficiency naturally arises. As any artist knows, when used appropriately, tension deepens and enriches beauty and life. A dancer depends on gravity to enhance the beauty of seeming to overcome its pull. Only through incorporating this tension into the heart of existence can new and deeper ways of loving emerge.

The pull of our material and psychological needs can, and often does, get in the way of our awareness of Spirit. The dance is not easy, but in dancing the tension through embracing it, we develop more powers of wisdom and depths of love and compassion than would otherwise be the case. Spirit as it manifests in matter uses need to create a beautiful world that is complete in itself, but that also creates the preconditions for even more inclusive and varied manifestations of love to arise.

In the sacred cycle of physical existence what appear to be the world's "imperfections" take on added dimensions of meaning that fulfill them and raise them into blessings, for they generate new patterns that enable the deeper pattern more completely to fulfill itself. Good music is always more beautiful than even the purest note repeated over and over again. But for music to exist, that note must "die."

1. A. H. Armstrong, "The Ancient and Continuing Pieties of the Greek World," in *Classical Mediterranean Spirituality: Egyptian, Greek, Roman*, A. H. Armstrong, ed. (New York: Crossroads, 1989), p. 98.

2. Charles Hartshorne, *Omnipotence and Other Theological Mistakes* (Albany: State University of New York Press, 1984).

3. Ibid., p. v.

4. Rainer Maria Rilke, "Just as the Winged Energy of Delight," *Selected Poems of Rainer Maria Rilke: A Translation from the German and Commentary by Robert Bly*, Robert Bly, trans. (New York: Harper and Row, 1981), p. 175.

5. Gerald Gardner, *Witchcraft Today*, (New York: Magickal Childe, 1954) p. 41; Janet and Stewart Farrar, *The Witches' Way: Principles, Rituals and Beliefs of Modern Witchcraft* (London: Robert Hale, 1984), p. 30.

6. Gary Snyder, *The Practice of the Wild: Essays by Gary Snyder* (Berkeley, CA: North Point Press, 1990), p. 19.

7. Robinson Jeffers, "The Inhumanist," *The Double Axe* (New York: Liveright, 1977), p. 57.

8. This insight in the context of Classical Paganism is explored by Michael Hornum, "The Availability of the One: An Interpretive Essay," *Alexandria: The Journal of the Western Cosmological Traditions*, 2, 1993.

9. Yevgeny Yevtushenko, *Selected Poems* (Baltimore: Penguin, 1962), p. 85.

10. D. H. Lawrence, "Love," *Sex, Literature and Censorship*, Harry T. Moore, ed. (New York: Twayne Publishers, 1953), pp. 35–36.

11. Aldo Leopold, *A Sand County Almanac* (New York: Ballentine, 1966), p. 117.

# Malice, Suffering, and Evil

Any person born in the twentieth century cannot have missed the challenge to spiritual world views arising from the carnage of two world wars, holocausts against the Armenians in Turkey, Jews, Gypsies, and others in much of Europe, and more recent genocides in Bosnia and Rwanda. Additional millions have been slaughtered for their politics or religion by criminal rulers. Anyone with a spiritual perspective, whatever it may be, has to try and make sense of crimes and dangers on such a vast scale, along with individual acts of extraordinary cruelty and malevolence. Even if the suffering of physical existence is compatible with the existence of divine love, what are we to make of these events?

If evil is anything at all, it is malice, a desire to cause pain in others. Why does malice exist? In my experience, malice is one of the most powerful and painful results of ignorance combined with a closed heart. Errors of judgment by limited but free beings are inevitable. Their existence makes it possible for malice to arise.

Probably all of us have found on occasion that our anger toward another evaporates completely when we learn we had been misinformed, or had misunderstood that person's actions. What if we had not learned we were wrong? And how often do errors of this kind remain undiscovered? When we do not learn of our error our anger may fester and grow. If in consequence we then strike out verbally or in other ways, we in turn feed that person's own confusion, fear, and resentment. They now see *us* as malicious, and may strike back in return, confirming for us their nastiness. Pride, itself a form of ignorance, can magnify the impact of these errors. Over time, a self-centered enough individual can be turned to evil. People are not born consumed by malice, but some may end up that way as they walk a path of many false steps.

Pride and ignorance can feed on one another without any need for an outside supernatural agency to intervene. Wisdom, which is their remedy, can be acquired only through living life attentively. For most of us, I suspect, it often takes a hard knock up against our head to get our attention. Until our attitudes have been adjusted, our eyes and hearts opened, it is all too easy to feel resentment and anger. We lose sight of larger contexts that ameliorate or limit the significance of our suffering until the slights we believe we have suffered become mountains of resentment and anger.

Once I was so caught up in my own suffering and self-pity that when I saw strangers happily in love, or enjoying material prosperity, or otherwise experiencing obvious good fortune that seemed denied to me, I felt an upwelling of resentment and envy. I will always remember one time in particular when the intensity of my malice shocked me deeply. That episode became a turning point. I realized I had better not proceed farther down *that* path.

That was long ago. Looking back, it seems to have happened to another person, in another time and place. In a sense it did. But no outside forces generated that spiritual and psychological poison, although some may have been attracted by its existence. I managed all by myself. Far from evil being a fundamental aspect of the world, confronting us as an alien and hostile force, it is largely we, ourselves, who create evil.

With help from friends, teachers, and the Gods, I slowly, painfully, dissolved away much of that anger, and the resentment it fed. No evil spirit created my self-pity, depression, and anger during that dark time. It originated from out of my own ignorance. My narrow conception of self, with its corresponding self-centeredness, provided the most feeble of contexts for coping with pain and disappointment, and I blew my frustrations out of proportion.

These insights, drawn from my own life, can apply to understanding even the most depraved actions. When discussing the nature of evil, one Christian correspondent pointed to Richard Allen Davis as an example of human evil. Davis abducted a young girl, Polly Klaas, from her home during a slumber party, and later strangled her. What Davis did was certainly an act of malice. What he did was evil. But I have also felt malice toward those who did me no harm. Sometimes their very lack of awareness of me and of my suffering could add fire to my anger. "How dare they be so unconcerned, so selfish!" As I grew in understanding and openness of heart, resentment's strength diminished, and its flames withered.

What if I had not? What if additional events, real and imagined, had continued to feed my pain and ignorance? Might I ultimately have become so trapped by my anger that I would have lashed out? I cannot be confident that the gulf between me and the most depraved of individuals is not made up of many small steps, each a choice, but each strengthening one predisposition or another.

The roots of at least some of my anger and fear lay in a miserable childhood, and in mistaken interpretations I made of things which happened to me. The experiences that fed those emotions were not intended by those responsible to have such an impact. They would have been appalled had they known, but how can a child exercise the wisdom of an adult? Few adults can view the world from a child's eyes.

Yet we know the decisions and attitudes a child develops often carry over into adult life, serving as all but invisible filters through which their world is perceived and their life lived. Habits formed long ago in ignorance later become powerful challenges and barriers to our wisdom and happiness, often requiring enormous effort to overcome them. If they are not overcome, the person can commit evil acts.

Unless Richard Allen Davis is so alien that I cannot begin to understand him, I can only conclude that at bottom the differences between us, great as they are, are ultimately quantitative, not qualitative. From what I read of his childhood, his responses to life are comprehensible, though not defensible. Many people have had a horrible childhood and not gone on to murder, but to some extent I can grasp the long line of mistaken interpretations and bad decisions that ultimately led him to death row.

I, and many other Pagans, believe that mind creates and shapes energy. Such psychic energy reflects the quality of mind from which it came. We do not need the presence of bad spirits for very unpleasant things to manifest and happen on the level of nonmaterial existence. We can do it ourselves.

However, many Pagans, I among them, would also say that some spirit entities are capable of malice—and probably for the same reasons that people are. There is no reason to believe that just because a being exists in a nonmaterial way it must therefore be spiritually wise. Why should my death make me wiser than I am now? Maybe it will. Maybe it won't. Perhaps what appear to be malevolent entities are simply the tough drill sergeants educating us toward wisdom—but if they are, they are inspired actors. There do indeed seem to be malicious spiritual forces. But even if malevolent humans and spirits exist, failings such as theirs are not evidence of a deep flaw in existence or an ultimate demonic spiritual principle.

## A Final Christian Objection

Some Christians will raise a strong objection to arguments such as these. Because I have suggested that the likelihood of future lives puts suffering in this one into a larger context, they ask, if we accumulate wisdom over many lives, why isn't life significantly better today than in earlier times? In part, I believe that they are wrong, and life *is* significantly better.

We are so sensitive to the many failings of our society that we often do not fully appreciate what has been accomplished that is worthwhile. For the first time the majority of people on the earth, as a whole, are not poor. For the first time we appear to have developed political forms—representative democracies—which do not wage war on their own kind. Life spans continue to improve, as does the average condition of our health. Childbirth is rarely life threatening. Men and women now enter relationships based primarily upon friendship and love rather than economic need and family status. These are pretty big improvements. Even our sensitivity to our failings is an important step forward. In my view, the world is getting better, albeit if unevenly.

Yet this reply can be acknowledged without really setting this objection to rest. A Christian can agree that the factors I have mentioned are genuine improvements, but not signs that *people* are getting better. Wealth does not necessarily make anyone more kind, generous, or loving. Nor need poverty necessarily cause cruelty, selfishness, or hate. Certainly some of the poorer people I know are among the kindest and most giving and some of the wealthier people in our society are among the most cruel and self-centered.

As virtually everyone will grant, the conditions of family life can have a powerful impact upon the character of children, and these influences will last, in some cases, all their lives. The quality of family life does not make children's later behavior as adults completely predictable, but neither is it without weight. The same point holds for all other social institutions. Humane institutions encourage humane values. The steady improvement in human well-being institutionally has on the whole a beneficial impact upon individual character. That character is influenced by many other factors as well should not blind us to this fact.

Anyone reading early American history cannot help but be impressed with the ease with which many Americans slaughtered those who stood in their way, such as Indians. Bigotry toward immigrants extended to Italians, Irish, and many other European peoples. Non-European peoples were even farther beyond the pale. Segregation and lynching were taken for granted in many regions of our society.

Gradually these attitudes have withered. As we have become relatively secure in our livelihoods, many of us more easily pursue values of care and service for others or for nature. As we have become more democratic in our outlook we have become more loath to resort to violence, or to applaud it in others who oppose people and causes we dislike. In short, our society, and many others which are democratic, have been and are continuing to be transformed. In so doing the individuals who comprise those societies are also being changed. As a people we are more comfortable with variety and complexity than were our ancestors, largely because we have expanded the circle of those we regard as fellow human beings in a deep sense.

This is my perspective, but the answer to this Christian argument does not depend on whether the trend toward greater humanity that I am describing is a real trend or a momentary high point along the erratic road of human existence. I may be wrong, but even so, there is no reason to grant this Christian objection any validity. Ram Dass may be right, and we will ultimately graduate from the fourth grade rather than help the world as a whole enter the fifth. I, for one, hope we can take our classroom with us.

Regarding reincarnation, many Wiccans, myself included, have had vivid glimpses of what certainly appear to have been past lives, but we do not as a rule remember them in much detail. Perhaps we only experience the "big picture" in between our physical lives, rather than taking those learned lessons with us into our next earthly one. Enlightened spiritual traditions say it is only at or on the verge of enlightenment that people remember their past lives in great detail. I wouldn't know, not being enlightened, but clearly there is no shortage of reasonable responses to this Christian criticism. It does not appear to be particularly convincing.

## A Christian Alternative: Satan and God

Many monotheistic faiths explain life's evils by invoking a supreme force for evil. It seems the more that God's power is emphasized over His love, the more all earthly problems have to be attributed to a particularly nasty opponent. In the case of Evangelical Christians, even for those who are not Fundamentalists, this force is called Satan, a being many apparently regard as second only to the Creator Himself in power and implacably opposed to Him.

Not all Christians focus on Satan as a distinct entity in malicious rebellion against God. Many may find much with which to agree in my discussion of evil from a Pagan perspective. But the emphasis upon a distinct source of evil external from God is one of the biggest differences separating many Christians from Wiccans, and it inspires some Christians to consider all other religions, even other Christian denominations, as Satanically influenced.

It seems appropriate, then, to examine the widespread view that evil can be blamed on an external Satanic force of some sort. Is the Satan explanation as plausible as others I have suggested? Let us see.

The view of Satan as the malevolent opponent of God inevitably leads to a conception of an ongoing "war in heaven," with its contesting powers of Good and Evil, Light and Darkness, locked in an implacable struggle for ultimate dominance. Such a conception has been the source of enormous suffering, because it leads its adherents to oppose any diversity of views and practices on subjects they regard as spiritually significant. They also have a corresponding tendency to view anything different as inferior or evil. When we are at war those who question our views easily appear guilty of treason. Such attitudes often encourage a person in the silly pride that he or she is "on God's side," as if God were a needy embattled commander.

A view of spirituality that focuses *solely* on Divinity's transcendent aspect makes enormous demands upon the wisdom and spiritual clarity of its practitioners, *because* it separates the world of actual experience from the Divine. Nowhere is this demand for clarity more the case than when confronting the question of suffering in the world. As we have seen, there *is* a tension between Spirit and matter. When this tension is embodied into two utterly different realms of Spirit and Matter, it is all too easy to make evil a separate principle radically opposed to God. Evil then naturally gravitates to being ruler of the material world. Indeed, through the centuries Christianity has continually battled a heretical tendency to evolve into theological dualism, where the universe is characterized by a battle between two basic forces: good and evil.

Nowhere is the utter arbitrariness of absolutist interpretations of Scripture more apparent than in this common Biblical understanding of Satan. However, the Bible itself is anything but clear on the matter. Its lack of clarity is why Christians disagree with one another even while, in so many cases, condemning other faiths for not being biblical.

From a biblical perspective, it is the Christian God, *by His own admission*, who created and controls evil, which therefore does His will. Amos 3:6 asks, "shall there be evil in a city, and the Lord hath not done it?" 1 Samuel 18:10 describes "the evil spirit from God [that] came upon Saul . . . ." Lamentations 3:38 tells us, "Out of the mouth of the most High proceedeth not evil and good?" If God controls evil, it can scarcely be said to be in rebellion to him. Biblically speaking, God's relationship to evil may be even closer than this. 2 Samuel 24:1 finds God inciting David to number Israel, that is, to take a census. 1 Chronicles 21:1 finds Satan inciting David to do the same thing. The passages appear to be about the same episode (although the census takers report different summations).

These passages suggest that either God and Satan are in a close working relationship, and so are hardly implacable enemies, or that the chief difference between God and Satan is not what they do but who does it. Either explanation challenges many Christian accounts of evil. The latter is the most unsettling since it defines goodness as a derivative of God's power. From such a perspective Satan's real failing is in being weak, not in being bad.

I would think these Biblical passages should deeply trouble Christians who believe other faiths are Satanically inspired. If evil is necessary for God to finish His creation, as these passages suggest, does this imply a limit on God's goodness and power? Or is the ultimate source of spiritual evil, at bottom, not really evil? This latter interpretation is in harmony with the view I am presenting here, that evil does not exist in any fundamental form, but instead is rooted in fear and ignorance.

The Christian Satan appears to be a far more paradoxical being than most believing in him have been willing to admit. Originally Satan appeared as something less than the Lord's implacable opponent. In the Book of Job he is on at least speaking terms with God, and is at least occasionally present in Heaven. Satan appears more as God's attorney general than a source of pure malevolence, but as time passed his role darkened. Perhaps this was because of the Jewish people's later exposure to Zoroastrian dualism, which conceived the world as a battleground between good and evil. Whatever the reason, Satan's Biblical status steadily changed for the worse.

Satan supposedly was second in heaven until his pride led him to rebel against God. A being second only to God would presumably have superhuman insight (or else God promotes very foolishly). And Satan's crime was supposedly rebellion. Now, if Satan is rebellious, and is also of superhuman intelligence, he would presumably be able to come to the following conclusions: "God has a plan to cope with my rebellion. This plan has been laid open to some extent in Scripture, where man and demon alike can read it." Satan should therefore be well aware that to the extent he encourages people to act in the fashion already described in the prophecies, he will in fact be *helping* God carry out His divine plan. Some rebel! It would be far more rebellious for him simply to go on strike. Do nothing. Force God to do His own dirty work.

For a superhuman power, second only to God in intelligence, to so conveniently and willingly play the role that God requires of him, while remaining His implacable foe, is absurd. This is especially the case if God continually rubs it in by publishing all over the world what Satan will do before Satan in fact does it. Many Christians believe this was the case in the prophecies they interpret as foretelling Jesus' arrival and death. They also believe the Book of Revelation is a reliable guide to Satan's future actions. Presumably Satan has read it as well.

If Satan is God's implacable enemy, he should have sought at all costs to have Jesus die of old age. If Jesus had died naturally, the standard theology would suggest we could not now be saved, for according to most Christian views it took Jesus' death as some sort of sacrifice to make God's forgiveness of our sins possible. Otherwise there was no point to it. What greater blow to God could Satan give? If Satan is ruler of "this world" he certainly had the power to save Jesus' life. Doing so would indefinitely perpetuate the bad effects of the Fall.

The alternative possibility is that Satan is a pretty stupid opponent.

Some Christians respond that Satan is blinded by his pride, the same pride that initially caused his rebellion. Maybe so—but it is a singularly stupid pride, one that has blinded him for millennia. As we know from prideful humans, pride is pretty good at blunting intelligence, but some prideful people eventually catch on. Again, Satan must be an extraordinarily stupid opponent if this explanation is true.

Since some human beings can see the ultimate hollowness of evil and its pleasures, compared to what is available when acting from love and kindness, it is impossible for me to conceive a super-intelligent Satan as being so blind as to continue being mired in malice. This is especially the case if mere humans, who can see the superiority of love and compassion, are themselves supposedly damned by Original Sin. That there are malevolent spirits is no great theological dilemma for either Christian or Pagan. It is little different from explaining why there are malevolent human beings. But that there be malevolent spirits of superhuman intelligence—intelligence second only to God's—*that* is a problem. If Satan is "in on it" with God, all these problems disappear. Satan as God's attorney general seems to be a more reasonable view of Satan's reality than Satan as God's implacable opponent.

If this observation is true, one major leg of the Christian claim to spiritual exclusivity is knocked away. It is no longer the case that just because a religion is not focused on Jesus it must be Satanic. In addition, a Pagan interpretation of evil, such as the one I have suggested, appears harmonious with this alternative perspective. It allows plenty of room for the likes of malignant spirits, as well as more ambivalent beings such as Coyote, Elegba, and Loki. Evil no longer becomes an inexplicable intrusion into the work of a master potter, but rather an important but ultimately not fundamental aspect of perfectly loving Spirit manifesting as matter.

## Suffering, Blessing, and Growth

The natural world provides many examples enabling us to see how what superficially appears agonizing and a struggle is often essential for the well being of the individual beings so "afflicted." If you help a butterfly struggling to emerge from its chrysalis, its wings will not develop. The butterfly will emerge crippled. The butterfly's long and exhausting struggle is essential to its becoming a strong and beautiful being. The chaparral-covered hillsides of California, stately groves of soaring sequoias in the Sierra, and lodgepole-mantled mountainsides of the Rockies all require the searing destruction of fire for their well-being. In a different but perhaps analogous way, the insights we gain from accepting and overcoming the suffering in our own lives can help us find its deeper significance—even in suffering from which it may seem we cannot recover, or in witnessing the apparently pointless suffering of others.

Socrates, the Buddha, and many other wise teachers have observed that ignorance leads to suffering. There are two kinds of ignorance: spiritual and profane. The first has to do with the ultimate nature of reality and how to live in harmony with it, the second with getting what we want in daily life. We have plenty of both.

For the suffering taking place within the body of the Divine to result in the ultimate benefit of those who suffer, suffering must help create some quality which would not otherwise arise. Otherwise it is needless. Occasions for suffering are so many, and in some cases apparently so uncompensated, that any argument here must be very tentative. After all, how can a human being know what qualities can arise from suffering that he or she has not undergone?

Yet we can humbly reflect upon the possible wider implications of our own ignorance. In my experience, even great suffering, once worked through, has always left me better off, and wiser. Some whom I know to have life-threatening diseases have told me their illnesses were good for them in very profound ways. I am therefore very hesitant simply to judge suffering as bad, much as I try to avoid it.

To be sure, in the midst of profound suffering arguments like mine give only a little solace. They do not make suffering go away. They only give it a more meaningful context, making it easier to endure.

Sometimes I have given thanks for things that once caused me to suffer but left me wiser, as well as for the blessings that have more gently brought me happiness. But in the midst of deep pain I give no more thanks than most people. Pain hides contexts and clouds judgment. Indeed, when we focus on them, even little pains have a distressing tendency to take on greater importance in our lives than they merit. I think we need a little distance from our greatest pains before we can begin to grasp how they have contributed to our lives, and so truly to give thanks.

I am not arguing our personal sufferings constitute foreordained lessons, like the inexorable march of tests in a math class. Maybe. But there seems to be real room in our world for freedom and choice, and therefore opportunities for unexpected accidents and errors. Bad things do happen to good people. However, if the fundamental ground of being is compassionate love, these bad things provide opportunities—both for those to whom they happen, and for those who know people who suffer—to practice manifesting love more perfectly themselves. While not preordained, these events need not destroy the deepest sacred patterns into which they intrude. Spirit can take them and turn them to other ultimately beneficial uses. The greatest artists integrate the unexpected into their rhythm, creating even more complex and beautiful art than would otherwise have existed. Every time a misstep occurs, there is an opportunity to take the dance into new directions of grace and beauty. If we fail, it is largely because we don't know the steps. And often we don't. We stumble a lot, but over time we become more sure-footed, as practice makes us into better dancers.

Many people I know report similar insights after passing through a period of suffering and emerging to the other side. We notice we have learned lessons leaving us better off than if we had never suffered at all. Given the very real likelihood of reincarnation or something like it, this observation may even apply to what, from the perspective of a single lifetime, seems undeserved and meaningless suffering.

Suffering is an enriching manure for the human spirit. It is a compost for the heart. Genuine empathy for others often arises most readily after we have suffered ourselves. Our hearts grow only when open. What opens them is often our suffering, which can first ignite the fire of care in our hearts. Until that fire is lit, we retain only the seed of a human spirit, closed in upon itself, without depth of understanding for either ourselves or others. The fire of care warms and softens its shell, enabling the spirit within to grow.

Such experiences widen our frame of concern, helping us put our personal desires within a larger context and set aside our demands that the world proceed as we desire. Given that we do not have anything near the wisdom required to order the world, or often even our own lives without the assistance of others, this nonattachment to outcomes takes us another step toward genuine wisdom—the integration of experience and love. Nonattachment in this sense is not ceasing to care, it is ceasing to demand, and ceasing to judge if our wishes are not met.

I think suffering is needed to develop depth of soul and wisdom. Many spiritual traditions, Pagan and Christian alike, have argued so. If I had never suffered, I doubt that I would much understand compassion, let alone practice it to the limited extent that I do. It is our compassion that opens us up to loving others for themselves, and therefore better attaining our potential as human beings. Perhaps like the butterfly, we need to struggle and suffer to reach our true potential.

## An Important Caveat

We can make judgments such as these in our own cases, once we see how we have ultimately benefited from such experiences. Remembering this insight can sustain us while we live through hard times. Extrapolating from our own and others' similar experiences can help us get a better handle on suffering in general, but it is arrogance and worse to make such judgments to others in the midst of their pain, particularly concerning suffering we have not experienced ourselves. I would never tell a reader who just suffered a great tragedy that this was a blessing. It is at most an opportunity *for them* to turn something into an ultimate blessing. The event itself is still bad and those responsible deserve no thanks, no matter how great in retrospect the blessing might be.

To the extent the argument I have presented is convincing it is because of my readers' personal experience, not my logic. Nothing is more personal than suffering, which is why we can lose sight of wider contexts when we are in its midst. A general argument such as mine helps alert us to these larger contexts, but at the cost of removing us to some extent from the immediacy of our experience. Abstraction, useful as it can be, distances us from the concrete and so can harden the heart when applied to others. Abstracting from the concrete suffering of others to anonymous generalities threatens the heart most because it removes our attention to what is unique about each person, focusing only on anonymous similarities. Abstraction is perhaps our most powerful intellectual tool. But when we allow our tools to define our reality, we are lost.

The suffering of others gives us the opportunity to act with love, compassion, and wisdom. On our part that is all that is truly appropriate at such times because we do not see the larger patterns at work. Discovering the deeper meaning of suffering is up to those who suffer. Discovering the deeper meaning of love is up to the rest of us.

## Conclusion

From a Wiccan perspective we can now conclude that while much suffering is unnecessary, in the sense that wise beings would neither inflict it nor suffer it, there is still an irreducible core of suffering inherent to physical existence as such. This irreducible core stems from our existing as mortal material beings who must meet our physical and psychological needs in order to live, and who have limited understandings about how to do so, and therefore cannot help but make mistakes. Some people may regard these conditions as signs of fallenness. I find them necessary aspects of being a human being in this beautiful world, and so, except in the depths of despair, judge the price worthwhile. Suffering is not evidence of radical failure. It goes with the package—and on balance the package is good. Indeed, often it is in confronting opposition and trouble that we, like the butterfly emerging from its cocoon, develop genuine spiritual strength, depth, and beauty.

With this final judgment we return to a major spiritual divide distinguishing those of us who want to live in harmony with our world from those who seek salvation from it. I have tried to show that there is valid insight in both perspectives. Each of us must answer for ourselves which speaks most directly to our hearts and lives. It is neither naive nor willfully blind to argue that our lives here are blessings, and that the world and the myriad relations that most fundamentally comprise it are worthy of our love and gratitude.

# Biblical Inerrancy
# and Scriptural Authority

A major difference between Christian spirituality and most Pagan spirituality is the presence or absence of sacred scriptures. This is particularly the case with Neopagan religion, where no writings are regarded as so divinely inspired as to be in any sense infallible. To be sure, Gardnerian and other Wiccan traditions have Books of Shadows, kept more or less successfully secret, and gradually revealed in their entirety to Wiccans as they advance within their traditions, but these materials are not scriptural in the Christian sense.

Interestingly, Books of Shadows are akin to most texts used by Greek and Roman Pagan traditions, which usually consisted of hymns and rituals rather than recitations of sacred dogma.[1] If someone ignores crucial parts of his or her tradition's Book of Shadows, that person will no longer be regarded as practicing that Wiccan tradition. They will not necessarily be regarded as spiritually deluded. What unites Pagans within a tradition is shared practice, not shared interpretation.

Nothing could be more different from the Christian tradition. The Bible defines what it is to be a Christian, and while the Bible is filled with stories and teachings, it is relatively empty of specific practices. The Sabbath and the Last Supper, which inspired Communion, are two notable exceptions. The Bible is regarded as sacred scripture in a way no Book of Shadows ever is.

Many Christians see our lack of scripture as a shortcoming. Without such texts, they argue, we are simply mired in our own self-interested subjectivity, judges in our own case, and so deprived of the objective guidance provided by God's word. Consequently Wiccan ethics cannot provide the spiritual bedrock that people require in this confusing life. Such a bedrock, we are told, can only be provided through revealed scripture. "Scripture" they insist, "is objective." All a Christian need do is follow the will of God as it is revealed there. They have text; we have opinion.

This argument is at its most impressive when it is not closely examined. From its very beginnings the Christian community has been filled with acrimonious arguments about what Scripture really means. Early Church history was repeatedly convulsed with sometimes violent debates between Marcionites, Montanists, Donatists, Arians, Pelagians, and the view that ultimately triumphed and came to be called Orthodox. Even here the Church fractured again and again, most notably in the great schism between Roman and Eastern Orthodox branches, and later between Protestant and Catholic Christianity in the West. These disputes show no signs of waning.

Mutual disagreement has never deterred those who claim knowledge of the One True Interpretation. Others may be in error, but they, at least, have been blessed with a clear understanding of God's will where others stumble blindly, deluded in darkness. Probably a sizable majority of Christians do not make such claims. They have a greater sense of their own human fallibility and of the dangers of pride, particularly the spiritual pride of believing that, compared to others, they are uniquely God's obedient servants. In their very humility these people are not vocal. They tend their own spiritual gardens and rarely walk on those of others. As a consequence, they are often drowned out by fewer, but louder, and more aggressive, voices. Those speaking most loudly within the Christian community generally claim the Bible is objectively inerrant, and they know its meaning. Loudest of all are those who call themselves Fundamentalists.

The apparent security stemming from the absolute confidence displayed by Biblical Fundamentalists can be unsettling to those of us less certain of our own judgment and aware of our own capacity for error. "How can they be so sure?"

Many of us grew up within the Christian tradition, learning at young ages that the Bible constitutes the Word of God. Impressed into our minds at such a young age, the message acquires a power not simply due to the quality of its reasoning. Usually no reasoning at all is offered to small children, nor could they evaluate it if it were. The Bible's early persuasiveness is more emotional than rational.

Fundamentalist Christianity is the fastest growing portion of the Christian community in the United States. They are also the noisiest critics of Wiccans. Therefore explicit confrontation with their doctrine of biblical inerrancy is necessary before we can penetrate further into understanding the character of genuine spiritual authority.

When I began working on this project some friends told me that addressing Fundamentalist arguments is a waste of time. Fundamentalists, they said, have largely cut themselves off from honest human dialogue. There is no "co" in their communication. Our views do not interest them, except as varieties of error to be overcome. This bitter judgment is often true, but it is not always true.

Other Fundamentalists I have encountered are deeply sincere and able to at least listen to and consider other perspectives. They are people who, like many Pagans, have found life without a serious spiritual commitment to be pretty superficial. When they actively criticize or attack contemporary Pagans, they merit our respectful engagement.

My point is to argue that Scripture is not objective, not to argue that Scripture is wrong. If Scripture is not objective we cannot be absolutely sure what it means. In order to understand Scripture, substantial interpretation of seemingly contradictory passages is required, and that interpretation must be done by fallible human minds. If we are intellectually honest we can never be sure we are right.

If Scripture is truly objective we can understand it with only the most minimal recourse to our own fallible judgment in weighing ambiguous passages. This, after all, is what "objective" means. *The more we must rely upon our judgment in accepting a proposition, the less objective it is.* This is why in physical science measurement and prediction are such powerful theoretical tools. As human things go, measurement and prediction are pretty unambiguous. They reduce personal judgment to a minimum.

If Scripture is objective in this sense, that would identify a genuine and important difference between Wiccan and Christian spirituality. If, on the other hand, it requires extensive and subtle interpretation, Scripture has no obvious superiority to the nature religions' sources of spiritual knowledge. The sources may differ but the means for interpretation are the same.

I will grant my Fundamentalist critics a point, although I think it will soon return to haunt them. If there is only one way to salvation, and if God wants us to take it, and hopes that everyone will be saved, *He will make that path clear.* He will so make His case that sincere seekers will be able to find it. He will make it as close to objective as possible, so that no error of judgment will lead to disaster. Only a refusal to abide by His instructions will lead to failure.

In the Bible, God explicitly grants that Abimelech's ignorance of doing wrong is adequate reason to expunge his guilt (Genesis 20). So scripture can reasonably be considered spiritually binding only if it is objectively true. After all, to refuse an instruction it must first be understood.

In the argument that follows I will rely on the King James version of the Bible because it is often the preferred translation for many Christian Fundamentalists. Sometimes other translations eliminate some apparent errors—for example, the Jehovah's Witnesses' version combines bats and birds into flying things, and so does not commit the apparent bloopers in the King James version (Leviticus 11:13, 19), but most of the problems I identify seem to exist regardless of the translation.

---

Interestingly, Scripture itself testifies that it is impossible to interpret it or the will of God with absolute confidence. In 1 Corinthians 13: 8–10, 12, Paul writes, "Charity never faileth: but whether there be prophecies, they shall fail; whether there be tongues, they shall cease; whether there be knowledge, it shall vanish away. For we know in part, and we prophesy in part. But when that which is perfect is come, then that which is in part shall be done away . . . For now we see through a glass, darkly. . . ." This seems to be a clear and straightforward admission by Paul of fallibility on the part of every Christian attempting to understand his faith.

Unfortunately, the literal meaning of Paul's words will not satisfy many biblical literalists. So I will supply additional biblical passages. Again, and I cannot overemphasize this point, my argument is not that Scripture is wrong. My point is that it is not obviously right. Consequently we must use our own fallible judgment in trying to understand its meaning. Our interpretation of Scripture *cannot* be objective. Therefore, Scripture has no stronger claim to objectivity than the personal spiritual experience provided within Pagan (and many other) spiritual traditions.

## The Second Coming

The textual evidence does not easily support the claim that Jesus knew more than two thousand years would elapse before He came again. Matthew 10:23 says, "But when they persecute you in this city, flee ye into another: For verily I say unto you, Ye shall not have gone over the cities of Israel till the Son of man be come." To my mind, nothing in Matthew 10 indicates that Jesus was thinking of his brief appearance after his resurrection when He said this. After all, between His death and resurrection, His disciples did little, if any, preaching. They were in despair. From a Fundamentalist perspective this despair was justified. As proof of Jesus' claims Fundamentalists emphasize the fact of His resurrection, which had not yet occurred. So there was no reason for the disciples to believe Jesus was anything else but dead. Even if the disciples had gone out and preached, there was no time for them to do any travel of the nature Jesus described. Nor were they apparently persecuted in the three-day span between the crucifixion and His reported resurrection. So why did He say it?

Mark 14:62 has Jesus saying to the chief priests, "Ye shall see the Son of man sitting on the right hand of power and coming in the clouds of heaven." Are these priests still alive? This certainly sounds like a reference to His second coming to me. So far, according to a literal interpretation of Scripture, Jesus may have left in the clouds of heaven, but He has not yet come in them.

Some of the critical texts I have consulted in researching the issue of Biblical objectivity have listed passages where the most reasonable reading indicates that the disciples and early Christians generally thought Jesus' second coming was near at hand. Among them are: John 21:22–23; Romans 13: 11–12; 16:20; 1 Corinthians 7:29–31; 10:11; 15:51–52; 1 Thessalonians 4:15–18; 1 Timothy 6:14, 2 Timothy 3:1; 2 Timothy 4:1–3; Hebrews 1:1–2; 8:13; 10:25; James 5:8–9; 1 Peter 1:20; 4:7, 17; Jude 17–23. Revelation 1:1, 3. In no way can a person easily get the sense that any of these writers thought the second coming was over 2,000 years away.

## Apparent Errors in Science

1. Bats are birds. (Leviticus 11:13, 19).
2. Birds have four legs, and so do locusts, beetles, grasshoppers, and other flying things. (Leviticus 11:20-23).
3. Pi = 3. (1 Kings 7:23).

## Ambiguities and Apparent Contradictions in the Nature of God

1. God cannot be seen (John 1:18; Exodus 33:20) and God has been seen (Genesis 18; Exodus 24:9–11, 33:11, 32:30, Isaiah 6:1).
2. God cannot and has never been heard by anybody (John 5:37) except that He speaks to Moses (Exodus 33:11).

3. No graven images may be made (Exodus 20:4), except that sometimes they should be made (Exodus 25: 18, 20).

4. 2 Samuel 24:1 finds God inciting David to number Israel, that is, to take a census. 1 Chronicles 21:1 finds Satan inciting David to do the same thing. (In both cases, David apparently sinned. Yet 1 Kings 15:5 says David only sinned with regard to Uriah, the Hittite.)

5. God repents (Gen. 6:6–7, Exodus 32:14, Jonah 3:10; Amos 7:6), but really He doesn't (Numbers 23:19).

6. God is no tempter (James 1:13), and yet He frequently hardens hearts in order to enable men to do evil they might not otherwise do (Joshua 11:20, Isaiah 63:17, John 12:40).

7. God punishes future generations for the sins of their fathers, (Exodus 20:5; Deuteronomy 23:2–3), except that He also tells us that children will not suffer from the iniquities of their fathers (Ezekiel 18:20).

## Apparent Contradictions and Ambiguities in the Story of Jesus and the Apostles[2]

1. Jesus has two genealogies: Matthew 1:1 and Luke 3:23. One lists twenty-seven ancestors, plus Jesus; the other totals forty-three. Six names are common to both lists. All the others are completely different. There is hardly any overlap between the two. Nor do the different lengths of these lists permit the otherwise conceivable interpretation that Jesus' ancestors branched off and then came back together again.

If Jesus was born of a virgin, why is his genealogy traced through Joseph in both cases? If His conception was immaculate this makes no sense. Joseph had *nothing* to do with it. God did. Jesus' human descent would have to be through Mary. But descent through Joseph appears necessary for him to meet the prophetic requirement that he be from the line descending from David.

2. Luke links Jesus's birth with Quirinius's governorship of Syria and Herod's kingship. But Quirinius took office in A.D. 6, whereas Herod died in B.C. 4 or 5.[3]

3. Matthew 2:13–15 says that immediately after his birth, Jesus and his family fled to Egypt to avoid Herod's massacre, but Luke 2:21–39 gives a radically different account of the days following Jesus' birth, having the family go to Jerusalem after his circumcision and then returning to Nazareth. They returned to Jerusalem "every year" after that.

4. Jesus delivered his first recorded sermon after choosing his disciples while on a mount (Matthew 5:1–2), but it really happened on a plain (Luke 6:17).

5. In John 7:38 Jesus refers to a scripture that has never been clearly located. The closest approximation refers to Jerusalem, not Jesus (Zechariah 14:8).

6. Jesus apparently predicted that the Queen of Sheba would reappear in his own lifetime. She didn't (Luke 11:31).

7. In the Synoptic Gospels of Matthew, Mark, and Luke, the Last Supper took place on Passover. In John it is reported to have occurred on the day before (John 13:1; 18:28).

8. Judas hanged himself (Matthew 27:5) and did not hang himself. Instead he fell and split himself open (Acts 1:18).

9. Matthew 27:32, Mark 15:21, and Luke 23:26 all say Simon of Cyrene carried the cross. John 19:17 says Jesus did.

10. Two thieves reviled Jesus on the cross (Matthew 27:38, 44; Mark 15:32), but really, only one did (Luke 23:39–43).

11. Jesus' last words were different in every Gospel (Matthew 27:46; Mark 15:34; Luke 23:46; John 19:30). Which account is correct?

12. According to Matthew 28:9 and Luke 24:39, Mary was able to touch Jesus after the resurrection. Indeed, he *tells* her to do so in Luke. But John 20:17 says he *forbade* her to do so!

13. Matthew says the two Marys were the first to see Jesus while on their way to Jerusalem after leaving the tomb. (Matthew 28:9). Mark says it was only Mary Magdelene who saw Jesus sometime after she left the tomb (Mark 16:8–9). Luke says it was Cleopas and another in the village of Emmaus (Luke 24:13, 18). John says it was only Mary Magdelene, at the tomb (John 20:1, 11–14). Paul left Mary out of it completely, reporting instead that it was Cephas, but doesn't say where (1 Corinthians 15:5).

14. Paul gives three different accounts of his conversion. In Acts 9:7 Paul says his companions heard a voice. He himself is told to go to a city where he will receive instructions, which are given him by Ananias. In Acts 22:9 his companions saw a light but heard no voice. Again, he is told to go to Damascus. In Acts 26:13 Ananias has disappeared, and Paul reports he received his instructions directly from Jesus at the time of his vision.

## Contradictions and Ambiguities in Biblical Theology

1. We can fall from grace (2 Peter 2:20–21), and not fall from grace (John 10:28).

2. One sin cannot be forgiven (Mark 3:29), except that it can (Acts 13:39).

3. Jesus tells us to honor our father and mother (Matthew 15:4), but if we want to be his disciple we must hate them (Luke 14:26).

4. Jesus says that everyone who asks receives and everyone who seeks will find (Matthew 7:8–11), yet he also says few will be saved, even when they try (Matthew 7:14–23, Luke 13:24, John 12:40).

5. Good works should be done openly (Matthew 5:16), but only in secret (Matthew 6:1–4).
6. Hatred is permitted, even demanded (Luke 14:26), but is simultaneously not permitted (1 John 3:15).
7. Jesus' yoke is light (Matthew 11:28–30), but it is accompanied by chastisement (Hebrews 12: 6–8).

## Did God Forget?

In some ways the oddest passages in all Scripture are 2 Kings 19 and Isaiah 37. They are identical. In the King James version the translations are word for word the same through verse 14. After that there is a minor change in the numbering of verses so that, for instance, Isaiah 37:21 is the same as 2 Kings: 20. After verse 14 there are occasionally very minor differences in the wording, probably because both are translations into English, but the stories remain identical. The only "significant" differences between the two is that "fenced cities" are laid waste in 2 Kings 19:25 and "defenced cities" are laid waste in Isaiah 37:26. To be laid waste, a fenced city had to be "defenced," so even here there is no difference.

The same repetitive pattern occurs, albeit for a shorter span, in 2 Chronicles 36:22–23 and Ezra 1:1–2. At least these passages are sequential. Are these repeated passages more important than any of the Bible's unrepeated passages?

## A Challenge to the Fundamentalists

The Book of Matthew, chapter 10, is famous in Christian circles and is frequently cited. There Jesus calls His disciples together and gives them instructions about spreading His message. Two elements of that chapter, taken together, demolish any possible "objective" interpretation by contemporary Christians. In Matthew 10:5–8 Jesus commands his disciples to go to the scattered "lost sheep of the house of Israel," but not to the Gentiles and Samaritans. They are to preach that, "The kingdom of heaven is at hand."

Among other things, they are to, "Heal the sick, cleanse the lepers, raise the dead, cast out devils: freely have ye received, freely give."

Literally, Jesus is commanding His disciples to preach only to Jews and, among other things, to raise the dead. I know of no cases anywhere, then or later, where His disciples were reliably reported to have raised the dead. This chapter is now freely quoted as teaching how Christians should spread the Gospel, but when it is cited the prohibition against preaching to non-Jews is never mentioned, nor is the command to raise the dead. How is this objective?

I am sure that many literalist Christians will be confident they know the correct interpretation of these apparently contradictory passages. Some may even be able to figure out how in God's eyes beetles have four legs and pi equals three, but I really do not care if Fundamentalists can figure out a way to preserve their claims of truth in these passages.

My argument here is not that the Bible is wrong, except in a *literal* sense. It need not be spiritually wrong. Validated by nearly 2,000 years of Church history, no matter how sure individual Christians will be that their interpretation is the correct one, they will encounter other Christians with different interpretations who are equally sure theirs is correct—*and no objective means exists to distinguish between them.*

Clearly, the Bible's meaning is not straightforward, even on crucial questions such as whether all sins can really be forgiven or what really happened at the resurrection. There is not even agreement among Christians as to whether grace, or good works and grace, are necessary for salvation. Taken literally, the Bible says both.

Some psychologists use standardized ink blots, called Rorschach blots, to try and diagnose their clients' problems. Depending on the client's state of mind, the same blot can elicit a number of possible interpretations. I suspect that for many people the Bible is a kind of spiritual Rorschach blot, whose interpretation says much more about the person explicating its meaning than about what it "really" means.

In seeking spiritual guidance Christians cannot ignore the need to interpret Scripture, and in doing so must take personal responsibility for their judgments. As soon as they do, they also have to admit the possibility of error, and search for means to reduce both its likelihood and seriousness, while acknowledging that neither can ever be reduced to zero by fallible men and women. Never, ever, are they justified in saying its meaning is "objective." Those claiming otherwise only demonstrate they do not understand the term.

## Hebrew, Greek, and Objectivity

An interesting discussion regarding Spirit and authority arose from an exchange in which I was told by a Christian Fundamentalist that Greek is intrinsically superior to Hebrew for transmitting the word of God because it is more precise. I disagreed. On matters such as interpreting the written word of God I would vote for ancient Hebrew.

I am more than skeptical of people's capacity to have precise understandings of spiritual matters. Others' words are always descriptions twice removed from the event. First the person has the encounter, and tries to make sense of it. He or she then puts this description and interpretation into words with greater or lesser skill. Finally, those words are interpreted again, often by people far removed in place, time, and experience from the person who originally wrote them or the audience he or she addressed. (Even our own language can be a poor vehicle for describing what is most important to us. Words are certainly an inadequate means to communicate our feelings to those we love most, unless we resort to poetry and metaphor.)

In my experience spiritual insight does not arrive through words. God, thank God, is not a college professor giving a lecture. As a result the task of translating insight into words in order to communicate it to others inevitably leaves room for unintentional misunderstandings and subsequent distortions. There is no way I can accurately portray to others my encounters with the

Wiccan Goddess or the Godhead. I have done my best, but all my words are so many candles seeking to demonstrate by analogy and metaphor the brightness of the sun. Poetry would be better than prose, if only I had the gift, but poetry is far from "objective."

These considerations explain why, if a religion's insights are to be written down, I think ancient Hebrew is better than Greek. Describing ancient Hebrew scripture in his extraordinary *The Spell of the Sensuous*, David Abram writes:

> The traditional Hebrew text . . . overtly demanded the reader's conscious participation. The text was never complete in itself; it had to be actively engaged by a reader who, by this engagement, gave rise to a particular reading. Only in relation—only by being taken up and actively interpreted by a particular reader—did the text become meaningful. And there was no single, definitive meaning; the ambiguity entailed by the lack of written vowels ensured that diverse readings, diverse shades of meaning, were always possible.[4]

I would add to Abram's account that this active interpretation would serve to transform the reader while simultaneously helping to insulate him or herself from the arrogant certainty that God's meaning is crystal clear. Such an attitude towards spiritual texts would be in keeping with Paul's admonition that on matters spiritual we see through a glass darkly.

Abram adds that "The [traditional] Hebrew Bible is not a set of finished stories and unchanging laws; it is not a static body of dogmatic truths but a living enigma that must be questioned, grappled with, and interpreted afresh in every generation. For, as it is said, the guidance that the Torah can offer in one generation is very different from that which it waits to offer in another."[5] Ancient Hebrew remained in perpetual dialogue with its readers.

The spirit of written Greek was and is very different. In the *Phaedrus*, Plato has Socrates state that written words "seem to talk to you as though they were intelligent, but if you ask them anything about what they say, from a desire to be instructed, they go on telling you just the same thing forever." Socrates' observation is the opposite from that made of the Torah by Abram. In Greek there is a monologue, not a dialogue. According to Abram, the reason for this difference is rooted in Greek's very precision as a written language—the same characteristics which appealed to my Fundamentalist correspondent. This precision was not characteristic of traditional Hebrew. Even the most fluent Hebrew reader "encounters a relatively high degree of ambiguity when reading a traditional text without vowel marks; it is this ambiguity that forces the reader of Hebrew to actively grapple with conflicting meanings, conflicting ways of sounding the text."[6]

If Abram is correct, traditional Hebrew leaves the reader much more room for personal judgment, interpretation, argument, and responsibility. (By contrast, modern Hebrew has been standardized, and no longer possesses those characteristics.) On matters such as spirituality, ancient Hebrew treats us more as adults, requiring us to bring to bear our intellect, our intuition, and our hearts. On the same matters Greek treats us more like math students learning the correct theorem. Perhaps that is why debate and discussion occupy such an honored place in Jewish teaching, whereas in Christianity the sermon seems to be what counts. If our heart and intuition do not play a role, we cannot understand spirit—and so Greek's very precision encourages a spurious certainty on matters such as this, thereby obscuring the true meaning of its words on spiritual subjects.

If a Christian argues that the Old Testament is a sacred revealed text, it follows that God did not necessarily want to present His people with a precise set of lessons because written Hebrew was not then a precise language, as it later became, and written Greek always was. He wanted them to use their minds, hearts, and intuitions. Since Jesus spoke a Semitic language, perhaps the same would have transpired had His words been written down in Aramaic. Greek was the language of the cities of Jesus' time and place, Aramaic the language of the countryside. Jesus certainly spoke Aramaic. He may or may not have spoken Greek.

Written Aramaic might have better preserved the Hebrew tradition of critical thinking than would written Greek. Greek may well have gotten the message wrong precisely *because* it was more precise. It gave people the opportunity not only to put their faith in God's word, it also allowed them to deposit their minds there as well, predisposing them to commit a new form of idolatry: the worship of texts.

Approached fairly, then, the evidence cannot possibly support a fundamentalist reading of objective inerrancy. Potentially mistaken human interpretation must always be a part of *any* Christian point of view. Once we admit our understanding can be in error, and that we might be wrong, true *communication* with others can take place. Aware of our own fallibility, we are open to other points of view. Until then, communication is simply a matter of waving placards and shouting slogans, like the "missionaries" who, standing on street corners with bullhorns, are totally unconcerned with whether anyone really listens to them. If there is no scriptural "objectivity," there is no justification for this way of behaving.

The Bible is no more objective than Wiccan teachings. To be sure, there is a physical book with a text unreasonably claimed by some to be objectively true. Wiccans do not have the equivalent. But we have nature, and our own personal experience with the Divine. Nature is our primary spiritual text. In this sense we have an advantage over the Christian community. Our text does not require our relying on the sometimes fallible translations of others. Further, while we generally agree about Nature's sacred status, there is no agreement among Christians as to what qualifies as a biblical text. To this day Protestants and Catholics argue about which texts truly qualify as divinely inspired. We generally agree as to what qualify as the core characteristics of Nature: our focus on the turning of the seasons, phases of the moon, cycles of life and death, all fundamental processes free from human control.

Christians read the texts of Scripture, Pagans read the texts of Nature. Both require fallible human beings to exercise their understanding to the best of their ability in a humble and open way.

Neither is obvious in its meaning. It is a matter of opinion, experience, and a person's spiritual calling, as to which is most easily understood.

In both the Christian and Wiccan cases, each of us can find our spiritual path through the many possibilities for misinterpretation and confusion by our knowledge that the basic character of the Divine is love, aided by our own experience and intuition, with the assistance of others within our spiritual community. In every case our spiritual community provides a powerful check against too quickly confusing our own ideas with those of the Divine. It remains everyone's personal responsibility to seek understanding of his or her proper relationship with the Divine, and for any acts committed on the basis of that understanding. Each of us must also constantly be aware that our understanding and our actions may be in error.

ENDNOTES

1. Robin Lane Fox, *The Unauthorized Version: Truth and Fiction in the Bible* (New York: Vintage, 1993), p. 92.

2. Many of these concerning the Resurrection were assembled by the Rabbi Tovia Singer, whose list is actually far longer than those I pass on. See Tovia Singer, "The Resurrection: What is the Evidence?" *The Book Your Church Doesn't Want You to Read*, Tim C. Leedom, ed. (Dubuque, Iowa: Kendall Hunt Pub. Co., 1993), pp. 219–221. Many of the other examples are taken from Robin Lane Fox's *Unauthorized Edition*.

3. Fox, Unauthorized Edition, pp. 28–9.

4. David Abram, *The Spell of the Sensuous: Perception and Language in a More-than-Human World* (New York: Pantheon Books, 1996), p. 243.

5. Ibid., p. 244.

6. Ibid., p. 300.

# Spiritual Truth
# and Human Experience

Frequently I have encountered a Christian criticism that we Pagans confuse the products of our minds for Divine inspiration, and so have no solid anchor against spiritual error. In short, there is no spiritual depth to Wiccan religion. Initially I responded that our basic ethical principle is the Wiccan Rede's powerful sounding injunction "An it harm none, do as ye will."[1] At the time I took the Rede to be, as many Wiccans still believe, an absolute prohibition against harming others.

Far from being ethically flabby, the more I pondered the interpretation of Wiccan ethics the more I thought it *too* demanding. How can we possibly do anything significant without in some sense harming others? Any change in the status quo discomfits someone. For example, if I get a job, that almost always means someone else did not get it. Was that person therefore harmed? They might think so.

Based on my previous discussion of evil, we might respond that the suffering experienced by others' not getting the job was really a blessing. I believe that may be true, but, as I also emphasized, as an aid for determining how to treat our fellow beings, this observation is irrelevant. I do not know how my getting a job will be a blessing for someone else who therefore doesn't get it. If I do not know how it will be a blessing, it is absurd for me to argue I am helping that person by taking the job they desire.

The usual interpretation of "An it harm none, do as ye will" is too strong to be of much help in guiding us in actions that may have significant impact upon others. Strictly speaking, "An it harm none . . ." really says *nothing* about what you should do regarding actions that do in fact harm others! If your action doesn't harm another, go ahead. If it does, advice from the principle is unclear except to try to minimize harm.

Often it is not clear how to minimize harm. We can never know the full results of our actions. The person whose life I save may go on to take the lives of many others. Or save many others. The person I refuse to assist in a time of need may, as a result, call upon reserves of strength and creativity they did not realize they possessed in order to solve their crisis themselves. Or they may sink even more deeply into despair. Our ignorance of the larger patterns to which our actions contribute means we cannot reliably use "minimize harm" as a clear principle for guiding our actions, particularly in complex situations. In the absence of Divine commandments, what is a Wiccan to do?

A deeper understanding of this question then suggested itself to me. Also central to Wiccan spirituality is the principle of "perfect love and perfect trust." In some traditions this principle plays a fundamental role enabling a person to be accepted into the Wiccan spiritual community. To be sure, I have never yet met a Pagan, or anyone else, who embodied perfect love, and therefore merited perfect trust. But the Gods certainly do, and we can learn from them.

In conscientiously attempting to follow our Rede, we quickly become aware we often cannot act so as to be sure of harming no one. Even the most committed pacifist vegan, who refuses to use animal products of any sort, will eat vegetables, whose production normally requires farmers to destroy hungry animals threatening their harvest. To live is to take life.

Thinking about the Rede's meaning and its applicability to our daily lives leads us into recognizing the interrelatedness of all life, and that beings cannot live without hurting other beings, even if only inadvertently, but we are also shown, sometimes through direct encounter with Divinity in our rituals, that perfect love is the fundamental spiritual power. These lessons lead to awareness that harming others is a necessary dimension to embodied existence, combined with a deep reluctance to inflict such harm, and an acceptance that there are times when we have little reasonable choice in the matter.

To act lovingly, then, is to try and act for the benefit of others, and to treat all beings, even those we must harm, with respect. When we do cause another harm, it is always with regret. Anything we do regretfully we will not do thoughtlessly, and so we will act only for what we believe to be good reasons that are sensitive to the well-being of others than ourselves. We also act with humility, for we are all deeply ignorant regarding the larger patters to which our actions contribute. We have ultimately to learn to subordinate our power to our love.

Some readers may think this principle simply readmits the "minimize harm" injunction through the back door. But there is an importance difference between this and the earlier injunction. A rule such as "minimize harm" is an external prohibition, akin to "Thou shalt not kill." As such, it is fundamentally impersonal. Everything that falls under the required category should not be killed, regardless of what we think about it. We need care only for the principle and not for those to whom it applies, but an ethic rooted in respect for others requires us to consider them as beings, not objects, as "Thous" and not "Its." In doing so, our hearts are potentially opened to others. In opening our hearts we are led to grasp the inevitable suffering that accompanies physical existence, and so, our compassion deepens. Deepened compassion opens us to love.

I believe an ethic of respect is more directly transformational to those seeking to practice it than are impersonal commands. Commands work when there is no need to understand the reason for the command, but only to obey it. A dog can follow commands, but its reason for doing so—perhaps to be rewarded—has nothing to do with why the command exists. Not killing in order to avoid punishment falls into the same category, but as soon as we respect another we *want* to act thoughtfully towards them, and automatically take their interests into consideration. If we must, we override their interests thoughtfully and with genuine regret.

The ethic of respect is a deeply Pagan ethic. It is found among hunting and gathering peoples in many places who recognize that they live in an inspirited world, that all beings in that world require respect, and that some beings in that world need to die so that others can live. This is not moral relativism, but neither can it be broken down into a series of do's and don'ts engraved upon a tablet. How we act with respect cannot be put into a rulebook because the form respect most appropriately takes is so context specific. How to act respectfully depends upon our relationship with another. In acting respectfully we treat family members differently than strangers, and strangers differently than animals—without in any sense failing to show appropriate respect in every case.

While human beings may not be able always to act with love for others, we can all reasonably be expected to act with respect for them. It is hard not to do so when we really grasp the meaning of Yevtushenko's poem. As soon as we do, we have entered into a path that, when followed with wisdom, finds our respect for others opening us to finding compassion for them, a compassion deepening into love for all beings. This is a morality for adults, not children.

So the usual Pagan response is not as mistaken or naive as it first seemed to me. Taken superficially, the common Wiccan interpretation to do no harm is closer to the true implication of the Wiccan Rede than the relativistic one. The deeper interpretation focusing on the Rede's weaknesses points to a more profound insight, an insight clarified by the other primary Wiccan principle honoring perfect love and perfect trust. That insight is that harm can never be eliminated, and so we need always to act with respect and compassion, the better to ensure that harm is minimized.

## Are Pagans Living Off the Christian Moral Heritage?

There is another Christian supremacist argument. Some critics have argued that while contemporary Neopagans are in many ways an ethical lot, their ethics have Christian roots. Scripture's basic ethical teachings have penetrated deeply into our common cultural heritage, but, unlike Christians, by taking up the Pagan path we have supposedly cut ourselves off from the spring of eternal truth. The water we once drank, that nourished our ethical roots, is no longer renewed. The farther we move from that unfailing spiritual well, the more open we will be to influence by darker motives.

The reasoning behind this argument is based upon a particular interpretation of humankind's "Fall," and a deep ignorance of other cultures and times. The Fall supposedly rendered us so confused by evil, so prone to error, so much the dupes of Satan, that left to our own devices we will continually slide further down into degradation. The premise is that, on their own, human beings cannot sustain or perhaps even discover standards of ethical decency.

My account of my encounter with the Goddess should give pause to those making this argument, but they might respond that this was simply my subjective interpretation based upon my expectations of what a divinity would be like—that I interpreted Her through a Christian-inspired image of what constitutes goodness. I find such an argument silly. But what about Pagans who did not have my experience or something similar to it? What of future Pagans far less influenced by Christianity? Might Pagan spirituality eventually drift, as one evangelical critic suggested to me, back into committing acts of human sacrifice and the like?

These objections need to be addressed at two levels: the history of Paganism and comparative histories of Christian interactions with Pagans. Most fundamentally, it is simply not true that without the Bible human beings would be left in moral and ethical darkness, or tend in any sense to degenerate morally. Christian behavior is also not noticeably superior to that of non-Christians.

It is well known that the golden rule, which Jesus emphasized, emerged worldwide. The same holds with the injunction to love God. This or something very like it is found in widely spread spiritual traditions. And, as Jesus said, "On these two commandments hang all the law and the prophets" (Matthew 22:40). Deeply sublime ethical teachings are the monopoly of no people and no faith.

To further illustrate this point I refer to a small book by the well-known Christian writer, C. S. Lewis. In *The Abolition of Man* Lewis argued that a universal ethical sensibility exists which he revealingly called the Tao, or Way. Its principles characterize traditional wisdom worldwide. Here are a few of the quotations Lewis gives from pre-Christian Pagan sources:[2]

> "There are two kinds of injustice: the first is found in those who do an injury, the second in those who fail to protect another from injury when they can."—Cicero (Roman Pagan)

> "Utter not a word by which anyone could be wounded."—Law of Manu

> "Never do to others what you would not like them to do to you."—Confucius

> "What good man regards any misfortune as no concern of his?"—Juvenal (Roman Pagan)

> "Is it only the sons of Atreus who love their wives? For every good man who is right-minded loves and cherishes his own."—Homer

> "He who is asked for alms should always give."—Hindu

Over 1,500 years ago, Julian, the last Pagan emperor of Rome, addressed the claim that Christians have a uniquely enlightened moral perspective. Discussing the Ten Commandments, Julian asked rhetorically, "What nation is there by the gods, exclusive of the mandates 'Thou shalt worship no other gods,' and 'Remember the Sabbath,' which does not think it requisite to observe the other commandments? Hence punishments are established in all nations for those that transgress them . . ."[3]

Charity, benevolence, mercy, and love are all prominent themes in Pagan thought. If it took God to give us such insights, since they are taught in the Bible, maybe He was speaking to more than one group? Alternatively, perhaps, only those depending on the Bible were *incapable* of discovering for themselves truths of which many peoples and cultures were well aware? The first possibility seems to me far the most likely.

There are certainly no grounds for the claim that Christian ethics are so new that a Pagan society could not comprehend them on its own. In late Classical civilization there was not much difference between the ethics promoted by the early church and that of many Pagan philosophers. The argument between Christians and Classical-era Pagans was over the spiritual status of Jesus and the Gods, not over ethical insights. It is entirely false to suggest that Christian ethics are fundamentally different from those of Pagans, or that Pagans today must depend on Christianity's moral heritage to refrain from human sacrifice.

There is another, more disturbing, dimension to this issue. Many times, Christians (or at least those influenced by Christian culture) took actions far *worse* than the Pagans they encountered. When the Spanish first arrived in the Western hemisphere they encountered cultures completely unacquainted with biblical teachings. It was during this time that the Catholic priest Bartolomé de las Casas participated in the Spanish subjugation of the people of Cuba. Unlike most of his countrymen, however, he apparently took seriously biblical injunctions about treating others well. Las Casas ultimately became a vehement critic of Spain's inhuman policies towards the island's inhabitants. He wrote:

> Endless testimonies . . . prove the mild and pacific temperament of the natives. . . . But our work was to exasperate, ravage, kill, mangle and destroy; small wonder,

then, if they tried to kill one of us now and then. . . .
The admiral, [Columbus] it is true, was blind as those
who came after him, and he was so anxious to please
the King that he committed irreparable crimes against
the Indians. . . .[4]

English Protestants were no better than Spanish Catholics. In
Virginia John Smith, leader of the Jamestown colony, endorsed
the Spanish method of dealing with Indians, for they "forced the
treacherous and rebellious Infidels to doe all manner of drudgery
worke and slavery for them, themselves living like Soldiers upon
the fruits of their labours."[5] My examples are not taken out of
context, nor are they isolated. Genghis Khan's treatment of his
subjugated peoples was no more depraved than Christian treatment of the Indians upon their arrival in the New World.

So on the one hand Christian ethics are hardly unique, and on
the other, societies where Christianity was far more central to people's beliefs than is the case today acted with extraordinary sav-
agery against peaceful peoples who had committed no acts of
aggression against them. No Pagan, or Christian, need assume that
the decency and kindness we encounter in our lives today rests
only upon Christian foundations.

## Love, Objectivity, and Subjectivity

There is a fundamental error in arguing that spiritual authority is
objective. When we labor under that illusion Spirit becomes, in
Martin Buber's sense, an "It" rather than a "Thou." That Buber's
views come from deep within the Judaic tradition, and that he
writes with enormous respect of the Christian tradition, will, I
hope, reassure my Christian readers that in making this point I
am not importing something utterly antithetical to their own understanding. Speaking of God, Buber writes:

The eternal *Thou* can by its nature not become *It*; for by
its nature it cannot be established in measure and

bounds, not even in the measure of the immeasurable, or the bounds of boundless being; for by its nature it cannot be understood as a sum of qualities raised to a transcendental level; for it can be found neither in nor out of the world; for it cannot be experienced, or thought; for we miss Him, Him who is, if we say "I believe that He is"— "He" is also a metaphor, but Thou is not.[6]

and:

Although we earthly beings never look at God without the world, but only look at the world in God, yet as we look we shape eternally the form of God.

Form is also a mixture of *Thou* and *It*. In belief and in a cult form can harden into an object; but, in virtue of the essential quality of relation that lives on in it, it continually becomes present again. God is near His forms so long as man does not remove them from Him. In true prayer belief and cult are united and purified to enter into the living relation. The fact that true prayer lives in the religions witnesses to their true life: they live so long as it lives in them. Degeneration of the religions means degeneration of prayer in them. Their power to enter into relation is buried under increasing objectification, it becomes increasingly difficult for them to say *Thou* with the whole undivided being . . .

All direct experience of the Divine is a revelation. Any revelation and the resulting interpretation of that revelation, either for oneself, or as a teaching and guide for others, must preserve the relation of Thou, not as simple subjectivism, but as a personal relationship with that which is most real. An essential dimension of this relationship is love, but a love which is neither rooted in my preferences and wishes, which would be subjective, nor turned into a word without real content, which results from the attempt to make it objective. For those who experience it, this kind of love is neither simply subjective nor merely objective. It is instead an encounter with reality in its most fundamental sense, an ultimate reality better grasped as a Thou than an It.

This quality of Divine love is attested to, in one form or another, throughout humanity's religious heritage. Previously I argued that it was the most uniquely human capacity among physical beings, even if it is initially only embryonic within us. This power attracts us solely by its complete fulfillment of all that we are and can ever hope to be. During such an experience there is no sense of need or lack. We are fulfilled. Completely.

Allowing the written word to come between ourselves and this experience of divine love is to blind ourselves. Scripture (and Nature) can only point to what is beyond both, but that includes both. Only in that sense is either kind of revelation useful. We must not be like the dog who, when we point, looks at our finger and ignores that to which we are pointing.

From a Traditional Wiccan perspective, those who focus only on God or Goddess are in some ways akin to Christians who focus only on Scripture, and do not look at what manifests through them. Perhaps because I am a Pagan, it seems to me that the perfect love of the Goddess is a far more reliable means for grasping that Source than any printed words, no matter how wise. She loves us unconditionally. Paper pages, obscure passages, and printer's ink do not—and have a long history of being interpreted in such a way as to minimize any of the love they do describe. I believe a Wiccan focusing solely on the polytheistic dimension of our tradition, while in error, is not in serious error so long as that focus emphasizes the Goddess's love, as indeed most do.

I will take this point farther. Those who focus simply on Nature as divine, rather than deities, also have a closer appreciation of the Ultimate than do those who similarly focus upon texts. Nature precedes, enfolds, and sustains humanity. Its presence is direct and, when the mind is clear and the person in solitude, little mediated by our preconceptions. That is why even Christians often call it "God's Country." Texts, by comparison, are human creations, accounts mediated through another, and likely to keep our thinking at abstract rather than concrete levels. When we think abstractly we cannot experience a Thou. We can only experience an It. Consequently, the danger of spiritual error is greater when reading a text than when experiencing Nature.

Sacred texts have a special appeal to people seeking certainty without responsibility, morality without understanding, and truth without humility. The concreteness of the words gives the illusion of the concreteness of their meaning. Believers can all too easily give up personal responsibility, reduce morality to rigid rules, and convince themselves that they speak and act for God.

Sacred texts interpose the words of others between ourselves and the Sacred. This creates two sources of error. On the one hand, people who have had no personal encounter with the numinous arrogate to themselves a claim to spiritual understanding based upon their ability to read. On the other hand, those seeking spiritual insight are encouraged to turn their backs on personal experience in favor of the words of others. Supposedly such words are more "objective." This latter is a double error—equating the spiritual with the objective, and therefore as an object, while simultaneously ignoring those dimensions of awareness that cannot adequately be captured in words.

However valuable when used appropriately as pointers to something beyond themselves, sacred texts run a strong risk of becoming idols. Christians are very sensitive to the idolatry of graven images. What about the idolatry of written ones? Words can no more encompass the sacred than can images and, in a very subtle way, can be even more misleading to those who come across them naively.

D. H. Lawrence, whom I have earlier quoted on quite different matters, captured this point beautifully, observing that:

> When it comes to the meaning of anything, even the simplest word, then you must pause. Because there are two great categories of meaning, forever separate. There

is mob-meaning, and there is individual meaning. Take even the word *bread*. The mob-meaning is merely: stuff made with white flour into loaves that you eat. But take the individual meaning of the word bread: the white, the brown, the corn-pone, the homemade, the smell of bread just out of the oven, the crust, the crumb, the un-leavened bread, the shew-bread, the staff of life, sour-dough bread, cottage loaves, French bread, Viennese bread, black bread, a yesterday's loaf, rye, Graham, bar-ley, rolls, Bretzeln, Kringeln, scones, damper, matsen— there is no end to it all, and the word bread will take you to the ends of time and space, and far-off down av-enues of memory. But this is individual. The word bread will take the individual off on his own journey, and its meaning will be in his own meaning, based on his own genuine imaginative reactions. And when a word comes to us in its individual character, and starts in us the indi-vidual responses, it is a great pleasure to us.[7]

If the word "bread" cannot do justice to what it means to us as individuals, how much more frustrating must words be when we try to speak and write of that which is most sacred? We *cannot* describe the sacred accurately in what Lawrence calls "mob-meaning" because when the Sacred speaks to us, it speaks to us *as individuals*. As a Thou, the Sacred speaks directly to our heart. Any words we then use to describe our experience are derivative.

Too often more effort goes into squeezing meaning from printed words than into opening the heart. This approach breeds fanaticism, legalistic obsession with forms over substance, and a wholly unwar-ranted sense of spiritual understanding and mission. The text be-comes the source of truth, and Truth is obscured. As Paul observed: "the letter killeth, but the spirit giveth life" (2 Corinthians 3:6).

Leonard Shlain contrasts Christianity when literacy was wide-spread, and when it was not. His argument is fascinating. In late Classical times textual arguments dominated the early Church, and with them, a concern for rooting out heresy, meaning any who read Scripture differently from those with temporal power. In the Middle Ages, when literacy in Christian cultures reached an all-time low, the Christian mystical traditions flowered, women were more visible in positions of spiritual authority, and in the secular world the ideal of chivalry blossomed. Compared to centuries to come, religious persecutions were fairly rare. Later, as literacy grew, more attention was paid to the supposed letter of the text, and unusually harsh interpretations of God's nature and message arose. These problems appear to have been exacerbated with the invention of the printing press. Many people could now read Scripture, and in so doing be naively sure that they knew God's will. Persecution and religious wars grew in severity and extent.

To this day there seems to be a curious connection between an extreme concern for capturing the literal meaning of a text and a harsh and punitive conception of the Divine. In my judgment this penchant for violence is at least partly because the intellect alone is utterly incapable of grasping the most fundamental spiritual truths. No matter how subtle, intellect alone cannot help but miss their point.[8] Biblical literalism is simply modern idolatry.

The illusion of objectivity carried within sacred texts allows us to read shades of meaning into a manuscript that are, in fact, products of our own minds. This truth is easily grasped by those placing total faith in the objectivity of texts when they encounter interpretations at variance with their own, but they fail to apply the same discernment to themselves.

Words do not speak for themselves, whether spoken or printed. All words occur in contexts, and all contexts occur within still larger contexts. It is we, and the members of our spiritual community, who choose which contexts to attend, and which to ignore. In doing so we place our fallible human judgment at the very *core* of our task of spiritual interpretation.

Having done this, we import into an inspired text—for I do not doubt that texts can be inspired—far more of ourselves than we like to admit. That is why for many the Bible is a kind of spiritual

Rorschach blot. Interestingly, I think, those claiming to be most "fundamental" and "literal" in their interpretation are likely to *most* color the texts they cite with the characteristics of their own minds because they are *least* aware of the role contexts play in interpretation.

When we mistake the product of our own understanding with the word of the Divine, we commit the errors of pride and idolatry. The idolatrous worship of words, and the pride-filled certainty that those words are uniquely clear, has led to great foolishness and greater crimes. This potent and poisonous error has led many to claim absolute certainty that those who differ from themselves are heretics or infidels who, as God's enemies, deserve the harshest treatment. And so, idolaters make war on idolaters because alternative idols are perceived as defective by those captivated by the creations of their own minds into thinking they honor the superhuman. In fact, none worship anything beyond themselves.

The best evidence that these supposed devotees of objective truth are worshipping their own desires disguised as God's commandments is that they so often personally profit from their harsh treatment of so-called heretics and infidels. Witness, for example, the common argument that Christians were justified in seizing the lands of native peoples because they were Pagans! Even those who do not profit materially puff themselves up in self-righteousness, looking down on those they regard as "fallen."

## Human Authority: Pagan Priestesses and Priests and Christian Clergy

How we obtain knowledge of spiritual truth, and of appropriate relationships with the spirit realm, powerfully shapes the nature of spiritual authority among human beings. A religion deriving its spiritual guidance from sacred texts relies on different talents and training than one obtaining spiritual guidance from spirit and spiritual encounters, mediated through the contactee and the spiritual community. Among Traditional Wiccans, founders of our tradition such as Gerald Gardner are not so much considered divinely inspired teachers of revelation as divinely inspired discoverers and creators of a tradition within which revelation can happen to anyone.

Superficially, Pagan priests, Protestant ministers and Catholic priests have much in common. All specialize in bridging the gap between our day-to-day existence and our relationships with the sacred, and in assisting others to do so as well. However, in other ways the differences between Christian and Pagan spiritual leaders are deeper than their similarities.

A list of synonyms for clergyman includes: ecclesiastic, churchman, cleric, divine, man of the cloth, man of God, holy man, priest, minister, chaplain, father, pastor, parson, preacher, rector, vicar, dean, bishop, canon, presbyter, deacon, reverend, and clerk in holy orders. A few, but only a very few, easily cross over into a list of roles performed by Pagan spiritual leaders: priestess, priest, high priestess, high priest, Witch Queen, Magus, healer, medium, shaman, and diviner. Understanding why the two lists are so different is illuminating.

In most instances the Christian titles are descriptions of a person's relationship to an organized body. The Catholic priest possesses his authority not from any personal character of his own, but rather from investiture by the Church. Consequently, even if the priest himself turns out to be corrupt, or worse, the functions he performs remain valid for his parishioners. He carries on the Church's mission, which is derived from God. As an ordained priest he is a qualified intermediary between God and the people, regardless of his personal morality.

A Protestant minister holds a different role. Every Protestant stands in a completely personal relationship with God. The minister is therefore in no sense an intermediary. However, he or she is charged with leading the congregation, teaching its members, preaching God's word, and generally being the primary human authority for interpreting Scripture within the Church. Ministerial authority largely derives from the freely given recognition by members of the congregation of his or her abilities as a preacher, in interpreting Scripture, and in living by Christian precepts. Sometimes he or she is even hired and fired by the congregation. The variety of Protestant churches is so great that there are many variations, but this picture is broadly accurate.

A traditional Wiccan priestess or priest does not preach. If she or he tried to give a sermon to coven mates, or to an assembled crowd gathered to celebrate a Sabbat, most would find it offensive. Neopagan priestesses and priests are often teachers, but what they teach is not primarily doctrine. Rather, it is how to act within a small group that, as a coven, works with the world of spirits and Spirit. In Traditional Wicca, the high priestess is usually the most skilled and experienced female member of the group, and the high priest is the male member she chooses to perform in that role. Oftentimes their authority is greater than a minister in a Protestant church because they can expel members unilaterally. On the other hand, they do not possess anything like the institutionalized authority of a Catholic priest or a minister appointed by one of the more institutionalized Protestant churches. Nor are they paid for their services.

While the high priestess and high priest possess only minimal institutional authority (other coveners may well possess as high a formal initiation as they) they are expected to be the most adept or at least most experienced at working with the world of spirits and of Spirit. This is why despite possessing legal similarities with some Christian clergy (such as the authority to marry others), they are primarily judged by their ability to work with spiritual powers. For example, the most highly regarded Traditional Wiccan high priestesses and priests are able to incorporate the presence of the gods into their own body, a mediumistic skill with almost no Christian equivalent. It is this "hands on" aspect of their job that most differentiates Wiccan high priestesses and priests from *most* Christian ministers. (The exception would be some charismatics and their relationship with the Holy Spirit. Significantly, this relationship leads to charismatics being regarded with distrust by more mainstream Christian ministers).

These abilities link traditional Wiccan priestesses and priests with healers, diviners, mediums, and shamans in many other Pagan traditions. In all these cases, a person's spiritual influence rests primarily in their personal connection with the realm of spirit. Next in importance, (and for sensible people just as important), is their personal spiritual maturity. Last, and often distantly so, is their institutional affiliation. I am a Third-Degree Gardnerian priest. In Gardnerian circles that means something, but my formal rank does not mean nearly as much within that community as my personal reputation both as a human being and as someone who works with the world of spirit. That is as it should be.

As with Christian clergy, the abilities of individual Pagan high priestesses and priests vary widely, but the skills and qualities by which they are judged differ significantly from those of their Christian cohorts, though there is some overlap. For example, coveners may well go to their high priestess or priest for advice on spiritual matters and tough decisions, just as a Christian might consult their priest or minister, but these instances of overlap occur within very different theological and institutional universes. Christianity promises salvation in the next life, and the priest or minister is charged with helping his "flock" attain that goal. The Pagan approach seeks to attain and maintain greater harmony with the spiritual dimension of this life. High priestesses and priests are charged with helping people in this task.

Pagan ceremonies and ritual are quite distinct from a Catholic Mass or Episcopal communion service because they are celebrating the spiritual dimensions of physical existence rather than a specific historical event enabling people to be saved. In a Pagan context, healing, divining, and the like can be used to restore balance with the powers that surround us. Preaching is much less efficacious for that task. From a Christian perspective preaching can help us concentrate on the goal of salvation, or better grasp the meaning of a text, things for which spiritual healing and divining are of little use.

Some Pagans use the term "clergy" in defining their community responsibilities, emphasizing their performing marriages and public Sabbats for the larger Pagan community, conducting funerals, memorials, baby blessings, and helping the dying to pass over. These services are vitally important to all Pagans who take their religion seriously, and they have near or exact analogues within the Christian context. Because of this overlap, the temptation is strong to appropriate the term "clergy" within a Pagan context. But, if for no other reason than the very different sizes of covens and congregations, these responsibilities will be performed frequently by Christian priests and ministers and very rarely by Wiccan priests. They play a larger role in the life of Christian clergy than they do for Pagan priests and priestesses.

Pagan and Christian spiritual leaders work within very different religious communities, are expected to be able to do different things, and stand in different relationships to the world of Spirit and spirits. Just as most synonyms for clergy do not fit Pagan spiritual leadership, expertise, and authority, so terms like healer, diviner, shaman, and medium do not fit easily within the category of clergy. In my judgment, the terms "priestess" and "priest" are probably the best general terms we can use for our roles because there is already widespread awareness that many different religions have priests and priestesses who do many different kinds of things. Keeping titles distinct helps sensitize us, and others as well, that there are different spiritual paths of value and beauty in this world.

## In Conclusion

The ethical teachings derived from Pagan traditions and insights are as profound and valid as any found within a revealed text. Indeed, the ethics described in revealed Scriptures are in no way greatly different from those that have arisen within Pagan traditions, except insofar as they refer to specific spiritual practices demanded by a specific deity, such as honoring the Sabbath. Far from people having an innate tendency to degenerate morally when not taught by the Bible, we find worldwide a remarkable area of agreement among major spiritual traditions as to how a good person should behave. Worldwide, we find within every spiritual community a wide variation in how well specific members exemplify their principles.

Actions, of course, speak louder than words. Those who walk their talk are the ones most appropriately taken seriously on matters such as these in any tradition, Pagan or Christian. In these respects the ethical practices of Pagan societies vary as widely as those of Christian societies, with some falling well below the standards we regard today as minimal and others that look, from our present vantage point, as deeply admirable. There is therefore no basis in fact or in logic, in experience or in dogma, for arguing that Pagan religions or their Wiccan variant are in any sense at all ethically inferior to Christianity or have a weaker claim to spiritual authority. All these Christian criticisms of Pagan belief and practice are, without exception, invalid.

Nevertheless, the very different spiritual outlooks of these two communities lead inevitably to different ways of judging valid spiritual insight. This is the immense barrier making mutual comprehension and respect so difficult between followers of these spiritual paths. Because we are happy with the way the Divine speaks to us, it is often hard to appreciate that others may be equally happy when the Divine speaks differently to them.

When we enjoy a diversity of interpretations within a community of common practices, as is the case with Pagan religion, the meaning of spiritual community changes from its Christian meaning. Rather than supporting one another in our search for salvation, or seeking to bring others into the fold, the Pagan community provides a framework of stability within which individuals seek to grow in harmony spiritually. Our sense both of individuality and of community is different from dominant Christian conceptions.

In traditional Pagan societies change was perpetual because spiritual experience was ongoing. A person might have a vision that inaugurated a new practice or insight, but change was moderated within any particular community by the influence of individuals recognized by their neighbors as spiritually wise. This is as it should be. Each of us is fallible, and even if our personal revelation is valid for us, translating it into the community's framework and practice is by no means straightforward, easy, or appropriate.

Traditional Wiccan communities are far more fluid than those within traditional Pagan societies, for we do not comprise a tribal society. The modern world consists of impersonal and fluid networks comprised mostly of strangers. Spiritual institutions and practices are influenced by their environment, even as they in turn influence it. Covens come together, flourish, and often then disperse or divide.

Spiritually, the result is a more individualized and eclectic kind of practice as ongoing revelations of varying degrees of universality influence individuals within relatively unstructured environments. One result is a lot of silly or superficial practice, and in some cases the subordinating of spiritual practice to other goals, social and political. Another result is creativity and vitality. The future of Neopagan spirituality will rest in part on whether this creativity is able to reach out in good ways to a variety of people, or whether individual eccentricities, self-indulgence, and secular causes come to dominate and obscure genuine spiritual insights. Given the similarly mixed record of religious hierarchies, Pagan fluidity is not obviously inferior to Scriptural stability. I suspect the flux and flow of contemporary Wicca and other Neopagan traditions will prove spiritually very fruitful within the context of the modern world.

ENDNOTES

1. Many Neopagans also believe in the law of three fold return. This means, as ye sow, so shall ye reap—with a very high rate of interest!
2. C. S. Lewis, *The Abolition of Man* (New York: Macmillan, 1947). Lewis's entire list is on pp. 97–121.
3. Julian, *The Arguments of the Emperor Julian Against the Christians* (Chicago: Hermetic Pub. Co., 1809), p. 46.

4. Bartolomé de las Casas, *History of the Indies,* (New York: Harper and Row, 1971) quoted in Howard Zinn, *A People's History of the United States: 1492 to Present.* Rev. ed. (New York: Harper Collins, 1995), p. 6.

5. Quoted in Edmund S. Morgan, *American Slavery American Freedom: The Ordeal of Colonial Virginia* (New York: W. W. Norton, 1975), p. 77.

6. Martin Buber, *I and Thou,* 2nd. ed. (New York: Charles Scribner and sons, 1958), pp. 112, 118.

7. D. H. Lawrence, "Pornography and Obscenity," Harry T. Moore, ed., *D. H. Lawrence: Sex, Literature and Censorship* (New York: Twayne Publishers, 1953), pp. 70–71.

8. Leonard Shlain, *The Alphabet Versus the Goddess* (New York: Viking, 1998), 236–361. I do not endorse his frequently faulty historical accounts, but this point seems well taken.

# PART III

# Pagan Criticisms of Christianity

# Spirit and Nature

## A Christian Blindness

## Spirit and Nature

Christianity originally appealed with particular force to people who were poor or of modest means, or who were disillusioned by the hypocrisy and cruelty of Classical society. Frequently these people were city dwellers. Given the often-appalling living conditions and brutal politics of those places, any sensitive person could easily conclude that earthly life was a vale of tears. Only later did the Church put down firm roots in the countryside where, even if life was far from easy, people's daily connection to natural forces reinforced spiritual practices with Pagan sensibilities.

By late Classical times many Classical Pagans had come to emphasize salvation as the greatest spiritual good because of such widespread harshness and misery. However, their perspective still reflected the original Pagan insight that the spiritual could be approached through the sacred within natural phenomena. Even in those dark times, from a Pagan perspective, salvation involved not so much a rejection of the world as escaping the bonds of fate.

Early Christians would probably have had a difficult time sympathizing with views conceiving the material world as sacred. Their beliefs, even if not so world-denying as the Gnostics, usually strengthened pre-existing attitudes about the undesirability of physical existence. The doctrine of the Fall as interpreted through Saint Augustine's conception of Original Sin created a deep gulf between two spiritual worlds. For Christianity, misfortunes were evidence the world was a truly defective place. Misery was so great in those times that, for many, the Christian view seemed reasonable.

Much has happened since then. Rome withered away and a new civilization arose in its place, many of its roots explicitly Christian. For many reasons the Christian West entered into a process of profound transformation, one unlike any earlier society. This transformation has changed the circumstances of peoples' lives and, in so doing, changed many of their spiritual concerns.

If the Middle Ages were particularly conducive to sustaining a Christian civilization, Western modernity is not. In important respects the modern world has produced an environment conducive to a renaissance of Pagan spirituality. Modern societies are the first since hunting and gathering times where most people are not poor by the standards of their time. The necessities of human life have been met with unparalleled success. The elderly make up a greater proportion of the population than at any time in history. Modern Westerners are reasonably prosperous, enjoy relatively secure social and political rights, and are literate. The old perception that life for most people is poor, brutish, and short has been decisively changed in the developed countries, and increasingly in others.

Further, we moderns live in societies that have become secularized to a degree that would have once been unthinkable. The privileged political positions of some Christian denominations have been greatly weakened or abolished. Today in the United States and other democratic societies, extraordinary religious freedom generally prevails. Religious leaders can no longer take their practitioners for granted. More than at any time during the past 1,500 years or so, today religions have to survive solely on the freely offered allegiance of people who are aware they have alternatives.

If Spirit is immanent as well as transcendent we might well expect a diversity of religious practices to arise under modern conditions, and this is what we do observe. In the United States Christianity itself evolved into a wide variety of denominations and sects. Some people have become skeptical of the whole idea of revealed scripture, while maintaining an interest in spirituality. Along with Neopaganism, increasingly indigenous spiritual practices, and those of new immigrants, are finding interested audiences. Non-Christian spirituality is attracting more and more people for whom traditional American Christian practices fail to resonate.

From a spiritual perspective the modern world is deeply paradoxical. Its achievements in bettering human life are very real, but simultaneously we are surrounded by a society where virtually everything has its price and almost nothing is respected as holding intrinsic value. Today our poverty is not often in material wealth or physical security. It is a poverty of meaning and value. Many people lack a context that gives significance to their lives, their society, and their world. The slogan "He Who Dies With The Most Toys Wins" does not satisfy many people.

This widespread poverty of meaning is rooted in our common dissociation from anything but human society. Surrounded as we usually are by a largely manufactured and controlled environment, human purposes and desires can seem the ultimate locus of value. But because they are usually rooted in our incompleteness and need, by themselves these expressions of the narrowly human are incapable of fulfilling our deepest longing. When taken as ultimate standards they deprives us of a context to make deeper sense of our lives.

Our society's disconnection from the natural and spiritual worlds that sustain it is perfectly illustrated in the common argument by many economists and business people that the market should determine how we use the world. Consumer choice and profit should be our guide. From this perspective old growth trees should be "harvested" if it is the most profitable use to which they can be put, even though it makes no economic sense to invest in a new old-growth forest to replace the trees that were cut, because no conceivable interest rates would justify an investment taking at least 300 years to realize. The most rational use the logic of our culture can come up with for something we cannot "afford" to replace is to cut it down.

Wherever this logic penetrates nothing is recognized as worthy of respect, nothing counts for anything except for how it contributes as a resource to someone's plans. Trees, animals, air, water, earth, and even human beings are valued for their convertibility into cash—the ultimate idol before which the modern world prostrates itself. Small wonder so many people find the contemporary world, even with its very real benefits and blessings, ultimately insufficient to provide the basis for a satisfying life.

When everything has a price tag, nothing is valuable in itself. All "Thous" become "Its." Yet most of us know genuine value exists, at least when we think of our friends and loved ones. Very often we encounter it in nature as well, which is why terms like "pristine waters," "virgin forests," "unspoiled scenery," and "God's country" are so popular. These figures of speech point to a directly *experienced* reality of beauty and value, and to something qualitatively different from human society.

Compared to our daily routine of commuting, working, and being passively entertained, many of us encounter greater meaning when immersing ourselves in the changing of the seasons, viewing the play of evening light across hills, or watching a herd of deer emerge from the woods. It is within the embrace of nature's rhythms that we are freed from our preoccupation with the perpetual calculation that powers our society, teaching us the price of everything and the value of nothing.

It is within nature that we most easily encounter a reality far greater than human plans and aspirations. Wild nature first demonstrated to me, and to many others as well, the limitations of our society's dominant outlook. In nature our socially derived preconceptions and prejudices are most easily quieted, for they are not continually reinforced by encounters with others in a similar frame of mind. In quiet alertness, our senses open to meaning and goodness unconnected with human ends. Spirit in nature reaches out through beauty, peace, and the openness of heart it evokes within us.

While Christianity is genuinely capable of honoring nature, historically it has not to any great degree. This failing continues to the present. For example, ChristianityToday.com published an article respectfully critical of Neopaganism, written by Loren Wilkinson, a Canadian Christian theologian. In his article, Wilkinson writes of participating in a demonstration defending old-growth forests on Vancouver Island. He explained, "We were persuaded to participate by a new Christian who was impressed by the spiritual seriousness of the protest and the complete lack of Christian presence there."[1]

Despite honorable exceptions such as Loren Wilkinson, today Christianity's loudest representatives emphasize the opposite view: that nature is to be dominated and used up. This appears to be particularly the case with Fundamentalists and evangelicals who see themselves as the front line against Wiccan Paganism, and who are sometimes active in the so-called "Christian" Right. Anyone who believes in nature's intrinsic value, they contend, is "Pagan." Flattering as this claim is, it nevertheless evidences enormous ignorance of biblical Scripture on their part.[2]

These people are incredibly selective in their use of scripture. Even more significantly, they are also cutting themselves off from appreciating one of the strongest sources for spiritual awareness available to many Americans today. In my judgment, this is one major reason why there is a growing renaissance of Pagan spirituality within the United States, and in Western Europe as well.

The sacred is in everything, but it can be apprehended most easily when we are removed from our preoccupation with human purposes. Wild nature helps free us from them. Seasons, solstices, equinoxes, and the lunar cycle are free from human manipulation, and so are truly wild. That is why they can offer us a more satisfactory context and healing presence than is present in secular pursuits. So is the rest of nature allowed to speak to us in its own way.

With their emphasis on harmony and experience, the Pagan nature religions enable us to enter into a deep and profound relationship with the immanent aspect of the Divine. In doing so, like all genuine religion, they open up the possibility of personal transformation, away from egoism and toward love, away from selfishness and toward compassion, away from spiritual need and toward spiritual abundance. This is perhaps the deepest message of Henry David Thoreau's profound observation that: "In wildness is the preservation of the world."

Pagan nature religion is today a particularly powerful and appropriate spiritual path, for it teaches us lovingly to accept and embrace our world, and enter into an I-Thou relationship with it. Even as our sacred earth refreshes and uplifts our spirit, the world also needs our love. The oceans, rivers, and lakes are degraded. Forests, savannas, and prairies are degraded. The air is degraded. The great silence that speaks to us so powerfully is degraded. There is a great need for healing on both sides, a healing that can only result from our hearts and minds, guided by Spirit.

Where does Christianity stand with respect to all this? As befits our times, it takes many stands. But again and as usual, its loudest practitioners disapprove of and fear any efforts to find Spirit in nature.

## The Bible and Nature

Many Christians have criticized Wiccans for denying the gulf supposedly separating humankind from nature. Even Christians who accept the reality of evolution, and happily most now do, are bothered by Pagans finding divinity in nature, and not just in a transcendent God alone. Man, they tell us, was created in God's image, unlike the rest of creation. Creation is therefore fundamentally inferior. For example, one Christian wrote me that "man [alone] is described as having the breath of God, not just the breath of life, since the Bible says God breathed the breath of life into man."

Who, I wrote back, breathed life into animals? One of the two Genesis accounts says the earth brought forth the land animals, which might lead some Christians to suggest that animals are one step removed from God, compared to human beings, but there is no similar wiggle room when considering birds and whales, who are described as directly created. Are birds and whales closer to God than land animals? Adam, we read, was constructed out of dust, which is of the earth. God, however, created the whales and birds directly. Dust is not mentioned. Are they closer to God than Adam was? Even in strictly Biblical terms, these passages in Genesis fail to establish a deeper separation between animals and God than between human beings and God. From a Biblical perspective, perhaps the separation between God and earth is not quite so stark as most Christians believe.

Job 12:7–10 clearly says that animals have souls. Genesis 7: 21–22 explicitly says that animals received their life in exactly the same way as people: through the breath of life. The Hebrew word for soul, *nephesh*, is used to refer to both animals and humans, although it is usually translated differently in the King James version when referring to animals than when referring to us.[3] Even so, the distinction between the two cannot be maintained because sometimes Scripture *combines* reference to both human and animal souls, as in Job 12:10, which describes God: "in whose hand *is* the soul of every living thing, and the breath of all mankind."

Nor is this an isolated passage. Psalm 104:27–30 says of the animals of the earth and God "These wait all upon thee; that thou mayest give them their meat in due season. That Thou givest them they gather: Thou openest thine hand, they are filled with good. Thou hidest thy face, they are troubled: Thou takest away their breath, they die, and return to their dust. Thou sendest forth thy spirit, they are created: and thou renewest the face of the earth." Clearly there is little here to suggest we are so very different from animals in the eyes of the Lord.

God made a covenant with Noah after the flood, a covenant not to drown all life again. But while this covenant was with Noah and his descendants, it was not with them alone. Beginning with Genesis 9:10, God adds that His covenant is also "with every living creature that *is* with you, of the fowl, of the cattle, and of every beast of the earth with you; from all that go out of the ark, to every beast of the earth." In Genesis 9:12 God elaborates that the rainbow is "the token of the covenant which I make between me and you and every living creature that *is* with you, for perpetual generations . . ." Emphasizing this point, God again says in Genesis 9:15, "And I will remember my covenant "which is between me and you and every living creature of all flesh . . ." and in 9:16–17 He repeats this same point again and again.

Elsewhere, in Psalm 104:15–18, it is clear that God cares for far more than just the human race, and is actively involved with all other forms of life. For example: "The trees of the Lord are full of sap; the cedars of Lebanon, which he hath planted; Where the birds make their nests: as for the stork, the fir trees are her house. The high hills are a refuge for the wild goats; and the rocks for the conies." This passage could easily be interpreted as a command to preserve wilderness areas extensive enough to provide for all forms of life. Instead it is usually ignored.

My interpretation is strengthened when we read in the Bible that the destruction of wilderness is a *punishment* for bad behavior. According to Jeremiah 9:10, "For the mountains will I take up a weeping and wailing, and for the habitations of the wilderness a lamentation, because they are burned up, so that none can pass through them; neither can men hear the voice of the cattle, both the fowl of the heavens and the beast are fled; they are gone." Obviously, in a good world they are present.

Some Christians criticize the Endangered Species Act and environmentalism in general as "Pagan." While such attacks are a truly great compliment to us, nevertheless I have to wonder whether they have ever carefully read the text they supposedly revere. If *all* animals are valuable enough for God to covenant with, and voluntarily limit exercise of His power, and He even sets some parts of the earth aside for their use, on what possible scriptural basis can such people claim that determining the fate of animals is a *human* prerogative? How can Christians say they are a covenantal religion when they ignore the first of God's covenants?

The Church should be among the most enthusiastic advocates of preserving all life, as indeed some Christians are, but they struggle against the many who confuse their own convenience, greed, pride, and self-interested ignorance with what they claim to be God's will.

In response to this kind of argument, one Christian critic referred me to Job 12:8 as suggesting that the earth also has a soul. He argued that the obvious absurdity of this claim shows the inaccuracy of my interpretation. For me, and for many Pagans around the world, as well as for many pre-modern Christians, this point is not absurd. In my experience the land has a most definite presence. It is not inert. The earth is aware. Approached properly, it responds.

From this Pagan perspective the entire passage of Job 12:7–10 takes on a familiar meaning: "But ask now the beasts, and they shall teach thee; and the fowls of the air, and they shall tell thee: Or speak to the earth, and it shall teach thee: and the fishes of the sea shall declare unto thee. Who knoweth not in all these that the hand of the Lord hath wrought this? In whose hands is the soul of every living thing, and the breath of all mankind?" In Jeremiah 8:7 we read: "Yea, the stork in the heaven knoweth her appointed times; and the turtle and the crane and the swallow observe the time of their coming; but my people know not the judgment of the Lord." Here is direct scriptural agreement with a core Pagan insight that the world of nature, the living earth and all upon it, are *reliable* sources of spiritual wisdom.

## Nature, Text, and Spirit

I am continually amazed how what is in plain print is ignored by so many who claim to rely upon the Bible for spiritual guidance. I have long pondered why. I think the error comes from the capacity of printed texts to substitute for experience rather than helping us understand experience. The Bible's writers sought to integrate nature and text within a spiritual practice. Somewhere along the way the text came to obscure and dominate nature, despite the denunciations of scribes and pedants and praise of the world found in both testaments.

The contemporary denial by many Christians of Spirit in nature is related to an inadequate concept of deity arising from the heartless logic chopping that arises out of taking textual interpretation to an extreme. When we read about God rather than experience Spirit, and when we allow our understanding from reading to dominate or deny our experience, only our rational and abstracting mind is called into action. Separated from the heart, the mind reduces everything to objects of analysis. When Spirit is so separated from our experience we are led to conceive of God simply as power. Late medieval nominalism, followed by certain kinds of Protestantism, completely extracted Spirit from nature by substituting a highly selective interpretation of biblical text emphasizing the supremacy of God's will for thousands of years of shared experience.

Emphasizing God's arbitrary power as His defining quality made everything else, by comparison, an "it." Once this is done, even scriptural evidence to the contrary gets ignored—in the name of following Scripture. The world was increasingly banished from God.

The Pagan approach is more insightful. Spirit and awareness permeates everything. No yawning divide separates Spirit from Matter. In Classical times, from the Middle Platonists to the Neoplatonists, the World Soul was often conceived as the Goddess Hekate, and Hekate has for millennia has been considered, among other things, to be the Goddess of the Witches. From a Wiccan perspective, Job 12:8 is a powerful point in our favor. Awareness is everywhere. Consciousness is everywhere. It need not necessarily be connected to material metabolisms, as any Christian who believes in heaven or hell or souls or angels or God will have to grant. The Divine is immanent as well as transcendent. And everywhere the Divine is, awareness is.

# The Matter of God's Image

Some Christians attempt to rebut this argument about the sacredness of nature with the biblical claim that we were created in God's image whereas the rest of nature was not. Genesis does say that, but what does it, or we, mean by the "image" of God? Is it the point that God has a head, a navel, ten fingers and toes, and a bladder? There is little in Scripture to support this interpretation, and much to deny it. This view is childish.

Some Christians have suggested our free will is what makes us in the image of God. We share with Him a radical freedom. This is an improvement over a purely physical conception, but even so, suggests a pretty poor sort of God, one whose most defining capacity is to do whatever He desires. It elevates power over love and will over compassion. It is a conception of God suitable to a pouting three-year-old dreaming of doing anything he wants when he gets big enough. Conceptions such as these have led many people to conceive of God as a Divine despot, often with tragic results.

More to the point, from a strict Biblical viewpoint, especially one that emphasizes God's power, it is by no means clear that free will exists. Augustine apparently thought otherwise, and most Christians today emphasize that we cannot help but sin. That, after all, is why we need salvation. If we are inclined to sin, and God is not, from a Christian perspective how can our will be in His image? If God is free and we are not because we cannot help but sin, this argument equating God's image with free will is false.

Our will can be akin to God's only from our *desire* to choose the good. This desire may be continually thwarted by ignorance, but it persists nonetheless. This insight leads us to where the real "image of God" might be found. God desires the good, and so do we (sometimes) but God is far better at getting it right.

The "image of God," if it means anything at all, means our all-too-undeveloped capacity for unconditional love. Not only does my own spiritual experience tell me that such love is perhaps the most fundamental characteristic of what is Ultimate; this fact is also biblically attested. John writes that: "God is love, and he that dwelleth in love dwelleth in God, and God in him" (1 John 4:16). From this perspective, we act in God's spiritual image when we act with unconditional love.

On this point a great deal of Christian and Pagan thought, Classical and Traditional Wiccan alike, agrees. Much Classical Pagan philosophy has long considered love the essential binding force of reality. It is central to the Traditional Wiccan "Myth of the Goddess."[4] Without love, there would be no world. There does not seem to me to be much difference between John's observation and those of many Pagan philosophers on this very important point.

Unlike today, in Pagan times philosophers were also the theologians, who often explored and taught the deeper implications of popular spirituality. Like liberal Christian theologians of today, they sought to understand the deeper truths implicit within the popular religious practices of their day. For example, the Roman Cicero approvingly quotes a Stoic philosopher as saying that while the stories about the Gods in Homer are nonsense, so that, "we reject and scorn these myths, we shall be able to understand the identity and character of the deity which penetrates each element, Ceres the earth, Neptune the sea, and so forth; and we have a duty to honour and worship these gods by the name custom has given."[5] Many of these Pagan philosopher-theologians had a far better understanding of God than do many contemporary Christians.

Nor need we consider only liberal interpretations of Scripture to arrive at a loving awareness of the natural world from a biblical perspective. Even a more literal interpretation supports this observation. In the biblical story of the flood, God commanded Noah to save pairs of *every* creature, not simply those of utilitarian use to human beings. So spiders, snakes, and scorpions were presumably on the ark as well.

If God found the world good, how could any person of genuine spiritual knowledge *not* love it? God certainly does. If in fact our capacity to love is what brings us closest to the Divine, *then we relate most appropriately to nature when doing so in terms of our love for it*, whether as God's creation, such as Christian theology contends, or as a direct expression and manifestation of the Divine, as we Pagans believe. From a panentheist perspective, which views the Highest as both immanent and transcendent, these views are complementary. I would suggest that Pagans who find the Divine manifested through nature, and love it as sacred, possess a far more accurate perception of reality, including spiritual reality, than the common contemporary contention by so many Christians that nature is simply here for our use, even in biblical terms.

## Acting in a Sacred Way

Since, within the Biblical tradition, the whole creation supposedly fell because of disobedience by Adam and Eve, it seems to me that Christians, *above all others*, should take special care for the well-being of the vast abundance of life that, through no fault or action of its own, is now "fallen." To oppose protection of endangered species and wild areas because that would limit our ability to exploit them is, from a biblical perspective, rather akin to a thief objecting when asked to limit his use of ill-gotten gains. To treat other beings with less than kindness and respect is sin. There is plenty of scriptural evidence for this argument.

In Genesis 1:29–30 it is clear that God originally forbade human beings from eating meat. This passage occurs almost immediately *after* the granting of human dominion over nature. The "dominion" of which so many now boast when they try and convert the natural world to money was in fact that of a caretaker, refraining even from eating meat while dressing and keeping the Creation.

That the Bible can be selectively quoted out of context as granting "dominion" simply reflects the ability of a cagey con artist to quote his benefactor's words to justify his thievery, since such justifications never mention that people were also to "dress and keep" what God found good. For example, that passage would appear explicitly to forbid causing the extinction of anything. You don't "keep" something by wiping it out.

Biblically speaking, only after the flood were people given permission to eat meat, but this expansion of human prerogative did not thereby devalue the world. There are many "post-deluge" passages in the Bible that suggest the continued appropriateness of maintaining a respectful relationship with the earth, although certainly the major force of Christian development and interpretation took another path. Numbers 35:33–34 finds God commanding, "So ye shall not pollute the land wherein ye are. . . . Defile not therefore the land which ye shall inhabit, wherein I dwell; for I the Lord dwell among the children of Israel." Interestingly, God also commands that the land itself receive a Sabbath. In Leviticus 25:2–4 God is quoted as saying:

> When ye come into the land which I give you, then shall the land keep a sabbath unto the Lord. Six years thou shalt sow thy field, and six years thou shalt prune thy vineyard, and gather in the fruit thereof; But in the seventh year shall be a sabbath of rest unto the land, a sabbath for the Lord: thou shalt neither sow thy field nor prune thy vineyard. That which groweth of its own accord of thy harvest thou shalt not reap, neither gather the grapes of thy vine undressed: for it is a year of rest unto the land.

Leviticus verses 26:31–35 warn of the catastrophe that will follow if commandments such as these are not followed, concluding that "your land shall be desolate, and ye be in your enemies' land; even then shall the land rest, and enjoy her sabbaths. As long as it lieth desolate it shall rest; because it did not rest in your sabbaths, when ye dwelt upon it." God's reason for the Sabbath also extends to animals, apparently with equal force as it applies to humans. Exodus 24:12 commands, "Six days thou shalt do thy work, and on the seventh day thou shalt rest: that thine ox and thine ass may rest, and the son of thy handmaid, and the stranger, may be refreshed." In short, we are forbidden from treating animals as simply means to our ends. In the New Testament it is clear that God cares for sparrows that fall from the sky and lilies of the field. These passages demonstrate a deep concern with the natural world that is too often ignored by those claiming to take the Bible for guidance.

There is much more in the Bible that points to the special place the land plays in the eyes of the God of Israel. Land is never referred to as simply something to be put to our use. Thus, in Leviticus 25:23 God reportedly commands, "The land shall not be sold forever: for the land is mine: for ye are strangers and sojourners with me." This command is in sharp contrast to how the people of Israel could treat houses and other human-made things, which they could freely sell. For God, money can neither buy nor appropriately value land. We can use the land, but we must do so with respect, never treating it simply as our possession, for, "The earth is the Lord's and the fullness thereof; the world and they that dwell therein" (Psalm 24:1).

Isaiah 5:8 warns, "Woe unto them that join house to house, *that* lay field to field, till *there be* no place, that they may be placed alone in the midst of the earth!" It seems clear that from His perspective there should remain parts of the earth where anyone who wished could be alone, free from human contact. The Bible explicitly supports the primordial Pagan insight that the Great Silence is sacred. Isaiah condemns the usual implication of what so many Christians claim as their "right" of dominion.

The biblical God *commands* respect for animals, and for the land itself. He lives in the land, or at least in some of it. He speaks of the land as a living entity that needs rest, just as animals and people need rest. And, let us not forget, in the Bible, even before the creation of the first human beings, God said of His creation that it was good. These views are harmonious with a panentheist perspective that finds divinity within, but also in another sense transcendent to, the world. It is certainly in keeping with the Pagan perception of nature as sacred and worthy of respect.

One passage is endlessly cited to offset all these opposed views: that we supposedly have "dominion" over God's creation. However, the word read as "dominion" has alternate translations that bring it into harmony with the rest of these texts. One such term is "shepherding."[6]

Many Christians argue that pride was the basic sin for both Satan and the first couple. Any interpretation of Scripture that appeals to the human ego should therefore be treated with suspicion, particularly when other interpretations are equally possible. What could appeal to a self-centered ego more than the conceit that the entire world is ours to do with as we wish? What could give greater thrill to the little ego than the allure of dominion without obligation? Power without responsibility and will without heart! Over and over again the loudest Christians tell us the world is for our dominion and we have the right to do what God Himself refused to do.

A religion whose adherents claim the authority of sacred writings should pay more attention to what those writings actually say, rather than playing pick and choose among texts taken from context. Here, I think, thoughtful Christians can learn from many Pagans—not to become Pagan themselves, but to appreciate neglected elements within their own tradition—and so become better Christians.

ENDNOTES

1. Loren Wilkinson, "The Bewitching Charms of Neopaganism," Christianity-Today.com, January 19, 2000.

2. A pioneering attempt to recognize the role of nature and the environment within a evangelical Christian context is Francis A. Schaeffer, *Pollution and the Death of Man: The Christian View of Ecology* (Wheaton, IL: Tyndale House, 1972).

As I was completing this chapter I received an interesting magazine in the mail: *Religion and the Forests: Promoting Religious Responsibility for the*

*Forests*, RCFC, 409 Mendocino Avenue, Suite A, Santa Rosa, Calif. 05401. It is an impressive effort on the part of Christians and Jews to argue for respecting our forests, and nature in general.

3. Lewis Regenstein, *Replenish the Earth* (New York: Crossroad, 1991), pp. 43–44.

4. Gerald Gardner, *Witchcraft Today*, (New York: Magickal Childe, 1982), p. 41.

5. A. A. Long, "Epicureans and Stoics," A. H. Armstrong, ed., *Classical Mediterranean Spirituality: Egyptian, Greek, Roman* (New York: Crossroad, 1989), p. 147.

6. Robin Lane Fox, *The Unauthorized Version: Truth and Fiction in the Bible* (New York: Vintage, 1993), p. 177.

# Toleration and Violence
## A Christian Dilemma

## Hell and Tolerance

I have been saving the most difficult question separating Christians from Pagans for last, but it can no longer be avoided. Nearly two thousand years of Christian history stand united in the contention that the Christian way is the only spiritually valid way. I obviously argue otherwise. Some Christians will say that if I am correct, the Christian message is false. I am arguing the choice is not so melodramatic. But how are we to deal with what appear to be claims for religious exclusivity within the teachings of Jesus Himself? Claims which, if true, make Him our only Savior, and if not, simply deluded or a liar.

When advocates of a religion argue that anyone who does not believe its teachings is doomed to eternal damnation, it is hard for them to tolerate what they see as error in others. This is particularly true if they have the political power to suppress those they believe to be in error. The question of whether or not to tolerate error is doubly vexing when people thought to be mistaken are spreading their errors, causing others to stray from the path of eternal salvation. At that point the spiritually deluded become agents of evil, even if unknowing ones.

The question confronting contemporary Christian Evangelicals is both straightforward and brutal: are we showing love to our fellow human beings if we allow them to be swayed into eternal damnation by those who are leading them into error? We are to turn the other cheek when we are attacked, but are we to be similarly meek when we believe our passivity may injure others? The more a Christian cares about other people, the more excruciating the dilemma.

Loving Christians who take the exclusivity claim seriously must suffer grievously. On all sides they are surrounded by people for whom they care, often deeply, and who they also believe to be damned for eternity. To love God, and to love those damned by Him for eternity—even to be commanded by Him to love them—what an incredible and painful burden! How hard it must be to sustain their love for both God and human under such circumstances. And what kind of heaven awaits those who know that some loved ones simultaneously suffer eternal torment in hell?

Given the internal logic of the dominant Christian position, this tragic dilemma is unavoidable. Historically the implications flowing from this logic have been profound and tragic. It has repeatedly led to periods of bloody persecution of people deemed to be theologically beyond the pale. It is the ultimate contradiction to the meaning of "the Gospels," for this news is definitely not good.

The record of Christian persecution is very long and its roots are very deep. Ironically, the first victims of official intolerance were other Christians, who were believed by Christians with access to political power to "have it wrong" regarding what the Bible meant, but countless Pagans as well fell to the savage fury of the mob and the sword. As early as 317, only three years after Christianity was legalized throughout the Empire, the Roman state abrogated its decree of universal toleration in order to begin persecuting, albeit fitfully, Christian heretics! Roman religious toleration was revoked at the request of some Christians themselves.

About seventy years later Saint Augustine supported torturing and killing the Christian Donatists, whom he regarded as heretics, unless they accepted his views. Augustine's actions and reasoning established an ominous precedent. He argued that the true oppressors were not the Church but instead those whom the Church suppressed. In a masterpiece of rationalization, Augustine wrote: "It is rather the Catholic Church which suffers persecution through the pride and impiety of those carnal men whom it endeavours to correct by afflictions and terrors of a temporal kind."[1] The Biblical text Augustine cited to support political coercion, Luke 14:23: "And the lord said unto the servant, go out into the highways and hedges, and compel *them* to come in, that my house may be filled," was later used to justify the Inquisition. Once they enjoyed political power as officials of the state church, it took Christian leaders only a few decades to begin persecuting all Christians they believed to be in error.

It was not much later that Christian authorities turned on Pagans as well. In 392 Emperor Theodosius first outlawed the practice of Pagan religion throughout the Roman Empire. By the early part of the fifth century it had become dangerous to be an open Pagan in parts of the Empire. For example, Cyril, Bishop of Alexandria, enforced Christian orthodoxy upon Christian and Pagan alike. He closed the churches of Christians he deemed insufficiently orthodox, expelled the Jews from the city, and very likely instigated the bestial murder of Hypatia, a brilliant and prominent Pagan woman philosopher.

Hypatia was widely regarded as so extraordinary a philosopher that she was appointed to the chair of philosophy at Alexandria's top university. A Pagan, her teachings were regarded as so profound that even Christians were drawn to her. She represented virtually everything that Cyril disliked: a Pagan woman instructing men, even Christians. Worst of all, she was popular.

Cyril commanded a small army of lay monks, upon whom he relied to terrorize Pagans, Jews, and unorthodox Christians. In 415, during Lent, these monks seized Hypatia as she drove her chariot through Alexandria's streets. They stripped her naked, beat her to death with tiles, tore her body limb from limb, and burned her remains.

Cyril claimed not to be responsible, but did not condemn the killing by his men. Later he increased the number of his militant monks from 500 to 600. This thuggish man is universally regarded as a father of the Christian Church, and was later canonized as Saint Cyril.

Because Pagans could easily honor more than one deity, many "converted" to the Church. It was safer publicly, provided insurance against the possibility of Hell should the Christians be right, and they did not necessarily have to give up their private veneration of their own Gods. Most likely millions of Roman "Christians" continued to revere their old deities, rather like millions of contemporary Latin Americans. One surviving quotation reads: "I am thinking of the danger to my life, and so off I go now to the church, to evade the death that otherwise awaits me." This was no exaggeration, for in 435 the formal death penalty was instituted for practicing Pagan religion.

A constant readiness to resort to violence is a familiar theme in Church history. Saint Thomas Aquinas, for example, wrote of heretics that, "their sin deserves banishment, not only from the Church by excommunication, but also from this world by death." To be sure, Aquinas argued conversions should be voluntary, and he did tolerate the right of Jews to practice their faith. However, "The rites of other infidels, which bear no truth or profit, are not to be tolerated in the same way, except perhaps to avoid some evil, for instance the scandal or disturbance that might result, or the hindrance to the salvation of those who, were they unmolested, might gradually be converted to the faith."[2] A brilliant philosopher, Saint Thomas's intolerant positions were simply working out the implications of a faith that claimed spiritual exclusivity.

Today we take religious toleration so much for granted that we need to be reminded of what has always happened when there has been no separation of Christian church and state. For example, beginning in 1095 the Catholic Church began organizing "Crusades" against the enemies of its domination, both real and imagined. In 1099, in a scene to be repeated many times, Raymond of

Aguilers glowingly described a massacre of Moslems and Jews by Christians in Jerusalem:

> Wonderful things were to be seen. Numbers of the Saracens were beheaded . . . Others were shot with arrows or forced to jump from the towers; others were tortured for several days, then burned with flames. In the streets were seen piles of heads and hands and feet. One rode about everywhere amid the corpses of men and horses. In the [Jewish] Temple of Solomon, the horses waded in blood up to their knees, nay, up to the bridle. It was a just and marvelous judgment of God, that this place should be filled with the blood of unbelievers.[3]

In 1204 Crusaders sacked Constantinople, the center of Orthodox Christianity. Pope Innocent III justified mass murder, rape, arson, and pillaging in a Christian city by pointing out that the Orthodox Christians refused to acknowledge Rome as their superior. In 1208, the thirty-year Albigensian Crusade against the Cathars opened the way to a 500-year-long record of religious violence and persecution without parallel in Western history. The Albigensian Crusade decimated southern France, taking the lives of around one million people. The logic of Christian actions in Provence was captured in Papal Legate Arnaud's famous injunction: "Kill them all, for God knows his own!"[4] Nobody knows how many people were slaughtered during the Crusades, and close on their heels the Inquisition, as a whole, but it surely dwarfed the wholesale destruction in Provence.

The Inquisition cut a bloody swath of terror through Europe, the Americas, and parts of Asia. Catholic and Protestant alike participated in the Witch burnings, which in some villages left almost no women alive. Around 1600 a man wrote: "Germany is almost entirely occupied with building fires for the witches . . . Switzerland has been compelled to wipe out many of her villages on their account. Travelers in Lorraine may see thousands and thousands of the stakes to which witches are bound." The murder of witches and accused witches was practiced as official policy by both Catholic and Protestant churches. Luther and Calvin were as guilty of this crime against humanity as the pope.[5] Recent scholarship has reduced the numbers killed for "Witchcraft" during this period to a "mere" 40,000 or so, which is comforting only in that the earlier estimates have proven too high.[6]

Later the population of much of central Europe was annihilated in the wars between Catholics and Protestants. In Germany and Bohemia, where the worst of the fighting occurred, around 35 percent of the inhabitants, men, women, and children alike, were slaughtered. It took one hundred years for these populations to recover to their former numbers. Bloody civil wars motivated by sectarian hatreds also convulsed both England and France, as Christian neighbor slaughtered Christian neighbor in the name of a God both worshipped. The killers respected neither sex nor age. In England, Oliver Cromwell took the Biblical Joshua as his role model as he massacred countless Catholic Irish on that unfortunate island.

Such a record of violence in the name of religion is, I think, historically unequaled in length of time, in geographical breadth, and in numbers killed. This consistent record of destruction is why U.S. founding father James Madison wrote: "The separation of church and state is to keep forever from these shores the ceaseless strife that has soaked the soil of Europe with blood for centuries."

Christian apologists will challenge that such behavior could not be condoned by the Bible. Some have challenged me to show where, in the New Testament, scriptural authority for violence against unbelievers can be found. Saint Augustine found it in Luke 14:23. Taken in isolation, this passage virtually commands that believers "compel" others to come to services. If compelling is biblical, what should be done with those who resist compulsion? Augustine, and many after him, had no problem with relying upon the police and the sword.

The New Testament contains no explicit commandments to kill, but the Old Testament is another matter. It has repeatedly been used by some Christians to justify extensive violence and slaughter of Pagans. For example, the Israelites' extermination of the Pagan Canaanites was used to justify slaughtering Pagan American Indians who did not want to give their lands to Europeans. Many biblical passages justify the slaughter of women, the elderly, and even children, if they are Pagan. (For examples, see Exodus 32:27, 28; Numbers 21:35; Deuteronomy 2:34, 7:2; the entire book of Joshua; 1 Samuel 15:18.) From a biblical perspective it is not at all clear what parts of the Old Testament are no longer supposed to apply in the Christian era. There is a strong case that, taken literally, Scripture commands murder on a global scale.

The frequently heard claim that these killers were false Christians rings hollow. Why were there *so many* false Christians for so long, and in such *leading* positions? Advocates of violence constituted virtually *all* the Church's leaders at the time, Catholic and Protestant alike. It included Saint Augustine and Cyril of Alexandria, it included Saint Thomas Aquinas, Martin Luther and John Calvin and, as far as I know, every pope who had the power to get away with violence against those he believed to be in error. Most of these people certainly thought of themselves, and were considered by others of the time, to be good Christians. If they were the bad Christians, where were the good ones?

The basic spiritual error that led these Christians along the path to persecution and murder is, in my view, still committed by most evangelicals today. The chief distinction between then and now is the differences in their power to act on their beliefs, not in the beliefs themselves. Since some Christian readers may think I exaggerate, I ask them to consider the following words by one of their own, presidential candidate and long-time prominent religious leader, Pat Buchanan:

> . . . If God is king, men have a duty to try, as best they can, to conform their lives to His will and shape society in accordance with His law. Defection and indifferentism are not options. We are commanded to fight.

. . . We can no more walk away from the culture war than we could walk away from the Cold War. For the culture war is at its heart a religious war about whether God or man shall be exalted, whose moral beliefs shall be enshrined in law, and what children shall be taught to value and abhor. With those stakes, to walk away is to abandon your post in time of war.[7]

Even in the United States, as recently as a few decades ago, Native Americans were forbidden to practice essential elements of their religions, while missionary schools simultaneously worked hard to convert Indian children to Christianity. In many cases children were taken forcibly from their families to Christian boarding schools where this religious persecution took place, despite the Bill of Rights. Freedom of religion did not exist for these Pagans, and most Christian churches made no effort to end this injustice. The Fundamentalist ones certainly did not. It was not until 1978 that Congress passed the American Religious Freedom Act, promising to protect the spiritual traditions of our native peoples, but even then conservatives on the Supreme Court declared it unconstitutional. The disease of persecution is deeply embedded within the very fabric of the traditional understanding of Christian doctrines.

Today, fortunately, the Church controls neither police nor military, but both then and now the same monopolistic spiritual claim is made: that only through the Church is salvation possible. Historically we see a sustained juxtaposition of unprecedented claims about salvation with unprecedented violence against those regarded as spiritually in error whenever the opportunity arises. It seems impossible to me for anyone reasonably and honestly to deny a connection between the attitude and the deeds.[8]

I have emphasized this bloody record realizing full well that many Christians may be deeply offended, and tempted to enumerate cases of bloody practices by other religions in response. I will save them the trouble. We know that Pagan Carthaginians, Celts,

Mayans, and Aztecs all practiced human sacrifice, sometimes on an appalling scale. So did the Greeks and Romans at one time. It is very likely that no religious tradition is without blood on its hands.

Who can stack the pile of bodies highest is not my main point in bringing up this brief overview of Christian violence. I have not argued that the Christians' stack of bodies is higher in order to claim that Pagan insights are intrinsically better, or discredit Christianity's spiritual value. I have done so to try and break through the enormous *arrogance* and *pride* of those so smugly confident that they, and only they, possess spiritual truth, and that all others are demonically inspired.

To my Christian readers I ask: if your truth is so much better, why have your compatriots killed so many more in its name? Why is it that earlier Christians have been so woefully inept in preventing so much carnage in the name of your God, and for so long? For it is a sad fact that every step towards religious peace in the modern West has been disproportionately advocated for secular reasons, not religious ones, and usually by people who were unorthodox in their spiritual beliefs.

It is important to ask *why* religious violence is perpetrated. Many Pagan societies once practiced human sacrifice in the mistaken belief that the gods demanded such offerings in order to maintain the land's fertility and the like. However, as the the Greeks, Romans, and others demonstrated, when Pagan religious traditions discovered this was unnecessary, the sacrifices came to an end. When the Romans discovered the Gods would not punish communities where Christian citizens refused to honor them, most lost interest in persecuting the early Church. Much more recently the same breakthrough happened among the Skidi Pawnee. Without missionary intervention they abandoned the "Morning Star" ritual wherein annually a maiden had been sacrificed. In Pagan practice, when people learned that the letting of blood was not necessary for the perpetuation of fertility or prosperity, they simply stopped.

The same problem, and same ultimate solution, confronts Christians. They are as intelligent as Pagans. The bloody Christian record exists because of the common Christian belief in the theological exclusivity of their faith.

## A Way Out

For the threat of sectarian violence to end without simultaneously ending Christianity, a reasonable biblical case must be made that other faiths play spiritually legitimate roles as well. I will suggest here one way in which this may be done. There are others developed by more liberal Christians.

So far as I am aware, the New Testament gives only one certain test of spiritual value. Jesus said, "by their fruits ye shall know them."(Matthew 7:20) What are the fruits of valid spiritual practice? Galatians 5:22–3 tells us that "the fruit of the Spirit is love, joy, peace, long-suffering, gentleness, goodness, faith, meekness, temperance. . . ." But the fruits of those who have emphasized the errors of other faiths, when offered the power of state or mob to enforce their beliefs, have been vile, murderous, evil, and as far removed from these fruits of spirit in Biblical terms as a person can get.

Practicing one's own faith, and thereby setting an appealing example for others, does seem in keeping with the fruits of Spirit. Jesus was continually critical of those who made a public spectacle of their piety. In His eyes praying in closets was superior to praying on street corners, (a teaching which I wish more evangelicals would heed). Often He emphasized that He would not judge others for their actions. These actions certainly suggest that Jesus found more important things to do spiritually than aggressively confronting those with whom He disagreed. The chief exception was the money changers in the temple itself, who profaned the Sacred with cash.

It is noteworthy that there is no record of Jesus attacking Pagan temples in word or in deed. He debated the Pharisees, not

Pagan priests and philosophers. Nor was He apparently concerned with spreading His message to the gentiles. I have already referred to Matthew 10. As is apparent in Acts, even after His crucifixion there was no belief among the apostles that Jesus desired such evangelizing. The apostles certainly interpreted His message more narrowly, and they had known Him.

An observation by Julian, the last Pagan Roman emperor, may shed some light on the reasons for Jesus' lack of concern with His Pagan neighbors: "The Jews accorded with [us] heathens, except in believing that there is only one God. For that is peculiar to them, but foreign to us. Everything else, indeed, is common to us, temples, sacred groves, altars, illustrations, and certain things to be observed; in which we either do not at all, or but little, differ from each other."[9] As we have seen, this common foundation included a common belief in a single Divine Source of all. Plotinus, the great late Classical Pagan philosopher, put the relationship of Pagan polytheism to their awareness of the one source of all very clearly when criticizing the Gnostics' rejection of the world and its deities in the name of a higher deity:

> Every evildoer began by despising the Gods; and one not previously corrupt, taking to this contempt, even though in other respects not wholly bad, becomes an evildoer by the very fact.
>
> Besides, in this slighting of the Mundane Gods, and the world, the honour they profess for the [higher] gods of the Intellectual Sphere becomes an inconsistency; where we love, our hearts are warm also to the kin of the beloved; we are not indifferent to the children of our friend. Now every soul is a child of that Father, but in the heavenly bodies there are souls, intellective, holy, much closer to the Supernal Beings than are ours; for how can this Cosmos be a thing cut off from That and how imagine the gods in it to stand apart?

. . . here we urge that where there is contempt for the Kin of the Supreme the knowledge of the Supreme itself is purely verbal.[10]

Significantly, in Rome many early Christians argued that the God they worshipped was *the same* as the ultimate God worshipped by Classical Pagans. For example, in *The City of God*, Saint Augustine said that the God we worship "is the God whom Porphyry, the most learned of philosophers, although the fiercest enemy of the Christian, acknowledges to be a great God . . . ." And the Christian Theophilus of Antioch described the Christian God as "ineffable . . . inexpressible . . . uncontainable . . . incomprehensible . . . inconceivable . . . incomparable . . . unteachable . . . immutable . . . inexpressible . . . without beginning because he was uncreated, immutable because he is immortal."[11] This example of "negative theology," which attempts to describe the Highest by emphasizing that it cannot truly be put into words, was a common way of describing the Highest in Classical Pagan philosophy.

Christians and Classical Pagans alike, when they tried to describe the Highest in positive terms, used largely the same terminology of superlatives. Such descriptions of the Highest are also in perfect harmony with the traditional Wiccan conception of the Ultimate Source. As the Dryghtyn blessing, said in all traditional Wiccan circles, goes: "In the name of Dryghtyn, the ancient providence, which was from the beginning, and is for all eternity male and female, the original source of all things; all knowing, all pervading, all powerful, changeless, eternal. . . ."[12] Save only the unfamiliar term "Dryghtyn," this description of the Highest should be familiar to all Christians as according with their conception of God.

The Pagan Maximus of Tyre, wrote: "In the midst of such contention, strife, and disagreement [on other matters] you would see in all the earth one harmonious law and principle that there is one God, king and father of all, and many gods, sons of God, fellow rulers with God. The Greek says this and the barbarian says it, the mainlander and the seafarer, the wise and the unwise."[13] Pagans believed God was honored in part by honoring those who were created by Him. They found no tension here.

In Classical times many Pagans, and sometimes their oracles as well, accorded Jesus very high status, as high as any person who had ever lived. They often said He had even become immortal because of His spiritual goodness. In short, the issue was not that Pagans denied that the Highest existed or even the spiritual value of Jesus' teachings. They were simply unconvinced that Jesus was a Divinity and that their own Divinities were evil. Thoughtful Christians today concede that belief in Jesus' divinity is entirely a matter of faith. There is no compelling proof.

From this vantage point, Jesus' apparent disinterest in attacking Classical Paganism takes on a new light. Pagans largely acknowledged that there was a single Divine source of all, and they were more free from the extremes of scriptural legalism that Jesus criticized in His fellow Jews. As a teacher He focused on His Jewish countrymen even while teaching the spiritual worth of all people (Matthew 16:24). He emphasized over and over again the errors of neglecting the spirit in the name of the text. These legalistic perversions of Spirituality were far more characteristic of scriptural Judaism than of Paganism. The practices Jesus attacked most were least true of the Pagans. Whereas sacred Scripture could be treated so legalistically that the letter replaced its spirit— a criticism Jesus often leveled against the Pharisees—the texts of Pagan philosophers were far less subject to this error (although they were not immune). The contemporary philosopher Pierre Hadot explains why:

> Ancient philosophy, at least beginning from the sophists and Socrates, intended . . . to form people and to transform souls. That is why, in Antiquity, philosophical teaching is given above all in oral form, because only the living word, in dialogues, in conversations pursued for a long time, can accomplish such an action. The

written work, considerable as it is, is therefore most of the time only an echo or a complement of this oral teaching.[14]

It seems to me these arguments provide good scriptural grounds for suggesting that Christians may have misunderstood something pretty important when they attacked Pagan views and practices. And they still do.

A big stumbling block still confronts even the most sympathetic Christian in considering the validity of my argument. What alternative interpretation can be made of Jesus' statement that, "No man comes to the Father but by me" (John 14:6), a passage continually cited to prove Christian claims to exclusivity? Some scholars point out that Jesus' words were written down by others, long after He said them. True as this is, the observation has little weight in convincing Christians who believe in their spiritual exclusivity to re-evaluate their assumptions. So I will attach no great importance to the fact that these passages are, at best, others' recollections of Jesus' sayings. Instead, let us keep our attention focused solely upon Scripture as it has come down to us.

I find it impossible to believe that Jesus meant this statement the way He has been most commonly interpreted. The fruits of this interpretation of theological exclusivity, in terms of human suffering and murder, have been truly horrible. If He means the usual interpretation, Jesus contradicted himself, for then the fruit of His own teaching on this issue has been bitter indeed, and so *by His own criteria, absolutely worthless.* But if not that, and if the quotation is accurate (it appears only in John) what might He have meant?

In my view, the critical question in interpreting this passage is to what "me" did Jesus refer? Was it the historical man, Jesus, or was it some other aspect or dimension of Himself that was more timeless? I think Matthew 25:31–45 makes it clear that, from a biblical perspective, Jesus could speak in this latter way when making very important theological points. To me, it clearly says that Jesus is in some sense within everyone.

When the Son of man shall come in his glory . . . and before him shall be gathered all nations: and he shall separate them one from another, as a shepherd divideth *his* sheep from the goats . . . . Then shall the King say unto them on his right hand, Come, ye blessed of my Father, inherit the kingdom prepared for you from the foundation of the world: For when I was an hungered, and ye gave me meat: I was thirsty, and ye gave me drink: I was a stranger, and ye took me in: Naked and ye clothed me: I was sick, and ye visited me: I was in prison, and ye came unto me. Then shall the righteous answer him, saying, Lord, when saw we thee an hungered, and fed *thee* . . . . And the King shall answer . . . Verily I say unto you, Inasmuch as ye have done *it* unto one of the least of these my brethren, ye have done *it* unto me. . . . [And to those he rejects for not acting in this manner] Inasmuch as ye did *it* not to one of the least of these, ye did *it* not to me.

This passage explicitly says treating others with kindness and charity is treating *Jesus* with kindness and charity. It also says that those who acted kindly were chosen and those who did not were not. *Kindness, not belief or faith, is what counts most.* A person serves God best, according to Jesus, not when his or her theology is right, (such are the "righteous") but when others are treated kindly, compassionately, and lovingly. This passage also sheds light on the enigmatic parts of (John 14:10–20). As is said in Romans, "Love worketh no ill to his neighbor: therefore love is the fulfillment of the law." (Romans 13:6)

Significantly, little of Jesus' debates with priests has survived for us. His disciples were not the learned or publicly righteous. Those people with whom Jesus had least concern and most scorn were obsessed with forms and letters of the law, but not its spirit. As indicated by their response to his healing of people on the Sabbath, they were idolaters of the word rather than practitioners of the

Spirit. According to Jesus, they did not come even close to spiritual understanding—but a centurion, a Pagan Roman soldier, did (Luke 7:9). There is nothing in scripture to suggest that Jesus was ever impressed by those claiming a deep knowledge of theology.

Obviously my interpretation of Scripture is unorthodox, and I am not a Christian, but I ask every Christian reader to ponder what the fruits of the Orthodox interpretation claiming religious exclusivity have been. What would be the fruits of a religious teaching that urged all to be treated well, since Jesus was in some sense within all people? To juxtapose these two alternatives seems to me to demonstrate the clear superiority of one over the other, given that the passage can clearly be interpreted in such different ways.

Despite being presented by a Wiccan, this interpretation in no way belittles Jesus' message and is absolutely neutral with respect to the reality of the Resurrection. Where we stand on that issue will always remain a matter of faith. But not only is my argument biblically based, it demonstrates that Jesus' message is deeply, even fundamentally, in harmony with the most basic teachings of *all* the world's major religious traditions. The preoccupation of many Christians with the spiritual motes in others' eyes has led to their ignoring a long and bloody beam within their own. It is time they removed it, and learned to see more clearly.

If God is everywhere, I think one strong criteria for spiritual truth is how harmonious the insights of one tradition are with those of others. Those teachings that are in greatest harmony with the core of other faiths are most likely to be those where we all, more or less, finally got it right. Those beliefs denying the truths of most other religions are most likely to be false and require the most cautious and critical evaluation. When in doubt, "By their fruits shall ye know them." Only such an approach can hope to give adequate protection against our own fallibility.

If Jesus' message can survive only because people fear the hellish consequences of not believing, what sort of "good news" is this to *anybody*? This cannot be its meaning. The First Epistle of John says, "There is no fear in love; but perfect love casteth out fear: because fear hath torment. He that feareth is not made perfect in love" (I John 4:18). If Christianity is to survive it needs to win over and keep its believers due to the attractiveness of its message, not the fearfulness of its threats. Many people are Christians because they interpret Jesus as teaching love and forgiveness, not terror and violence. These people would not fall away were an interpretation such as the one I offer widely accepted. The only ones who might fall away are those who remain Christian through fear of hellfire, and, if John is right, they are not really Christians anyway. Another spiritual path would be far better for them, for then they might learn better to love, and less to fear.

ENDNOTES

1. St. Augustine, *The Political Writings of St. Augustine* (Chicago: Regnery, 1962), p. 195.
2. St. Thomas Aquinas, Article 3, Question 11, *Secunda Secundae*. I discovered these passages when reading Michael Novak, "Aquinas and the Heretics," *First Things*, Dec. 1995, pp. 35–36.
3. Helen Ellerbe, *The Dark Side of Christian History* (San Rafael, Calif.: Morningstar Books, 1995), p. 65.
4. Quotation cited by Ellerbe, Ibid., p. 74.
5. Quotation cited by Ellerbe, Ibid., pp. 136–137.
6. See Jenny Gibbons, "Recent Developments in the Study of The Great European Witch Hunt," *The Pomegranate*, no. 5, August, 1998, pp. 2–16.
7. Pat Buchanan, "Onward, conservative soldiers," *San Francisco Examiner*, February 21, 1999, editorial page.
8. A brief overview of these events and the reasons for them can be found in Helen Ellerbe, *The Dark Side of Christian History* (San Rafael, Calif.: Morningstar Books, 1995).
9. Julian, *The Arguments of the Emperor Julian Against the Christians*, Thomas Taylor (trans.) (Chicago: Hermetic Pub. Co., 1809), p. 84.
10. Plotinus, *The Enneads*, Stephen MacKenna, trans., John Dillon abr. (London: Penguin, 1991), p. 128.
11. Both passages quoted from Robert L. Wilken, *The Christians as the Romans Saw Them* (New Haven: Yale, 1984), p. 151.
12. This version of the Dryghtyn may be found in its entirety in Patricia Crowther, *Witchblood: Diary of a Witch High Priestess* (New York: House of Collectibles, 1974).

13. Robert Wilken, *The Christians as the Romans Saw Them* (New Haven: Yale University Press, 1984), p. 107.

14. Pierre Hadot, *Philosophy as a Way of Life* (Cambridge: Mass.: Blackwell, 1995), p. 20. See also 63–64.

# PART IV

# Conclusion

# Spiritual Truth
# for Christians and Pagans
## *A Pagan Perspective*

When we look at history it is difficult not to be struck by the incredible variety of spiritual paths taken by human beings, but if Spirit is immanent, they all deal more or less successfully with a common core reality. This reality is so rich, so multifaceted, that no human institution can do justice to it. No expression can be complete.

Some of us experience the world as fundamentally blessed, and wish to root our spirituality in practices helping us to grow into greater harmony with it. Such people will find themselves drawn toward Pagan insights, whatever their formal religious tradition. Others see the world and life as deeply flawed, and are attracted to spiritual paths promising ultimate salvation. Like those who see the glass as half-full and others who see it as half-empty, we may be dealing with basic differences in temperament. Referring back to my Grand Canyon analogy, not everyone likes backpacking into the Grand Canyon.

A loving and creative Divine Source might offer paths emphasizing spiritual immanence and loving harmony with the world, along with paths emphasizing spiritual transcendence, and loving separation from the world. Neither need be intrinsically better than the other, so long as they are followed with a good heart.

I believe that ultimately the most fundamental differences between legitimate religions rests with what they emphasize as most central to their particular path, rather than to actual contradictions in ultimate spiritual teachings, and these differing emphases were worthy of being made. All peoples are richer for their contributions.

## The Truth of Christianity

In the midst of writing this work I took some time off to visit the Colorado Rockies, a tumbling sea of high peaks, flowery meadows, and cold, clear lakes that has been especially dear to me since my childhood. One day dawned with a low dreary overcast sky, a bad sign for hiking. I decided, instead, to explore back roads I had not yet visited. My choice that day was the dirt road over Shrine Pass, with its view of the Mount of the Holy Cross, a 14,000-foot giant nestled so far back in the mountains that most views were reserved for hard-core backpackers.

Leaving a friend's cabin, where I was staying, I traveled south to meet up with Interstate 70. Turning west, I drove through gradually rising forests and expanding vistas, finally turning off at the sign for Shrine Pass. I followed the good dirt road up through wide meadows nearly to timberline. At the pass I saw my first view of Mount of the Holy Cross, with its long vertical coulior filled with snow and, crossing that fissure, a horizontal ledge also covered by snow. Together they formed a giant snowy cross, giving the peak its name. Because that vista was partially obscured by trees, and I wanted a better view, I turned up another, rougher, dirt road winding its way still higher along an adjoining ridge to the north. My efforts were soon rewarded by a breathtaking expanse of peaks to the west and, towering over them all, the Mount of the Holy Cross.

It was mostly overcast where I stood, and the intervening valley was deep in shadow, but the mountain itself was incandescent in the sunlight. The light seemed to come from within the rock itself, kindling a glow in my heart, illuminating both it and my mind. My understanding soared and expanded, embracing a lesson, a teaching, a vision that was entirely unexpected as Spirit communicated with me. Although a Pagan, I was granted a beautiful insight as to the true meaning of the Christian message, an insight of such strength, clarity, and impact that, were I not already devoted to the Wiccan Goddess, I might have embraced the Christian path on the spot. As it was, my experience gave me a deeper appreciation of Jesus and his message than any I had known before, penetrating to the core of my being, blessing and enriching it.

Christianity's message, I realized, focused on love and forgiveness, but not so much on God's forgiveness of us as on our own capacity to forgive one another. God's son had walked, taught, and healed among men and women, and had been cruelly murdered. Even so, God's love for humankind had not weakened. "Forgive them Father, they know not what they do," is perhaps the most famous account of Jesus' last words, words He had spoken while in agony on the cross. The entire Christian message seemed to be summed up in the insight that as God could forgive the murder of His innocent son, so we were called upon to forgive the wrongs done to us. And if we truly forgave, we would be freed from the poisons of resentment and malice. Our hearts would be opened more fully to love and compassion, and so more fully to God. The central lesson of Christianity was a lesson about unconditional love. I finally understood that the Christian message was a true gospel, a genuine good news for human kind.

To be sure, my insight was hardly orthodox. My experience in the mountains had no use for the bizarre notion that the only way God could forgive us was if we murdered His innocent Son. Any such extraordinary limitation on God's power and love was absent from this experience, as it seemed to me it had always been absent from logic and good sense. Also absent was any notion that one had to be a professing Christian to live in a spiritually valid manner. Nor did there appear to be any threat of eternal damnation, for a God of unconditional love is not a God of eternal damnation. This was instead a call to enter more fully into God's love, not a way to avoid His wrath.

This particular spiritual gift was perfectly timed, as it seems they always are. While I no longer harbored any feelings of ill will toward Christianity, as I once had, I still often wondered about the nature of its spiritual truth. I did not much doubt that Christianity had spiritual validity of some sort. It did, after all, provide a powerful religious foundation for millions of people. But I wondered what it was.

Most Christians I had spoken with simply argued that their religion was true because of the physical Resurrection of Jesus. Maybe the Resurrection happened, maybe it didn't. I have no way of knowing, and neither, ultimately, does anyone else today. Belief in the Resurrection is a matter of faith, as even most Christians will attest, but to base a claim for spiritual truth about God's love and forgiveness on a possible occurrence that demonstrated only God's power had always seemed strange to me. It also always seemed amiss to focus more on Jesus' death than on his life and teachings, and on his promised future appearance rather than what he did while here the first time.

As a result of my experience in the presence of Mount of the Holy Cross, Jesus now has an honored place in my heart, and sometimes on my altar as well, but I remain a Pagan and a Wiccan, not a Christian. The spiritual truths unveiled for me that afternoon amid beautiful mountains high above Shrine pass have given me a greater appreciation of how to live in a sacred manner—and of my own substantial shortcomings in that regard, for I am no saint. These insights also deepened my practice of Wicca, providing still more profound dimensions of meaning to my celebrations of the full moon, and the eight Sabbats of the wheel of the year.

In retrospect this experience was necessary in order to give this small book genuine weight as an effort at interfaith dialogue. Before it occurred much of this volume had already been written, but I possessed only an intellectual appreciation of Christianity's spiritual depth. And no spiritual path can be adequately appreciated by intellectual means alone, for Spirit exceeds intellect the way a symphony exceeds a single note. On that Colorado mountainside I experienced Christianity's message with my heart as well. Where better to be blessed with a sacred teaching than alone, amid gardens of flowers and groves of trees, beneath high soaring peaks and still higher flying clouds? Where better to receive a teaching about the deeper meaning of Christianity than in a place any Pagan would recognize as especially blessed by the Gods?

Here indeed was a revelation worthy of a world religion: that God so loved the world that even the death of his innocent son could not shake that love. From this it follows that no person can ever justify not forgiving another when truly asked, nor harbor resentment toward those too benighted to realize what they have done. Failure to forgive and resentment over past wrongs reflects our weaknesses, not our strengths, and from forgiveness can come love, harmony, and peace. Love opens us to understanding, and greater understanding deepens our love.

Classical Pagan philosophers of many schools had a similar concept of nonattachment to outcomes, and of living in harmony with whatever life brought to one's path.[1] To forgive the wrongs of others also seems remarkably similar to the Buddhist ideal of nonattachment as a way of eliminating karma. So the basic idea is a common one. But even so, the explicit focus on forgiveness as a high virtue is particularly connected with the teachings of Jesus. Given the long history of injustice and oppression practiced in the name of whatever religion happened to catch the favor of those with power, forgiveness is a uniquely important spiritual value today, for Christian and Pagan alike.

In my opinion, the connection between unconditional love and forgiveness has been obscured by the Christian claim to exclusivity. Nevertheless, it has proven powerfully transformative for those who take it to heart, and has had a profound impact upon Western ethics and society. At a time when focusing on past grievances, both real and imagined, has become a national industry, one exercising the attention and imagination of many people who would be far better occupied doing other things, who could doubt that this message is as powerfully relevant today?

It seems to me that there are additional areas of spiritual insight where Christianity has made genuine contributions to the religious heritage of humankind; contributions that all discerning Pagans can endorse. In making these contributions, Christianity provided new insights and enhanced sensitivity on points that, while not absent in other faith traditions, were not central to their message.

First is the spiritual worth of the individual. In the long run, Christianity has strengthened our regard for the worth of all human beings. Paul emphasized that in the Church there was neither slave nor free, neither male nor female, neither Jew nor Gentile. All, whatever their worldly status, were equally children of God, equally worthy of receiving Jesus' word. In late Classical times early Christianity often offered more spiritually to many women than was usually the case in Pagan Rome, although that early promise was almost immediately broken. Subsequent elaborations of Christian doctrine have varied in their emphasis on the worth of the individual, but Protestants in particular have emphasized that every person have a direct personal relationship with Jesus.

While Christian practice too rarely lived up to its ideals, this failure does not invalidate its core insights. No spiritual path perfectly fulfills its teaching, particularly after becoming institutionalized into hierarchies and political bodies. Christianity labored—and often still labors—under the enormous burden of believing in its monopoly of ultimate spiritual truth.

Even so, more than most of its predecessors in the West, the Christian message emphasized spiritual equality among all human beings, and the world has benefited greatly whenever this insight has been acted upon in any spiritual context. To give but one vital example, Christians in the nineteenth century were in the forefront of the movement to abolish slavery. To be sure, other Christians found plenty of passages in the Bible to justify slavery, but those who took its message to heart, rather than heartlessly reading printed words, helped end an institution that had been with humanity since the dawn of "civilization."

Growing out of this central insight as to the worth of the individual is the additional Christian emphasis upon charitable works. Charity was not a major value in late Classical Pagan society. It was not that charity was unknown. I have already quoted Juvenal, who asked, "What good man regards any misfortune as no concern of his?" And there are many other examples, such as Plotinus raising many orphans within his home and Jesus' story of the good Samaritan. Pagan temples also provided food to the poor on a large scale, but, generally speaking, Pagan practice did not *emphasize* the spiritual role of charity. Because pre-Christian Paganism did not focus as much attention on the worth of all individuals it was more rarely concerned with the fate of the unfortunate.[2] In my opinion, this was a spiritual shortcoming of Classical Paganism, and one the Church to some extent addressed.

Another contribution, one underlying these first two principles, consists of those teachings of Jesus that are most obviously in harmony with John's observation that God is love. They provide a foundation applicable to any spiritual insight, but again one that was too little appreciated in many earlier Pagan practices. Like the principle of charity, this was not because the idea was absent. It was not. But daily Pagan practice in Classical times did not usually focus on transcendent deity. Because Christianity emphasized the transcendent, it could continue to teach God's love even if its usual practice fell far below its words. In societies of enormous brutality and poverty this focus was very important because Spirit as immanent was so thoroughly obscured by suffering and injustice.

These insights, so central to Christian teachings, are of spiritual importance to all people, and the Church did more than any other Western religious tradition to make them a prominent part of the common spiritual heritage of all people. It should be honored for it, and encouraged better to exemplify it by giving up its smugly conceited claim to universal superiority.

Some of my Pagan readers will object that often these values were honored in words and violated in practice. True enough. But there is hypocrisy enough to go around for all religions, including our own. We often fall far short of our highest principles as well, but these principles still carry great weight in our practice, and influences many of us to strive better to exemplify them. The same point holds for Christianity.

## The Truth of Pagan Spirituality

Hunter-gatherers had a different kind of spirituality than did Neolithic farming peoples, although both were Pagan. In Classical times, the Pagan practices of the countryside were often different in emphasis from the Pagan practices of urban intellectuals. Secular scholars have sometimes tried to use this diversity as evidence that spiritual practices are nothing more than the product of their societies. They are wrong.

Spirit provides the ultimate sustaining context for daily life. As the conditions of that life change, so will the manifestations of Spirit that are most readily accessible and meaningful to people. Spirit's manifestations are a kaleidoscope of beauty emanating from its Source, that Great Mystery that underlies all things. It is within this framework that we can understand today's resurgence of Pagan spirituality. As the chant goes, "We are an old people, we are a new people, we are the same people, deeper than before." I'm not absolutely convinced we're deeper, but the rest is true.

The current renaissance of Pagan religion in the modern West is not simply a return to the spirituality of early times, however much it may have in common with it. Today's cultural context is entirely different. Modern Neopagans deal with nature not so much because they have to, as did the Pagans of the past, but because they want to. Most of us are both urban and prosperous. Being urban, we do not wrestle with nature the way many farmers once did. Even those of us who have moved to the country, or who are organic farmers, experience nature in more cooperative ways than many of our farmer ancestors. In these respects our relationship with the natural world more closely resembles that of hunter-gatherers, where nature was home, than as an adversary against whom we must struggle to survive. We turn to Nature for spiritual and psychological well-being.

Neopagans focus on spirit in nature as a source of meaning, because the society in which we live so thoroughly denies such meaning and renewal, and is so psychologically draining. Our Pagan ancestors lived in societies where religion and daily life were completely integrated, so that even the most utilitarian activities had spiritual dimensions. Contemporary practitioners of nature religions are rediscovering this primordial truth in a very different context, and so it manifests differently with us.

There is another difference with the Pagan past.

Unlike even a hundred years ago, today virtually everyone has a vivid image of humanity as a whole, and some awareness that alternative spiritualities exist. For nearly everyone today there is an irreducible element of self-conscious choice in our spiritual path. We are aware of alternatives we could have taken but did not. For most modern people this recognition is troubling, because the dominant religions have all claimed universal superiority on their part. Pagan religion today is uniquely equipped to appreciate spiritual diversity *and* our common humanity.

Yet these same characteristics have led some traditional Pagans to criticize modern Pagan spirituality. Native American Vine Deloria, Jr. writes: "American society, particularly its organized religions and its political institutions, is built on the idea of the solitary individual as the foundation of everything else." Because modern people are not immersed within the all-embracing community of the tribe, even their religious associations are simply "strings of people who are linked together by similar philosophies, experiences, or desires." He contrasts this pattern of relationships with tribal communities because "the community is held together by blood and common sets of experience."[3] In making this criticism, Deloria apparently includes Neopagans along with other modern Americans.

Deloria also emphasizes the vital role place plays in traditional Native American Paganism. "The essence of the Indian attitude towards peoples, lands, and other life forms is one of kinship relations in which no element of life can go unattached from human society. Thus lands are given a special status because they form a motherhood relationship with the peoples who live on them."[4] He explains in another essay that the traditional Indian clan structure "includes all possible relationships by blood and law, all important, lasting friendships, and all the special covenants established between plants, animals, and other forms of life through unique personal experiences."[5] Deloria grants that it is possible for Indian spirituality to be inclusive of everything encountered, but emphasizes its rootedness in both individual and tribal experience, rather than abstract universalistic teachings.

There are two interconnected elements to Deloria's observations. One has to do with choice, the other with relationship. Deloria is right in describing the difference between modern and traditional tribal spirituality, but in fact, today, everyone, including traditional Pagans such as Deloria himself, now practices modern spirituality. By this I mean that Deloria has *chosen* his spiritual path in a way his ancestors never did. Today even the most traditional Lakota medicine person is aware that he or she could have chosen otherwise, could have become a Christian, could have subordinated tribal and blood relationships to other values. Today there is an irreducible element of individual choice in religion, a degree of choice that is historically quite new.

Individual choice of this sort can, but need not, lead to egoistic individualism and religion as a consumer good. Just as Deloria in time returned to his tribe's spiritual traditions, so other modern people can choose spiritual contexts within which they feel at home, and in so doing enter into spiritual contexts larger that themselves. And insofar as the relationship is genuine, it is two-way. Spirit will respond in an appropriate fashion if a person enters onto a path good for her or himself.

Deloria can respond that while this is true in the abstract, it is less so in the concrete. Freely chosen relationships are inherently more fragile than unquestioned membership within a particular community. Spiritual practices are not always easy or pleasant, and at the first sign of significant discomfort people can leave rather that grow through their ordeals. This ease of exit strengthens self-will and discourages humility.

Deloria has a point, but by itself it is one-sided. The weakness and self-indulgence Deloria identifies are certainly present within Neopagan, and other, spiritual communities, sometimes appallingly so. But this is only half the story.

Traditional communities often provided environments where the powerful could lord it over the weak, who had nowhere to go and no choice but to submit. Like any other human institution, the public opinion of a small group was not always enlightened. It could support us in times of need, it could stifle us as well. The stability and support of traditional communities and the freedom of choice within modern ones are *both* two-sided coins. Each possesses strengths, but each also possesses weaknesses connected to those strengths. Comparing the strengths of one community form with the weaknesses of the other is always tempting, and always misleading.

Deloria's other point is, I believe, more fundamental, and poses a greater challenge to contemporary Neopagan spirituality. The God and Goddess of Neopagan practice are not deities of place, but rather are universal powers, present everywhere. Much Neopagan practice usually focuses only at this universal level. To be sure, elemental powers and guardians are invoked at every Esbat, and often at Sabbats, but again in universal garb rather than as powers associated with place. In most cases little attention is placed on the spirits of place, or of plants and animals. A Wiccan circle in England and another in California will follow the same basic format. There are both advantages and disadvantages to this situation.

The advantage, which Deloria neglects, is that we are aware of the all-embracing greater community of which we are all a part. The most important gift the modern world has bequeathed to humankind has been our recognition that all people have rights, simply by being people. But this universal community is necessarily a community of strangers. Our relationships with one another are completely abstract.

Traditional Paganism often was rooted in relationships with concrete spirits of place. Local places of power were known and honored. Local spirits were respected, honored, invoked, and included within the community. This dimension is largely absent in Neopagan practice.

This embeddedness within the concrete accomplished more than simply enrich one's spiritual relationships, although it certainly did that. It also meant that individuals were never free from involvement with others. A person had always to take into consideration the quality of his or her relationships with everything around themselves. Mother Earth, for example, was more than an abstraction because of this chain of spiritual relationships from the very small to the all encompassing. Few people seem gifted with frequent interactions with the highest deities, but all of us can knowingly interact within the web of spiritual relationships that surround us.

Neopagans need to become far more aware of their local spiritual connections with the land around them in particular, and with the forms of life and awareness with which they interact daily. It is here that the "bottom up" approach of many traditional Pagan societies, particularly hunting and gathering ones, is especially instructive. Once Pagan communities are situated within concrete spiritual communities, as well as the more abstract and universal ones, I suspect the quality of life within purely human communities will be transformed in good ways.

The reason is simple. In such contexts the needs and desires of individual Pagans will become situated within networks of relationships bigger than they, and quite concretely so. Such embeddedness will help us grow spiritually in profound ways, giving rootedness to our sometimes very top-down approach to a spirituality of the earth. I will give two examples from my own life. First, before every meal at home I make a small food offering, "sharing my abundance" with the spirits of the land where I live. Second, whenever photographing a flower or landscape, I say "thank you" and (if I remember—here I don't bat 1.000) leave an offering. Such courtesies do not go unnoticed.

## Pagans, Spirit, and Modernity

Some Christians believe that secular America is particularly receptive to Pagan beliefs. The truth is far more complex. A purely transcendental religion, such as much of today's Christianity, can to some extent survive within a rigidly secular society that is doing everything in its power to segregate the spiritual from the rest of life. A spirituality focusing primarily upon the Divine as immanent faces a more difficult challenge.

There is a strange aptness of fit between a purely transcendental religious fundamentalism that rejects the spiritual worth of the world, and a purely secular society that rejects Spirit. They simply do not intersect. Each can, in principle, go its own way without much influencing the other.

When the world around us is understood as sacred, ultimately there is no such thing as the purely secular. Everything is, in ultimate reality, a "Thou." The future of the nature religions will rest on their capacity to overcome this rigid dichotomy for the people within their communities. Thus, there is a deep irony when some Christians term modern secularism "pagan." Secular modernity, with its denial of ultimate value to anything on earth, is far more anti-Pagan than anti-Christian. It is we, and not contemporary Christians, who genuinely challenge secular modernity.

In another sense, however, Pagan religion *is* in harmony with modernity. Just as we are not at war with modern science, so we do not distrust the modern belief that human efforts can improve the quality of life. Because we believe the world is a sacred manifestation of the Divine, it is ultimately a good place and a beautiful home. Spiritually we are optimists. Our spiritual task is to work *with* the world rather than to subdue or dominate it. Consequently, to the extent we are true to our tradition we honor knowledge over power and experience over dogma. In this regard there is little tension between Neopaganism and the basic institutions of the modern world. And so, like every other spiritual perspective, we stand in a fascinating tension with the world of matter. We are within it, and honor it, but also (and here I can speak for only some of us) we see it within a context recognizing it as a beautiful and beloved dimension of the Sacred, a context where its most fundamental characteristic, need, is transmuted into the foundation for love expressed in material form.

Consequently, the Pagan spiritual perspective offers perhaps the most fitting corrective to the excesses of the Enlightenment and post-Enlightenment modernity. The seventeenth-century Enlightenment inaugurated the modern world. In many respects the changes it initiated have led to enormous blessings. We are all its heirs, and we owe to its founders virtually all that is best in the modern world, which is a great deal indeed. But the world is more vast and more profound than any human perspective can grasp, even one as fruitful as the European Enlightenment.

The Enlightenment emphasized the role of reason over faith and of investigation over authority. Compared to the brutal times that immediately preceded it, the Enlightenment's outlook was scientific and tolerant. But, like all perspectives, the men and women of the Enlightenment defined themselves in part by what they opposed.

The Enlightenment followed on the heels of a society dominated by institutionalized and politicized religion seeking a monopoly over all human thought and spirituality. The institutionalization of a single religious vision, to the exclusion of all others, narrowed the spiritual horizons of European civilization, rather like militant Islam does today in the Moslem world. This monopolization of faith and knowledge required violence to maintain its hold, and once secular power was invoked to serve a particular spiritual vision, Spirit itself became increasingly hidden by the exigencies of power.

When multiple sources of spiritual authority arose, as happened in the Reformation, the stage was set for bloodletting on an unprecedented scale. Neither Catholic nor Protestant authorities could allow the other to exist, since both claimed a spiritual monopoly. The result was the Thirty Years War. The Enlightenment was in significant part shaped by a horrified reaction to the terrors of that war.[6]

In reacting against the excesses of institutionalized religion, Enlightenment thinkers sought to define sources of authority free from any spiritual or "subjective" taint. For many of them, reason narrowly defined, the power of logic, and experiment and prediction became the only truly legitimate and reliable sources for knowledge. Little noticed was the subtle assumption incorporated into this outlook: that the world was ultimately comprehensible by these means alone.

This assumption implied that any qualities not amenable to investigation by these techniques did not really exist. Finding truth became following a method, one that was completely impersonal. There was no room here for "Thou" relationships along the path to truth.

For that dimension of physical reality amenable to human manipulation and control, the Enlightenment project succeeded beyond its founders' wildest dreams. It promises to provide still more benefits in the future, but these very successes obscured the fact that this view of reality was partial, and that much was excluded from it. In those areas of life where other forms of knowledge are more appropriate, the Enlightenment's bequests have been more ambiguous.

One reason these implications were obscured was that virtually everyone considered God solely in transcendental terms. From a spiritually transcendental perspective, there seemed little at stake in the Enlightenment's assumptions. While science steadily enlarged the scope of its knowledge, religion remained secure, over and above the material world. However, the extraordinary success of Enlightenment science seemed inexorably to shrink the importance of a transcendental Deity, who became progressively more insubstantial.

When Darwin convinced the scientific world of the truth of evolution, for many people the Enlightenment's compromise—bycompartmentalization that gave the world to science and Spirit to religion, broke down. If Darwin was right, Spirit seemed completely unnecessary to explain life and the incredible variety of plants and animals that flourished on earth. Worse yet, it seemed unnecessary to account for our own existence. Some Christians retreated into Fundamentalism, some gave up their faith entirely, and many continued with a bifurcated allegiance torn with doubt and uncertainty.

With this gradual marginalization of a purely transcendent Deity, the persuasiveness of moral principles once linked to that Deity began themselves to dissolve. In philosophy, the idea of natural rights dissolved into utilitarianism, the ideal that the good is that which benefits the greatest number. Utilitarianism itself sometimes dissolved into nihilism, the idea that nothing really matters. Today, so-called "post-modern" thought has degenerated into a nihilistic obsession with power and will, without any context of greater meaning.

Western modernity has reached a dead end, as it is unable to supply a vision for the future and a sense of meaning for human beings. The post-modernists have critiqued its theories of objective knowledge and value, ending in irrationality and nihilism. At the same time, they have proven laughably ignorant of the very scientific knowledge they claim to criticize.[7] On the other hand, orthodox science appears to offer us little more than reducing life to the blind interaction of "selfish genes" and/or selective pressures that produce organisms that need the illusion of meaning to live their lives.[8] The modern world cannot understand itself, or what is best about it, simply by relying on its own assumptions and values. The reason, of course, is that its context of understanding and experience is far too narrow.

The Pagan insight that Spirit is both transcendent and immanent offers us a way out of our modern dilemma, not by attacking or belittling science, but by rehabilitating consciousness and the values of love and compassion as fruitful guides to reality. Pagan religion therefore offers a message of great importance to all of us. That message is very simple, very profound, and very important. We are, everywhere and always, immersed in the sacred. Everything that exists is an expression and manifestation of the Divine. *All things* are worthy of care and respect. Nothing totally lacks value. Life itself, and its defining rhythms, are appropriately considered sacramental. Because today humankind's powers to destroy so vastly exceed its power to nurture and maintain, this is a spiritual message of utmost urgency for our time.

By conceiving our world as sacred and alive, we open ourselves up to experiencing it in ways ignored, denied, or belittled by our culture for countless generations. We find that when we do so, nature as Spirit answers. Sometimes those answers come in the form of spirits, forces, and Gods, and in encountering the high Gods, we learn what love truly is. Sometimes the veil is swept away even more completely, and we see through nature the full transcendent beauty and love that underlies, permeates, and transcends everything of which we can speak, and more. It is then that we learn a still deeper truth about living in harmony: that the most complete harmony comes from the most complete love, a love given completely without condition.

Spirit is not something removed from our experience. It continually speaks to us. We only become truly blind to it when we are convinced that our own world is so depraved and fallen that it obscures and defiles all that is good and true and beautiful. Withered and judgmental hearts are too closed easily to perceive the reality that surrounds and sustains them, like fish swimming everywhere in a frantic search for the water about which they have heard. In ceremony, in ritual and in ecstasy Pagan practice enables all who are called to it to encounter the sacred directly, and in so doing, gradually to learn to see it around them always.

To the degree we can incorporate these insights into our lives we come to a deeper harmony with the Divine. Such harmony teaches us patience, kindness, compassion, and understanding. From such a foundation deep and profound love can emerge.

## An Interfaith Perspective

Just as I argued that respect and regard for the world is contained within the Christian tradition, so Christianity's greatest insights are also in harmony with Paganism. Wicca is not Christianity, but they are complementary. They harmonize.

If history teaches us anything, it is that it is easy for religions to so fixate on the dimension of Spirit that speaks most directly to and through them that they lose sight of the rest. And Spirit transcends all religion. None of us are wise enough to honor all dimensions of Spirit in the ways they merit, but we can respect those traditions who can honor Spirit in ways that we do not. *We all need one another's spiritual traditions to help us keep our own in perspective.* The world's religions shine with a wealth of rays of Divine light that illuminate each of us. Each religious path selects from those rays the ones that cohere together in a way uniquely its own. Each ray, each color in the spectrum, adds to the beauty of the whole. And we need many traditions to have a sense of the glory of them all.

A story involving neither Christian nor Pagans helps demonstrate my point. In 1990, at the invitation of the Dalai Lama, a number of Jewish Rabbis traveled to the small town of Dharamsala, India, the center in exile of Tibetan Buddhist culture and religion. The Dalai Lama was interested in discovering how they had managed to preserve their religious tradition during almost two thousand years of exile. He was also interested in learning about Jewish meditation, mysticism, and the Kabbalah. Rodger

Kamenetz's marvelous *The Jew in the Lotus* is a delightful, as well as profound, account of that visit. But my reason for bringing Kamenetz's book up here is his report of the effect such interfaith dialogue had upon himself, and the other members of the Jewish delegation. It is in perfect keeping with the message of this book.

Kamenetz quotes Orthodox Rabbi Yitz Greenberg as saying:

> All religions, not just Judaism, are now being placed in a new situation. At first I thought the culture was forcing us. But I've come to believe this pluralism is God's will. Can you learn to propagate your religion without using stereotypes and negative images of the other? If we can't, all religions will go down the tubes—and good riddance—because we're a source of hatred and demolition of other people.

Greenberg elaborated that "Dialogue is an opportunity to learn the uniqueness and power of the other and then see if I can now reframe my religion to respect that power, to stop using negative reasons why I'm Jewish. It leaves me no choice but to be a Jew for positive reasons."[9]

Kamenetz himself, after leaving Dharamsala, concluded:

> My contact with Buddhism had opened me up. In Delhi, facing the multiplicity of religious expressions, and the obvious quality of devotion in several of them, I could feel the pressure of competing identities burst and melt—it was an emotional confrontation with pluralism that stripped away the need to feel one way was better than another.
>
> Paradoxically, this did not make me feel less a Jew. Rather, I had gained a much broader view of the power of all religions, including my own.[10]

What is true for these Jews and Buddhists of good will can be equally true of Pagans and Christians of good will. A Gregorian chant, a gospel song, a drumming ceremony, a Maypole dance, and a Sun Dance all honor the Divine. But they do not go together. Each is unique.

All the colors of the rainbow exist in white light, but who could deny that our world is enriched and blessed by rainbows, which give us kinds of beauty obscured when the spectrums are merged? And who can deny that a single color in the rainbow is enhanced because of the presence of all the others?

The world's most insightful religions are best understood through this metaphor. Each focuses on some spiritual values while not denying the others. No religion can do justice to all such values, but each can do a particularly good job of highlighting some. Together they enable humankind to truly honor Spirit in all the forms it manifests to us. By virtue of taking any one spiritual path we refrain from taking others. We cannot walk every path at once. But we can appreciate our own even more deeply as we come to honor others.

Interfaith work is that area of religious life where we can work with others of different faiths without having to justify our beliefs or worry about the validity of others' practices. Years ago I helped to organize an interfaith tree planting in the hills behind Berkeley, California. Christians and Pagans, Baha'is and Jews, Hindus, Sikhs, and Buddhists all came together to plant endangered oaks in what had once been their native habitat. Each faith community did its work with its own people. Each prayed and observed in its own way, a way appropriate to the teachings of that tradition. Each community worked side by side with the others. There was no watering down to a lowest common denominator, no "one world religion." Rather, each acted in a reverential fashion unique to its spiritual vision while helping the earth common to us all to bloom more abundantly.

No one talked theology or comparative religion. They were too deeply immersed in their own practices.

It was one of the high points of my life.

1. See for example, Hadot, *Philosophy as a Way of Life.*
2. Robin Lane Fox, *Pagans and Christian* (San Francisco: Harper and Row, 1988), p. 323.
3. Vine Deloria, Jr., "Secularism, Civil Religion, and the Religious Freedom of American Indians," *For This Land: Writings on Religion in America* (New York: Routledge, 1999), pp. 227–228.
4. Deloria, "Native American Spirituality," *For This Land,* p. 131.
5. Deloria, "American Indians and the Moral Community," *For This Land,* p. 178.
6. I owe this perspective to Stephen Toulmin. See his *Cosmopolis: The Hidden Agenda of Modernity* (Chicago: University of Chicago Press, 1990).
7. See for example, Noretta Koertge, ed., *A House Built on Sand: Exposing Postmodern Myths About Science* (Oxford: Oxford University Press, 1999); Alan Sokal and Jean Bricmont, *Fashionable Nonsense: Postmodern Intellectuals' Abuse of Science* (Picador USA, 1999); Paul Gross and Norman Levitt, *Higher Superstition: The Academic Left and Its Quarrels With Science* (Johns Hopkins University Press, 1994).
8. See the work of Richard Dawkins, *The Selfish Gene* (New York: Oxford University Press, 1976), and Edward O. Wilson, *Consilience* (New York: Knopf, 1998).
9. Rodger Kamenetz, *The Jew in the Lotus* (San Francisco: Harper, 1994), p. 110.
10. Ibid., p. 251.

# Bibliography

Abram, David. *The Spell of the Sensuous: Perception and Language in a More-than-Human World.* New York: Pantheon Books, 1996.

Apuleius of Madauros. "The Golden Ass," from Marvin W. Meyer, ed., *The Ancient Mysteries: A Sourcebook, Sacred Texts of the Mystery religions of the Ancient Mediterranean World.* San Francisco: Harper and Row, 1987.

Armstrong, A. H. "The Ancient and Continuing Pieties of the Greek World," A. H. Armstrong, ed., *Classical Mediterranean Spirituality.* New York: Crossroads, 1989.

Augustine. *The Political Writings of St. Augustine.* Chicago: Regnery 1962.

Brown, Dianna DeG. *Umbanda: Religion and Politics in Urban Brazil.* New York: Columbia University Press, 1994.

Buber, Martin. *I and Thou.* Walter Kaufmann, trans. New York: Charles Scribner's Sons, 1970.

Buchanan, Pat. "Onward Conservative Soldiers." *San Francisco Examiner,* February 21, 1999.

Carter, Forrest. *The Education of Little Tree.* Albuquerque: University of New Mexico Press, 1976.

Chuvin, Pierre. *A Chronicle of the Last Pagans.* Cambridge: Harvard University Press, 1990.

Clifton, Chas. "Leland's Aradia and the Revival of Modern Witchcraft." *The Pomegranate: A New Journal of Neopagan Thought,* February, 1997.

Crowley, Vivianne. *Wicca: The Old Religion in the New Age.* Wellingborough, England: Aquarian Press, 1989.

Crowther, Patricia. *Witchblood: Diary of a Witch Highpriestess.* New York: House of Collectibles, 1974.

Damielou, Alain. *The Gods of India.* New York: Inner Traditions International, 1985.

Davies, Paul. *The Cosmic Blueprint: New Discoveries in Nature's Creative Ability to Order the Universe.* New York: Simon and Schuster, 1988.

Dawkins, Richard. *The Selfish Gene.* New York: Oxford University Press, 1976.

De las Casas, Bartolomé. *History of the Indies.* New York: Harper and Row, 1971.

Deloria, Vine, Jr. *For This Land: Writings on Religion in America.* New York: Routledge, 1999.

Dodds, E. R. *The Greeks and the Irrational.* Berkeley: University of California, 1951.

Doniger, Wendy. "Who Lives, Who Survives?" *Parabola,* Winter, 1998.

Edwards, Jonathan. *A Jonathan Edwards Reader.* John E. Smith, Harry S. Stout, and Kenneth P. Minkema, eds. New Haven: Yale University Press, 1995.

Ellerbe, Helen. *The Dark Side of Christian History.* San Rafael, Calif.: Morningstar Books, 1995.

Farrar, Janet and Stewart. *The Witches' Way: Principles, Rituals and Beliefs of Modern Witchcraft.* London: Robert Hale, 1984.

Fitzgerald, Michael Oren. *Yellowtail: Crow Medicine Man and Sun Dance Chief: An Autobiography as Told to Michael Oren Fitzgerald.* Norman, Okla.: Univeristy of Oklahoma, 1991.

Fox, Robin Lane. *Pagans and Christians.* San Francisco: Harper and Row, 1986.

———. *The Unauthorized Version: Truth and Fiction in the Bible.* New York: Vintage, 1993.

Frey, Rodney. *The World of the Crow Indians: As Driftwood Lodges.* Norman, Okla.: University of Oklahoma Press, 1987.

Gardner, Gerald. *Witchcraft Today.* New York: Magickal Childe, 1954.

Gibbons, Jenny. "Recent Developments in the Study of the Great European Witch Hunt." *The Pomegranate: A New Journal of Neopagan Thought,* No. 5, 1998.

Gross, Paul and Norman Levitt. *Higher Superstition: The Academic Left and Its Quarrels With Science.* Baltimore: Johns Hopkins University Press, 1994.

Hadot, Pierre. *Philosophy as a Way of Life.* Cambridge, Mass.: Blackwell, 1995.

Hartshorne, Charles. *Omnipotence and Other Theological Mistakes.* Albany: State University of New York Press, 1984.

Herbert, Nick. *Quantum Reality: Beyond the New Physics.* New York: Anchor, 1985.

Hornum, Michael. "The Availability of the One: An Interpretive Essay," *Alexandria: The Journal of Western Cosmological Traditions,* 2, 1993.

Jeffers, Robinson. *The Inhumanist, The Double Axe.* New York: Liveright, 1977.

———. *Not Man Apart: Lines from Robinson Jeffers, Photographs of the Big Sur Coast.* David Brower, ed. New York: Sierra Club and Ballentine Books, 1965.

Julian, The Emperor. *The Arguments of the Emperor Julian Against the Christians.* Thomas Taylor, trans. Chicago: The Hermetic Pub. Co., 1809.

Koertge, Noretta, ed. *A House Built on Sand: Exposing Postmodern Myths About Science.* Oxford: Oxford University Press, 1999.

LaChapelle, Dolores. *Sacred Land, Sacred Sex, The Rapture of the Deep: Concerning Deep Ecology and Celebrating Life.* Silverton, Colo.: Finn Hill Arts, 1988.

Lawrence, D. H. "A Propos of Lady Chatterly's Lover," in Harry T. Moore, ed. *D. H. Lawrence: Sex, Literature and Censorship.* New York: Twayne Publishers, 1953.

———. *Sons and Lovers.* New York: Viking, 1958.

Leopold, Aldo. *A Sand County Almanac.* New York: Ballentine, 1966.

Lewis, C. S. *The Abolition of Man.* New York: Macmillan, 1947.

Long, A. A. "Epicureans and Stoics," A. H. Armstrong, ed. *Classical Mediterranean Spirituality, Egyptioan, Greek, Roman.* New York: Crossroads, 1989.

MacMullen, Ransay. *Christianity and Paganism in the Fourth to Eighth Centuries.* New Haven: Yale University Press, 1997.

Manchester, Peter. *The Religious Experience of Time and Eternity, Classical Mediterranean Spirituality, Egyptian, Greek, Roman.* A. H. Armstrong, ed. New York: Crossroads, 1989.

Martin, Luther H. *Hellenistic Religions: An Introduction.* New York: Oxford University Press, 1990.

Morgan, Edmund S. *American Slavery American Freedom: The Ordeal of Colonial Virginia.* New York: W. W. Norton, 1975.

Nisbet, Robert. *History of the Idea of Progress.* New York: Basic Books, 1980.

Pangle, Thomas L. *The Philosophic Understandings of Human Nature Informing the Constitution, Confronting the Constitution.* Alan Bloom, ed. Washington, D.C.: American Enterprise Institute Press, 1990.

Pépin, Jean. "Cosmic Piety," A. H. Armstrong, ed. *Classical Mediterranean Spirituality, Egyptian, Greek, Roman.* New York: Crossroad, 1989.

Plotinus. *The Enneads.* Stephen MacKenna, trans. John Dillon, abr. London: Penguin, 1991.

Prigogine, Ilya and Isabel Stengers. *Order Out of Chaos: Man's New Dialogue With Nature.* New York: Bantam, 1984.

Rilke, Rainer Maria. *Selected Poems of Rainer Maria Rilke: A Translation From the German and Commentary by Robert Bly.* New York: Harper and Row, 1981.

Regenstein, Lewis. *Replenish the Earth.* New York: Crossroad, 1991.

Schaeffer, Francis A. *Pollution and the Death of Man: A Christian View of Ecology.* Wheaton, Ill.: Tyndale House, 1972.

Shlain, Leonard. *The Alphabet Versus the Goddess.* New York: Viking, 1998.

Singer, Tovia. "The Resurrection: What Is The Evidence?" Tim C. Leedom, ed. *The Book Your Church Doesn't Want You to Read.* Dubuque, Iowa: Kendall Hunt Pub. Co., 1993.

Smith, John Holland. *The Death of Classical Paganism.* New York: Charles Scribner's Sons, 1976.

Snyder, Gary. *The Practice of the Wild: Essays By Gary Snyder.* Berkeley, Calif.: North Point Press, 1990.

Sokal, Alan and Jean Bricmont. *Fashionable Nonsense: Postmodern Intellectuals' Abuse of Science*. Picador USA, 1999.

Starhawk. *The Spiral Dance*. New York: Harper and Row, 1979.

Starkey, Peggy. "Agape: A Christian Criterion for Truth in the Other World Religions." *International Review of Mission,* vol. LXXIV, no. 296, October, 1985.

Thich Nhat Hanh. *Living Buddha, Living Christ*. New York: Riverside Books, 1995.

Toulmin, Stephen. *Cosmopolis: The Hidden Agenda of Modernity*. Chicago: University of Chicago Press, 1990.

Wilken, Robert L. *The Christians as the Romans Saw Them*. New Haven: Yale University Press, 1984.

Wilkinson, Loren. "The Bewitching Charms of Neopaganism," www.ChristianityToday.com, January 19, 2000.

Wilson, Edward O. *Consilience*. New York: Knopf, 1998.

Yevtushenko, Yevgeny. *Selected Poems*. Baltimore: Penguin, 1966.

Zinn, Howard. *A People's History of the United States: 1492 to Present*. Rev. ed. New York: Harper Collins, 1990.

# Index